ATTITUDES OF EDUCATORS
TOWARD EXCEPTIONAL CHILDREN

ATTITUDES OF EDUCATORS TOWARD EXCEPTIONAL CHILDREN

Norris G. Haring

George G. Stern

William M. Cruickshank

Including Lectures By:

Georgie Lee Abel, Rudolph J. Capobianco, Louis M. DiCarlo,

Vincent J. Glennon, G. Orville Johnson, Ruth Strang

SYRACUSE UNIVERSITY PRESS – 1958

SYRACUSE UNIVERSITY
SPECIAL EDUCATION AND REHABILITATION
MONOGRAPH SERIES 3

WILLIAM M. CRUICKSHANK, *editor*

Library of Congress Catalog Card Number: 58-7550

This study was financed by a generous grant from
THE FUND FOR THE ADVANCEMENT OF EDUCATION
City of New York

———————

The printing and publication of this monograph
is made possible through a grant from the
BENJAMIN ROSENTHAL FOUNDATION
City of New York

ACKNOWLEDGMENTS

Numerous individuals and organizations have participated in the research and publication of this study. More than one hundred teachers, administrators, and nonprofessional employees of the four schools mentioned in the report gave a large amount of time in the completion of the numerous tests and inquiry forms prepared by the research staff. The cooperation which was received from these groups of people as individuals was outstanding.

Appreciation of the authors is extended to the Fund for the Advancement of Education for financial support which made the study possible. Through the study, factors requisite to the integration of exceptional children in regular classrooms have been observed which should have important implications to practical public day school educational programs. Further research of this nature is needed and indicated, but the initial step, a significant one, has been made possible through this grant.

Further appreciation is extended to Carl M. Roters, Associate Professor of Design, School of Art, College of Fine Arts, Syracuse University, for his work in the development of thematic apperception plates. To the Syracuse University Research Institute and to the Syracuse University administration thanks are expressed for creating a climate wherein research is valued and where research activities are a possibility.

At the time the study was actively in process each of the authors was a member of the Syracuse University faculty. Dr. Norris G. Haring, then Research Associate and Instructor in Special Education at Syracuse University, is now Coordinator of Services to Exceptional Children, Arlington County Board of Education, Arlington, Virginia and Lecturer and Coordinator of Special Education at the University of Maryland. Dr. George G. Stern is Associate Professor of Psychology, Syracuse University. Dr. William M. Cruickshank is Professor of Education and Psychology and Director, Education for Exceptional Children, Syracuse University.

W. M. C.

CONTENTS

LIST OF FIGURES

LIST OF TABLES

CHAPTER ONE

INTRODUCTION

RECENT TRENDS IN THE EDUCATION OF EXCEPTIONAL children have prompted educators to provide many such children with part-time and/or full-time educational programs within the structure of regular public day schools. Several interdependent developments resulting from continuous research and educational planning have contributed to this trend. These are, among others:

1. the refinement of diagnostic instruments and procedures

2. the advancements in prosthetic devices for handicapped children

3. the increased training of specialists and itinerant personnel

4. the increased number of preschool training programs for handicapped children

5. the increased awareness on the part of educators of the educational, social, and emotional needs of exceptional children.

As a result of these developments, increased numbers of exceptional children are eligible for regular grade placement. The attitudes of the regular classroom teachers with whom these children are to be placed present a vital consideration which has not been explored. The success of any plan of integration depends largely upon how the teacher feels toward the exceptional child.

The problems under consideration in this investigation are:

1. to design instruments for measuring attitudes of teachers toward exceptional children

2. to determine to what extent teachers' attitudes can be modified toward greater acceptance of exceptional children

3. to determine to what extent increased attitudes of acceptance of exceptional children affect teachers' relationships with these children.

ADVANCES CONTRIBUTING TO THE INTEGRATION
OF EXCEPTIONAL CHILDREN

Major advances in the education of exceptional children have resulted in many new opportunities for diversification in educational programs, making it possible for an exceptional child to more nearly approach the goal of reaching his full potentiality. As professional people in medicine, education, and psychology have become more aware of the importance of early diagnosis for children who show symptoms of exceptionality, educational services have been strengthened and broadened. As a result, many exceptional children are being detected in time to take full advantage of early planning and training for education, care, and treatment.

Research has improved methods and instruments for diagnosing and assessing exceptionality in children and this in turn has increased the ability of psychologists and physicians to determine the existence and extent of exceptionality. The error of measurement in physical, intellectual, socioemotional, academic achievement, and aptitude areas has been reduced significantly and can be further reduced by continuous research (1). Diagnosis, psychological assessment, and educational planning are now being accomplished, in most instances, by case conferences which include teams of specialists such as physicians, educators, psychologists, therapists, and social workers. The educational planning and treatment which follow the case conferences are based upon a review of the reports of medical diagnostic and treatment specialists, psychological case studies, and educational and social histories. Integration of information and cooperation in planning has thus increased the accuracy of effective educational placement for exceptional children.

Continuous development and refinement of prosthetic devices for children with physical impairments have made it possible for these children to utilize more fully the abilities they have in spite of their disability. Recent developments in hearing aids and methods of amplification have increased the tonal qualities, power output, and fidelity to the extent that some children are now more fully able to participate in a normal situation. New developments in materials, equipment, and techniques for visually handicapped and blind children have increased their experiences to the extent that many of these children are educable in regular grades. Similar statements can be made about other areas of exceptionality.

Preschool training programs for children with impaired hearing and speech, for children with visual impairments, and for children with cerebral palsy have stepped up their training so that they are often qualified for regular classroom placement earlier in their educational program than was possible before.

The increase in the number of trained itinerant personnel in public schools in areas of speech and hearing impairments, visual impairments and emotional disturbances has made it practical to educate many children in the regular grades.

PHILOSOPHY OF INTEGRATION

Coincident with these advances in practice, the philosophy of educators concerning the educational placement of handicapped children has evolved toward a more integrative position. This philosophy states that exceptional children should have the benefit of experiences with their nonexceptional peers whenever possible. Because these children will eventually be required to achieve a satisfactory adjustment within a predominately normal society, the experiences they have as children with this society are invaluable to them. Furthermore, normal children should be given an opportunity to understand, accept and adjust to children with exceptionalities. Although it appears that the problem with children accepting the handicapped is not as great as with adults, having continuous and constructive experiences with these children throughout their formative years may assist normal children to accept and understand handicapped individuals as adults. In light of this philosophy plus the advancements made in the education of exceptional children, educators are becoming more favorable in their attitude toward the integrated placement of exceptional children which, of course, has resulted in more of these children being educated in the regular classroom.

CRITERIA FOR INTEGRATION OF
EXCEPTIONAL CHILDREN

Although this study deals with the attitudes of general educators and is concerned with the philosophy of integration, it is recognized that integration will not be the solution for all exceptional children. A program of selective placement is in reality being advocated with the recognition that regular class placement, special class placement, contact classes and resource rooms, and improved residential school programs each will play an important role in the educational life of individual exceptional children depending upon the latter's needs, capacities, and physical characteristics. The present study is concerned with only one of several plans for the education of exceptional children. The reader should keep in mind that the present stress on this one approach does not mean that other plans of special education are rejected by the authors. All of the above-mentioned plans of education need to be considered; all are necessary, and undoubtedly improvements are needed in each.

The integration of exceptional children in a regular classroom is an individual matter in all cases, and can be accomplished successfully only after a careful diagnosis and consideration of:

1. the extent to which the integrated placement can provide for the intellectual, social, emotional and physical needs of the child under consideration

2. the degree to which the exceptional child can become a contributing member of the group and compete on a fairly equal basis with the group

3. the extent to which the physical facilities of the school plant provide accessibility to the areas of the building to which he must go in the routine of his program

4. the degree to which the teacher with whom the child is to be placed accepts and understands him.

If the above criteria can be met to a high degree and if the exceptional child is physically and intellectually capable of dealing with the activities in or near his regular grade placement, he can be considered potentially competent of achieving a successful adjustment in the regular grades. Areas of exceptionality from which some candidates for integration may come include:

1. Children with poliomyelitis, cerebral palsy and orthopedic handicaps. These children may be placed in a building which will permit physiotherapy and integration in the regular classroom for the academic skills and social activities.

2. Children with cardiac disorders, congenital deformities, epilepsy, and endocrine disorders. These children who meet the above criteria may be integrated in a regular class in a building with minimum special facilities.

3. Children with partial vision may be placed in the regular grades of any school building providing special materials, resource library, and personnel are available.

4. Children who are blind may be integrated in a regular class for most of the day in any school building, providing personnel and the necessary special materials and equipment are available.

5. Children with impaired hearing who can attain functional hearing by amplification or who have developed efficient communicating skills and who can participate effectively with their nonhandicapped peers may be educated in the regular grades, providing equipment and personnel are available.

A re-evaluation in terms of the above considerations would reveal that many exceptional children who are now being educated in special classes are qualified for regular grade placement.

KNOWLEDGE AND UNDERSTANDING TEACHERS HAVE OF EXCEPTIONAL CHILDREN

The knowledge teachers have concerning exceptional children has a potent influence on the social and emotional adjustment of these children, both in terms of the teacher-child interaction and in terms of the relationships between the exceptional child and the other children. An adequate insight on the part of teachers into the potentialities, the limitations, and the problems of exceptional persons is essential to the teachers in their educational planning and interpretation. It is important for teachers to understand that the problems of basic adjustment of handicapped children are not different from nonhandicapped children of the same age, intelligence, and socioeconomic status. Moreover, fundamental psychological, social, and emotional needs which a handicapped individual has are the same as his nonhandicapped counterpart (2). The differences which occur in a handicapped individual's achievement of an adequate adjustment are a function of the additional frustrations he encounters surmounting the day-to-day barriers imposed by his limitation, the reaction of the people in his environment to his limitation, and his self-perception influenced by these frustrations and reactions.

ATTITUDES AND PERSONALITY OF TEACHERS

The attitudes, prejudices, needs, and conflicts which teachers have are reflected in their behavior and influence strongly the social growth of exceptional children (3). Ojemann and Wilkinson (4), Boynton *et al.* (5), and Baruch (6) have found a relationship between the personal adjustment of teachers and the adjustment of their pupils. Apparently, well-adjusted teachers are able to enhance the personal adjustment of the pupils whom they teach. Baruch (6) has demonstrated that student-teachers who have been able to achieve a better understanding of themselves can accept in a more positive way children who display deviant behavior.

Creating a friendly, accepting atmosphere in a classroom depends largely upon the teacher's capacity to accept wide variation in intelligence, emotional maturity, and physical characteristics. The ability on the part of teachers to produce this atmosphere of understanding and acceptance, so vital to the development of handicapped individuals in a classroom, exists in varying degrees. It is believed that this capacity of teachers to accept and to motivate acceptance in others toward handicapped children can be increased. The process involved in promoting this increase is not completely known. However, it is hypothesized for the purpose of this investigation that modifying attitudes toward acceptance of handicapped children involves:

1. a more accurate and realistic knowledge and understanding of handicapped children, including their educational, physical, emotional and social needs

2. a greater understanding of teachers' own needs and how these needs affect behavior and attitudes toward handicapped children

3. a greater opportunity for teachers to express freely their feelings toward children with impairments.

Increasing the level of knowledge that teachers have concerning exceptional children can be accomplished more readily than inducing teachers to come face-to-face with their own personalities. Providing an interpersonal setting in which teachers can come to grips with their own needs, conflicts, and attitudes will require very careful consideration.

Even though many children who have exceptionalities are educable in regular day schools as a result of the advancement in all facets of the education of exceptional children, hardly any research has been conducted with regard to the attitudes and knowledge teachers have toward these children. The knowledge and understanding a teacher has concerning exceptional children, the attitudes she has toward them, and the teacher's own personality characteristics are all essential considerations for investigation before the attempt is made to place any handicapped child in a regular classroom.

REFERENCES

1. Newland, T. Ernest. "Psychological Assessment of Exceptional Children," Chapter 2 of *Psychology of Exceptional Children and Youth*. Edited by William M. Cruickshank. Englewood Cliffs, New Jersey: Prentice-Hall Inc., 1955.

2. Cruickshank, William M. "Psychological Considerations with Crippled Children," Chapter 6 of *Psychology of Exceptional Children and Youth*. Edited by William M. Cruickshank. Englewood Cliffs, New Jersey: Prentice-Hall Inc., 1955.

3. Thompson, George G. *Child Psychology*. New York: Houghton Mifflin Co., 1952.

4. Ojemann, R. H., and Wilkinson. F. R. "The Effect on Pupil Growth of an Increase in Teachers' Understanding of Pupil Behavior," *Journal of Experimental Education*, VIII (1939), 143-66.

5. Boynton, P., Dugger, H. and Turner, M. "The Emotional Stability of Teachers and Pupils," *Journal of Juvenile Research*, XVIII (1934), 223-32.

6. Baruch, D. W. "Procedures in Training to Prevent and Reduce Mental Hygiene Problems," *Journal of Genetic Psychology*, LXVII (1945), 143-78.

CHAPTER TWO

REVIEW OF RELATED RESEARCH

A SUBSTANTIAL AMOUNT OF RESEARCH IS AVAILABLE IN the literature which pertains to the modification of attitudes and attitude measurement. The major portion of the research on attitudes appears to be in areas of socioeconomic status, race and religious prejudices. Published research dealing with attitudes of teachers toward exceptional children is almost completely lacking.

ATTITUDES TOWARD THE PHYSICALLY HANDICAPPED

The writers interviewed the teaching staffs of two grade schools, a total of forty-four teachers. The interview was structured only with the statement: "How would you react to the possibility of having a blind or crippled child in your class?" The teachers' responses were tabulated and classified in terms of the kinds of reactions expressed. Thirty-eight per cent of the teachers expressed feelings of pity for the handicapped child; 2 per cent fear; and 22 per cent other feelings of rejection. Out of the forty-four teachers who were interviewed, 59.1 per cent responded negatively to the interview question. Although few studies are available regarding the attitudes of teachers toward exceptional children, a number of studies have been reported on the attitudes of parents and other individuals toward the handicapped.

A study of the attitudes of parents toward their own orthopedically handicapped children has been reported by Coughlin (1). The fifty-one children she selected for the study were patients of the Detroit Orthopaedic Clinic. The attitudes of the parents of these children were grouped in the following four broad categories:

1. parents who had sufficient intellectual insight and were so well adjusted personally that they were able, while realizing the implication of the orthopedic problem, to accept it and turn their attention and energies toward finding means of compensating for it

2. parents who had a complete acceptance of a handicapped child on an emotional level with very little or no intellectual insight
3. parents who understood the problems intellectually, but could not accept the child on an emotional level
4. parents who could not accept their child either emotionally or intellectually.

The majority of the parents' reactions in Coughlin's study grouped in the third category and manifested behavior which was described by Coughlin as "overanxiety overprotection." This was coupled with an unrealistic level of aspiration for the accomplishments of their child. A substantial number of the parents' reactions fell in the fourth category. These parents demonstrated feelings of fear emanating from the amount of expense and social inconvenience which their orthopedically handicapped child would cause them.

A study on the attitudes of other people toward cripples was done by Mussen and Barker (2). The subjects, consisting of 117 college students, were asked to use a rating scale designed to assess the opinions of the students toward the behavior characteristics of crippled individuals. The ratings included twenty-four personality characteristics ranging from favorable to unfavorable. The ratings of the college students regarding their attitudes toward the crippled fell into the unfavorable range on the following personality dimensions: vitality, self-confidence, submissiveness, realism, aggressiveness, social adaptability, and sensitiveness.

From an exhaustive review of the literature, Barker et al. summarize the characteristics of the attitudes that other individuals have toward physically handicapped persons and the attitudes the handicapped have toward themselves in the following seven points:

1. Public, verbalized attitudes toward disabled persons are on the average mildly favorable; an appreciable minority openly express negative attitudes.

2. Indirect evidence suggests that deeper unverbalized attitudes are more frequently hostile. This point requires further investigation.

3. The evidence is rather clear that the attitudes of parents toward their disabled children tend to be extreme more often than toward normal children, centering about the following patterns: oversolicitude, rejection, pressing for accomplishments beyond the child's abilities, inconsistent attitudes. Overprotection appears to occur more frequently than overt rejection.

4. The speculation has been advanced that some favorable attitudes and some oversolicitousness on the part of parents mask deep, inadmissible hostile attitudes.

5. The attitudes of disabled persons toward their own disabilities have been inadequately studied. The available evidence suggests that these attitudes (a)

vary widely, (b) have little relation to the degree of disability, (c) are related to personality characteristics.

6. The attitudes of disabled persons and of their physically normal associates are frequently in conflict with respect to the meaning of help, curiosity, sympathy, and misfortune.

7. The attitudes of both the disabled person and his associates are influenced by the larger social situation in which interactions occur (3, pp. 84-85).

ATTITUDES TOWARD MENTALLY HANDICAPPED CHILDREN

One of the arguments that has been raised against special classes for mentally handicapped children is that these children are stigmatized because of segregated placement. The evidence that is reported would indicate that even though the mentally handicapped child is placed in the regular grades, he has little assurance of receiving greater acceptance from the other children. In a study by Johnson (4) which was concerned with the social position of the mentally handicapped child in the regular grades, children from twenty-five regular classrooms, each having one or more mentally handicapped children, were selected. The social position of the mentally handicapped children was studied by the sociometric technique. The author found that the mentally handicapped children were rejected by their classmates significantly more times than normal children. He also found that the rejection scores decreased steadily as intelligence increased.

Grebler (5), using the case study approach with parents of mentally retarded children, found that nine out of eleven parents studied felt either ambivalent or rejecting toward their retarded child. The parents, by and large, were extrapunitive in dealing with blame, *i.e.*, they were able to direct their hostile and aggressive attitudes toward the environment such as the other parent, teachers, professional groups, or toward the child.

McGehee and Lewis (6) asked teachers to rate attitudes of parents of gifted children, average children, and retarded children. The teachers rated parents of gifted children as having the highest degree of acceptance toward their children; the parents of mentally handicapped, the lowest degree of acceptance.

Miller (7), Lord (8), Kammerer (9), Oettinger (10), and Rosenbaum (11) have reported studies which give support to the idea that the attitudes of peers, siblings, parents, and society have a tremendous influence on the personality of the handicapped child.

IMPACT OF TEACHERS' ATTITUDES
ON ATTITUDES OF CHILDREN

Of particular relevance to the present research is the extent to which the attitudes of teachers influence the attitudes of children. Although there appears to be no research on the extent to which the attitudes of teachers toward exceptional children influence the attitudes of the children in their classes, available research with regard to teachers' attitudes toward socioeconomic classes, certain races and religions is important and meaningful.

Moffitt (12) found that 119 out of 634 high school pupils he studied attributed the cause of their prejudice against certain races to the instruction they had had in school. The degree to which the attitudes of teachers toward the Negro are reflected in the attitudes of their pupils was investigated by Manske (13). Ten schools located from southwest Oklahoma to northeast Rhode Island were selected to participate in the study. Both experimental and control groups of children were selected from ninth grade classes. The teachers and the pupils were given the revised Hinckley scale, using Form A before and Form B after special lessons on the Negro problem had been presented by the teachers to the experimental group of pupils. The pre-test and post-test results were compared. The results of the experiment showed that actual consideration of the Negro issue, irrespective of the expressed opinions by the teachers, modified the attitudes of the pupils toward a more liberal point of view. Six out of the twenty-two classes demonstrated more liberal attitudes, including two classes taught by the two most prejudiced teachers. Manske concluded that pupils do not necessarily reflect the attitudes of their teachers, particularly when teachers present the instructional material on an intellectual level.

A study by Mason (14) on the effect of the attitudes of high school teachers upon the attitudes of their pupils points up evidence somewhat conflicting with what Manske reported. In this study, twenty-five social-studies teachers were measured with the Harper Social Study Scale. Five of the most "liberal" teachers and five of the most "conservative" teachers, as measured by Harper's scale, were selected to teach social studies to two matched groups with seventy-seven pupils in each group from grades eleven and twelve. One group was taught by "liberal" teachers, the other group by "conservative" teachers. Both groups were pretested by a modified version of the Harper Social Study Scale and retested at the end of the semester. The pupils with the "liberal" teachers demonstrated a mean gain of 1.32 points on their liberalism score.

The group taught by "conservative" teachers showed a mean loss of 1.06 points. The difference proved to be statistically significant. Mason concluded that

> . . . association with liberal teachers furthers expression of liberal social attitudes upon the part of high school pupils, if the material studied concerns itself with present-day events and integrates study with current happenings (14, p. 57).

A second, similar experiment was conducted by Mason in twenty-three rural consolidated high schools in a Midwestern state using the Wrightstone Scale of Civic Beliefs especially constructed for use with high school pupils. The second experiment had some advantages over the first in that more adequate information was collected on the attitudes of teachers and an additional criterion was used with respect to teachers' effects upon pupils. In this study, twenty-nine teachers were divided into three groups called "liberal," "middle" and "conservative" as based upon their score from the Wrightstone Scale. Four hundred high school pupils were divided into three matched groups. The first group was taught by "liberal" teachers, the second group by "middle" teachers and the third by "conservative" teachers. The group of pupils assigned to "liberal" teachers showed a significantly greater gain in their attitudes toward liberalism.

Droba (15) completed a study in the same area as did Mason. In this investigation units of study on the problems of the Negro were presented to students at Ohio State University. The Hinckley Scale was administered before and after the presentation of the study units, revealing slightly more favorable attitudes toward the Negro.

MODIFICATION OF ATTITUDES

There appears to be enough evidence in past research to lend support to the assumption that the attitudes of teachers influence the attitudes of the children whom they teach. It is being assumed that if, through certain educational techniques, one can modify the attitudes of regular classroom teachers toward a realistic acceptance of exceptional children, these attitudes of acceptance on the part of teachers will also influence children in the direction of realistic acceptance. The present investigators are interested in educational methodology which has proved effective in modifying attitudes, in selecting the most effective methods, and in adapting them to the purposes stated above.

The most widely used methods for the modification of attitudes are films, group discussions, visitations, lectures, reading materials, or any combination of these. Some researchers (28, 29, 30) have concluded that one method is more effective than another. However, the evidence is not conclusive enough to suggest singling out any one method for all situations.

By far the greatest amount of research reports the use of instruction in some form or another as a means for modifying attitudes. The evidence at first glance seems somewhat contradictory as to the effectiveness of instruction in modifying attitudes. After closer inspection of the research one might conclude that the effectiveness of instruction in modifying attitudes is a function of the effort put forth by the instructor to modify attitudes in a given direction. Droba (15), Young (19), Bowden (20), Golub and Swahn (21) all report very slight, if any, changes in the attitudes of their students as a result of college courses during which no special effort was made to change attitudes.

On the other hand, in experiments where a special effort has been made to modify attitudes, significant changes are obtained. Longstreet (22) conducted an experiment in four public schools. In three of these schools the American history classes were taught by teachers in the usual way. In the fourth school a conscious effort was made in the classes to modify attitudes. The four schools were tested with a Thurstone scale at the beginning and at the end of the year. Statistically significant changes in attitudes were demonstrated by the students in the school where a conscious effort was made toward that end. The change in the other three schools was not significant. Weller (23), and Hurd (24) report significant changes in attitude toward certain aspects of science on the part of students as a result of special emphasis placed in this direction in science courses.

Campbell and Stover (25) conducted an experiment in which a short course was presented on the Negro to twenty-four ninth grade girls. The predominant methods used in the course were travel talks and films. The girls demonstrated an increased favorableness in their attitude toward Negroes on the Bogardus Social Distance Test and on the Hinckley test. Smith (26), Whisler (27), and Ford (28) further report significant changes in a favorable direction in the attitudes of white students toward Negroes resulting from college classes.

The results from several experiments indicate that lectures are a significant means of modifying attitudes. Binnewies (29) reports a slight change toward "liberalism" as the result of eight lectures. Cherrington and Miller (30) tested the results of a lecture and found a statistically significant change. A retest at the end of six months showed that the change had remained. Remmers (31) reports a significant change in attitude toward the League of Nations as a result of one lecture.

A most impressive study conducted by Peterson and Thurstone (32) indicates that motion pictures are an important influence on the attitudes of children. In this study 3,800 children were tested on certain attitudes before and after showing them a film. A significant change in attitude was demonstrated which was retained from ten to nineteen months. The authors also reported that two or more pictures on the same subject have a cumulative effect.

Several other investigators (33, 34, 17), have compared the effectiveness of the group discussion and the lecture methods and report results highly in favor of the group discussion method for changing attitudes toward certain foods. Zimet (35) conducted a study with fifteen New York State chief school administrators. Sixteen weekly sessions were held and were devoted to the discussion of human relations as related to administration. Each five-hour session was held in an atmosphere of free discussion. An eighteen-card picture story instrument was designed for the purpose of the study. Combs's Desires and Action Outcomes test (36) was also given. The school administrators were tested before and after the seminar. The picture story instrument was analyzed on a series of 19 five-point rating scales devised to measure attitudes toward self, other adults, children, and story endings. Zimet reports significant changes in attitude in a positive direction toward self, toward other adults and toward children. On the Desires List, the administrators changed in a "democratic direction."

SUMMARY

Research is grossly limited with regard to the attitudes of parents and other individuals toward physically and mentally handicapped persons. However, it is obvious from the existing studies that handicapped individuals are accepted to a lesser degree than those persons who are not handicapped. Although very little research has been conducted on the attitudes of teachers toward handicapped children, it is assumed that teachers, too, feel less accepting toward the handicapped than they do toward typical children.

The most widely used methods for modifying attitudes are lectures, films, visitations, group discussions and classroom instruction. The most conflicting evidence is reported by researchers in finding attitude changes using classroom instruction as the method for modification. It appears, however, that when a conscious effort has been made by the instructor to modify attitudes in a certain direction more substantial results are attained. By and large, effective methods for changing attitudes appear also to be favorable teaching methods. Certainly the method or methods used are not the only variables involved in the modification of attitudes. The instructor, lecturer, or group discussion leader as an individual plays a major role in this effort.

This review has been concerned with the research pertinent to this study in two areas: the attitudes toward handicapped individuals, and the methods of modifying attitudes.

REFERENCES

1. Coughlin, Ellen W. "Some Parental Attitudes Toward Handicapped Children," *The Child*, VI (1941), 41-45.

2. Mussen, P. H., and Barker, R. G. "Attitudes Toward Cripples," *Journal of Abnormal and Social Psychology*, XXXIX (1944), 351-55.

3. Barker, R. G., *et al. Adjustment to Physical Handicap and Illness: A Survey of the Social Psychology of Physique and Disability*. New York: Social Science Research Council, 1953 Revision, Bulletin 55.

4. Johnson, G. Orville. "A Study of the Social Position of Mentally-Handicapped Children in the Regular Grades," *American Journal of Mental Deficiency*, LV, (July, 1950), 60-88.

5. Grebler, Anne Marie. "Parental Attitude Toward Mentally Retarded Children," *American Journal of Mental Deficiency*, LVI (January, 1952), 475-83.

6. McGehee, William, and Lewis, W. Drayton. "Parental Attitudes of Mentally Superior, Average, and Retarded Children," *School and Society*, LI (April, 1940), 556-59.

7. Miller, Loretta M. *A Community Guidance Program to Meet More Fully the Needs of Crippled Youth in East Harlem*. New York: King's Crown Press, 1943.

8. Lord, Elizabeth E. *Children Handicapped by Cerebral Palsy*. New York: Commonwealth Fund, 1937.

9. Kammerer, R. C. "An Exploratory Psychological Study of Crippled Children," *Psychological Record*, IV (1940), 47-100.

10. Oettinger, K. B. "An Experiment in Teaching Physically Handicapped Children at Home," *Mental Hygiene*, XXII (1938), 245-64.

11. Rosenbaum, Betty B. "Neurotic Tendencies in Crippled Girls," *Journal of Abnormal and Social Psychology*, XXXI (1937), 423-29.

12. Moffitt, J. C. "An Analysis of Race Prejudice," *Educational Administration and Supervising*, XVIII (December, 1932), 641-48.

13. Manske, A. J. "The Reflection of Teachers Attitudes in the Attitudes of Their Pupils," *Contributions to Education*, No. 702 (New York: Bureau of Publications, Teachers College, Columbia University, 1936).

14. Mason, A. H. *Effects of Attitudes of High School Teachers of Social Studies upon Attitudes of Their Pupils*, Studies in Higher Education

XLV, Further Studies in Attitudes, Series V. Ed. H. H. Remmers, Lafayette, Indiana, Purdue University, June, 1942.

15. Droba, D. D. "Education and Negro Attitudes," *Sociology and Social Research*, XVII (November, 1932), 137-41.

16. French, R. V. "Retraining an Autocratic Leader," *Journal of Abnormal and Social Psychology*, XXXIX (1944), 224-37.

17. Willerman, B. "Forces Behind Food Habits and Methods of Change," In K. Lewis (Ed). Bulletin, National Research Council, CVIII (1943), 35-65.

18. Coch, L., and French, J. R. "Overcoming Resistance to Change," *Human Relations*, I (1948), 512-32.

19. Young, Donald R. "Some Effects of a Course in American Race Problems on the Race Prejudice of 450 Undergraduates at the University of Pennsylvania," *Journal of Abnormal and Social Psychology*, XXII (October, 1927), 235-42.

20. Bowden, A. O. "Change . . . The Test of Teaching," *School and Society*, XL (July 28, 1934), 133-36.

21. Golub, Jay, and Swahn, A. D. "Do American History Students Change Their Attitudes After One Term's Work?" *Historical Outlook*, XXIV (January, 1933), 25-28.

22. Longstreet, R. J. "An Experiment With the Thurstone Attitude Scales," *School Review*, XLIII (March, 1935), 202-208.

23. Weller, Florence. "Attitudes and Skills in Elementary Science," *Science Education*, XVII (April, 1933), 90-97.

24. Hurd, A. W. "Appreciational Objecting in Science Teaching," *School and Society*, XXXVII (January 28, 1933), 124-26.

25. Campbell, D. W., and Stover, G. F. "Teaching International-Mindedness in Social Studies," *Journal of Educational Sociology*, VII (1933), 244-48.

26. Smith, Mapheus. "A Study of Change of Attitudes toward the Negro," *School and Society*, LVII (April 3, 1943), 388-92.

27. Whisler, Laurence. "Changes in Attitudes toward Social Issues Accompanying a One-Year Freshman Social Science Course," *Journal of Psychology*, X (1940), 387-96.

28. Ford, Robert N. "Scaling Experience by a Multiple-Response Technique: A Study of White-Negro Contacts," *American Sociological Review*, VI (February, 1941), 9-23.

29. Binnewies, W. G. "Measuring Changes in Opinion," *Sociology and Social Research*, XVI (November-December, 1931), 143-48.

30. Cherrington, Ben J., and Miller, L. W. "Change in Attitude as the Result of a Lecture and of Reading Similar Material," *Journal of Sociological Psychology*, IV (November, 1933), 479-84.

31. Remmers, H. H. (ed.). *Further Studies in Attitudes*, Series II, Studies in Higher Education No. 31. Purdue University, 1936.

32. Peterson, Ruth C., and Thurstone, L. L. *Motion Picture and the Social Attitude of Children*. New York: The Macmillan Company, 1933.

33. Lewin, K. "Group Decision and Social Change," In T. Newcomb, and E. L. Hartley (eds.). *Readings in Social Psychology*. New York: Henry Holt, 1947.

34. Radke, Marian, and Klisweick, Dayna. "Experiments in Changing Food Habits," *Journal American Dietetic Association*, XXIII (1947), 403-409.

35. Zimet, Carl N. "An Investigation of Changes in Attitude and Motivation as a Result of a Group-Centered Social Action Technique," Unpublished doctoral dissertation, Syracuse University, 1953.

36. Combs, A. W. "A Method of Analysis for the Thematic Apperception Test and Autobiography," *Journal of Consulting Psychology*, II (1946), 167-74.

CHAPTER THREE

EXPERIMENTAL DESIGN AND PROCEDURES

THE PURPOSE OF THE STUDY

THE GENERAL PURPOSES OF THIS INVESTIGATION WERE (*a*) to determine the extent to which the attitudes of classroom teachers can be modified toward greater and more realistic acceptance of exceptional children, and (*b*) to attempt to modify the initial attitudes of these teachers in this direction by the utilization of a workshop. The resolution of these general purposes was sought through answering the following questions about the influence of the workshop:

1. Do teachers increase in the general knowledge they have about exceptional children?
2. Do teachers become more accepting of exceptional children?
3. Do teachers increase their abilities to determine the most accurate and realistic educational placement for exceptional children?
4. Do basic changes occur in the personality structure of teachers?
5. Do teachers become more positive in their responses to handicapped children?
6. Do teachers become more positive toward themselves and other individuals?
7. Do teachers use the understanding and acceptance they have gained in their relationships with exceptional children?

The purposes of this study are stated specifically as follows:

1. To measure the attitudes and knowledge of the teachers and administrators concerning children who are mentally retarded, acoustically handicapped, visually handicapped, physically handicapped, emotionally disturbed, academically retarded, and intellectually superior.
2. To attempt to modify attitudes in a positive direction and to increase understandings of teachers and administrators concerning

18

exceptional children through a series of fifteen meetings relating to the above-mentioned areas of exceptionality in children.

3. To determine the extent to which teachers and administrators can become more realistic in their judgments of the educational placement of exceptional children as a result of the workshop.

4. To determine the extent to which the workshop can influence, in a positive direction, the attitudes of teachers and administrators toward children with exceptionalities.

5. To attempt to provide an atmosphere within the structure of the workshop in which teachers and administrators can achieve a better self-understanding leading toward certain changes in their personality structure.

6. To determine the extent to which the workshop can change the personality structure of teachers and administrators.

7. To determine the extent to which teachers and administrators use the experiences gained from the workshop in their day-to-day re- relationships with exceptional children.

In seeking answers to these questions and to collect data in keeping with the above-stated purposes, it is the intent of this study, first, to determine the initial status of the teachers with regard to their information about exceptional children, their attitudes toward these children, their own personality characteristics, and their feelings toward themselves, other individuals, and exceptional children. Secondly, it is the intent of the study to reassess the teachers in the above areas after the presentation of a workshop and to determine the changes which occurred.

IMPLEMENTATION

In order to investigate the attitudes and understanding of regular classroom teachers concerning exceptional children and at the same time influence their attitudes toward a more realistic acceptance of these children, teachers and administrators from four schools in and near Syracuse, New York, were provided fifteen workshop sessions extending over a period of approximately thirty weeks. Throughout this period, eight areas of exceptionality were covered. Each meeting lasted two hours. During the first hour the teachers were given a lecture in a particular area of exceptionality. The second hour, they were asked to divide into small prearranged discussion groups not exceeding eighteen members. Discussions were conducted relevant to the area presented in the lecture. Films, demonstrations and visitations were distributed throughout the workshop. An attempt was made to provide at least one of each of these experiences in each of the eight areas.

The effect of the workshop in modifying the attitudes and understanding of the teachers toward exceptional children was evaluated by means of a test battery administered during the first and last sessions of the workshop. Five instruments were designed for this purpose: the General Information Inventory, the Classroom Integration Inventory, the Activities Index, the Picture Judgment Test, and the Critical Incident Test.

These five were selected in order to implement a multidimensional approach toward the assessment of attitude change on the part of the teachers. They incorporate breadth of coverage, ranging from the direct and structured evoking of factual information, to the indirect and relatively unstructured prompting of symptomatic attitudes by means of projective materials. At the same time, a certain amount of overlap has been provided, so that the General Information Inventory, the Classroom Integration Inventory, and the Critical Incident Test are explicitly and openly oriented toward the exceptional child, whereas the Activities Index and the Picture Judgment Test tap more grossly functional aspects of behavior.

Analyses of the pre-test and post-test results on these several instruments, and of the interrelationships between them, was expected to throw considerable light on the effects of the group workshop sessions in changing attitudes toward increased acceptance of the exceptional child.

SPECIFIC PROCEDURES

The foregoing paragraphs have discussed general procedures which were employed in the study. The remainder of this chapter will be devoted to a detailed description of (a) the selection of the participating schools, (b) the procedures utilized in the workshop, and (c) the instruments employed in measuring change.

SELECTION OF THE SCHOOLS

In selecting the schools to be included in the study, a good representation of schools with various educational problems was desired. It was believed that in order to achieve this representation, one school should be selected from each of the following types of school organizations:

1. a central school district in a rural area
2. a city school
3. a common school district in a suburban area
4. a parochial or private school.

In addition, it was required that the total staff of the school agree to participate in the workshop and that the school be within a radius of fifty miles of Syracuse, New York. The chief school administrators and principals from several schools meeting the above criteria were called together. At this meeting, it was explained that the complete supervisory, teaching, and custodial staff participating in the workshop would be granted two credit hours from Syracuse University in the Department of Education for Exceptional Children. It was emphasized that they would benefit from the opportunity of experience and training offered through the workshop in the area of exceptional children. In return, the total cooperation of the teaching and administrative staff was requested. The personnel from the several schools voted by secret ballot on whether or not they wanted to participate. In four of the schools the vote was 100 per cent in favor of participation. As a result of the expression of unanimous agreement for participation on the part of the total staffs, four schools were invited to participate in the study:

1. Union Springs School, an elementary and secondary centralized school district located in Union Springs, New York
2. Cherry Road School, an elementary common school district located in Geddes, New York
3. Seymour School, an elementary city school located in Syracuse, New York
4. St. John the Evangelist School, an elementary and secondary parochial school located in Syracuse, New York.

Incidence of Exceptionality in the Schools. In the schools utilized for the investigation considerable numbers of exceptional children were already enrolled as pupils. These included mentally retarded children, emotionally disturbed children, intellectually superior children, and some physically handicapped children of several different medical classifications. Altogether about 200 children were included in the several categories, the largest group being the children with retarded mental development, which accounted for nearly 50 per cent of the total. Among the physically handicapped children were pupils with cerebral palsy, poliomyelitis, scoliosis, epilepsy, hearing impairments, speech impairments, visual impairments, several children with visible congenital defects, cosmetic defects, and two children with severe disabilities following accidents. By far the majority of these children, however, came from two of the four schools. These two schools were Union Springs Central School and Seymour School.

Seymour School (School I), located in a lower socioeconomic area in the city, had enrolled in the school almost half of all of the exceptional children listed above. Three special classes for mentally handicapped children were located at School I. In addition, a considerable number of emotionally disturbed children were enrolled there at the time of the study. A higher incidence of children with speech and hearing handicaps attended School I than attended either Cherry Road or St. John the Evangelist Schools.

Cherry Road School (School II), located in a higher socioeconomic, suburban area, had relatively few handicapped children. Several children with physical handicaps were enrolled there, including one child who had had poliomyelitis. A very substantial number of gifted children, however, attended this school.

Union Springs Central School (School III), located in a rural area, had no special educational facilities for the relatively large number of exceptional children who were enrolled there. A considerable number of physically and mentally handicapped children were being educated in the regular classroom with itinerant services. With the exception of the emotionally disturbed children, this number was comparable to that of School I (City). The number of emotionally disturbed children was significantly lower as compared to School I (City).

St. John the Evangelist School (School IV), a parochial school located in an average socioeconomic area in the city, had a rather selective enrollment with very few exceptional children.

STRUCTURE OF WORKSHOP

The structure of each two-hour workshop was designed to provide one hour for a consultant to lecture to the workshop members in eight areas of exceptional children. The lecture group was then divided into smaller groups, each not exceeding eighteen teachers, and an hour of free discussion was held under the direction of discussion leaders. Fifteen sessions were held in each of the four schools extending over a period of approximately thirty weeks. The workshops began in October and ended in May. The purpose of the lectures was to increase knowledge and understanding by the participants of children with exceptionalities. The consultants were asked to define their area, discuss diagnosis and etiology of the exceptionality and give the current thinking with regard to special educational methodology. The second hour was left as unstructured as possible in order to give the teachers an opportunity to discuss the attitudes they had toward children with the particular exceptionality covered in the lecture. The discussion leaders were encouraged to provide an atmosphere of acceptance in their groups to allow the teachers to verbalize any misinformation, misunderstanding, or negative attitudes which they might have had.

The Program. The program included eight areas concerning exceptional children. These areas in order of presentation were:
1. children with intellectual retardation
2. children with orthopedic or neurological impairments
3. children with impaired hearing and/or speech
4. children with academic retardation
5. children with visual impairments
6. children with superior talent and/or intelligence
7. children with emotional disturbances
8. counseling for parents of exceptional children.

The first area, children with intellectual retardation, was subdivided into three lectures. They were:
1. mentally deficient children and clinical types
2. mentally handicapped children
3. children with slow learning ability.

Two lectures each were allotted to the areas of speech and hearing, academic retardation and emotional disturbances.

Teacher Visitations. The teachers were given one-half day during the period of the study for visiting a regular classroom, special class, residential school, private school or clinic in which exceptional children were having educational and/or therapeutic experiences. The educational situations selected for visitations were:
1. Syracuse State School (for the mentally handicapped)
2. Frank C. McCarthy School (for the mentally deficient)
3. United Cerebral Palsy and Handicapped Children Association of Syracuse, Inc.
4. Leonard C. Illingworth Nursery School for Blind Children
5. Reading Laboratory, Syracuse University
6. Special classes for mentally retarded children, Syracuse Public Schools.

Selection of Consultants. In selecting the consultants, it was desired to have a wide representation of several levels of experience and different points of view concerning exceptional children. The consultants were chosen from a national association, the New York State Department of Education, Syracuse University, Columbia University, and the local community. From the national level, Miss Georgia Lee Abel, Education Consultant, The American Foundation for the Blind, was the consultant in the area of children with visual impairments. Messrs. Charles Becker, Joseph Fenton, and Ray Simches from the Bureau for Handicapped Children, New York State Education Department, were consultants in the areas of mental retardation, orthopedically handicapped and emotionally disturbed, respectively. Dr. Ruth Strang, Teachers College, Columbia University, lectured in the area of children with superior talent and intellect. Consultants from Syracuse University were Drs. William M. Cruickshank, G. Orville Johnson, Louis M. Di Carlo, Walter W. Amster, William D. Sheldon, Rudolph Capobianco, Vincent J. Glennon, Mrs. Fern Root, and Dr. Norris G. Haring who lectured in the areas of children with orthopedic and cardiac impairments, children with mental retardation, children with speech and/or hearing impairments, remedial reading, remedial arithmetic, children with visual impairments, and emotionally disturbed children, respectively. Mr. Richard Greene, Chief Probation Officer, Onondaga County Children's Court, also participated as a speaker in the area of children with emotional disturbances. Summaries of the remarks of those consultants who made formal presentations are included in complete form in Appendix B.

Orientation for School Administrators. Two orientation meetings were held for the administrators prior to the workshop. In the first of these the history and background of the study were outlined. The importance of acceptance of exceptional children by the teacher and school administrator was discussed. It was further stressed that the success of a plan of integration depends largely upon the attitudes of teachers. Thus the purpose of the workshop phase of the experiment was to help the teachers understand the problems of the exceptional child and to correct any misunderstandings that might influence teachers' attitudes. In this meeting the administrators were asked to accept the attitudes of their teachers without criticism and to accept any negative feelings expressed toward children with exceptionalities. It was assumed that if the teachers expressed whatever negative feelings they might have, new insights might occur which in turn would increase attitudes of acceptance.

In addition, the following points were clarified:
1. Not all exceptional children can be educated in the regular grades

of the public schools. The purpose of this investigation was to gain information which would be useful in the present and future planning for the placement of exceptional children and, in addition, to prepare teachers for teaching in a regular classroom in which exceptional children might be integrated.

2. Another purpose of the workshop was to give teachers and other staff members a more realistic understanding of exceptional children and to rectify misunderstandings.

3. They were told the weekly program would require two hours of staff time, the first hour devoted to the major problems of exceptional children, the second hour designed for free discussion in small groups.

4. The results of the instruments used for evaluation of the teacher were to remain anonymous. The tests were not designed to evaluate the teachers individually, but to measure what changes might result in the total group as a result of the workshop.

5. The teachers were to be given the understanding that they would all receive the same grade and that their attitudes toward the exceptional child would have no influence on their grade in the workshop.

6. Teachers who had a special interest in certain areas of exceptional children were to be given an opportunity to visit special schools and rooms. The substitute teacher and transportation costs were to be provided through research funds.

Orientation for Consultants. A similar, second orientation meeting was conducted for the consultant and discussion leaders who had been selected to participate in the workshop. The following points were covered in this meeting:

1. The history and purposes of the study were explained.

2. The consultants were told the size of the groups at each school in which they were to lecture.

3. The consultants were asked to use nontechnical terms in their lectures whenever possible and to utilize concrete examples as often as they could.

4. The consultants were urged to give the teachers an understanding of the special educational considerations required for exceptional children.

5. The consultants were asked to define for the teachers those exceptional children who are potentially qualified for being integrated in the regular grades.

6. Each consultant was told that he would be responsible for an hour lecture and that he would also serve as discussion leader for one of the subgroups during the second hour. As discussion leaders the consultants were asked to stimulate free discussion relevant to the attitudes toward their particular area of exceptionality.

Registration. During the last week in September the coordinator and a representative from the Bureau of School Services, Syracuse University, registered the staff members of the four schools. The number of individuals registered were as follows:

School	Persons
Seymour School	25
Cherry Road School	36
St. John the Evangelist	14
Union Springs Central School	66
Total	141

Prior to the first meeting, all of the registrants were sent a letter of introduction and welcome to the workshop. Another purpose of the letter was to ask for the cooperation of the teachers in the program and in the evaluation materials which were to be administered. Because of the extensive nature of the testing material, it was believed necessary to explain to the teachers the value of this material to the success of the project.

Reference Material. A library of reference material concerned with exceptional children was ordered and placed in the four schools. The selection of the bulletins, reprints and books was made upon the recommendation of the consultants and included that which was believed to be a cross-section of the best thinking and most valid research available at the time.

Recording. A complete record of everything that was presented to the teachers and administrators of the workshop was believed to be of prime importance. Rather than to elect members of the group to serve as recorders, arrangements were made for mechanical recording. Two tape recorders were used to record all of the lectures and group discussions. Secretarial assistance was employed to transcribe the tapes.

EVALUATION INSTRUMENTS: PRELIMINARY CONSIDERATIONS

Only a few of the several instruments tentatively outlined for consideration at the beginning of this project actually survived preliminary discussion, development, pretesting, analysis and revision. Nevertheless, a description of each of the initially proposed devices, together with its eventual disposition, will be described briefly below, on the assumption that a summary of the blind alleys and failures which were encountered will prove as informative as the details of the more successful results.

Two criteria proposed by Campbell (1) were employed as an heuristic device for ensuring adequate breadth of coverage in the proposed test battery. The first of these, *disguise*, involves the degree to which the real purpose of the attitude measure is concealed from the respondent. A second aspect of the treatment of content in attitude tests is based upon the extent to which the task or response has been *structured*. A highly structured test is one in which the response alternatives are exhaustively specified and readily scorable, in contrast with the ambiguity of the task and the spontaneity of response characteristic of nonstructured instruments. The use of these two criteria directs attention to four general types of tests, for each of which we attempted to develop at least one example.

Nondisguised — Structured Devices. A Likert-type (2) distance or acceptance scale involving attitudes toward the integration of the exceptional child in the classroom was given top priority. This instrument is described more fully in the section which follows, under the name of the *Classroom Integration Inventory*.

Nondisguised — Nonstructured Devices. Open-end interviews, questionnaires, autobiographies, and essays typify the approach subsumed here. A biographical questionnaire was designed and pretested, but the necessity for conserving testing time required of the teachers participating in the discussions ruled out further consideration of this approach in the actual study. A nondisguised, partially structured procedure, requiring the teachers to cite instances in which they found themselves making use of workshop insights in their regular classrooms was developed instead, and will be described subsequently as the *Critical Incident Test*.

Disguised — Structured Devices. Structured tests with disguised purposes are of particular usefulness since the possibilities of deliberate distortion by the respondent are minimized with no sacrifice in the ease of administration or scoring. Five instruments of this type were considered.

1. A pseudo-objective information test, purporting to measure the

amount of knowledge the subject possessed regarding the exceptional child, while actually yielding information concerning his attitudinal orientation toward such children, was given early consideration. Such an instrument is based on the assumption that forced choices in an area characterized by a high degree of affect but little factual knowledge for the average respondent would elicit biased responses diagnostic of the subject's underlying attitudes. Under such circumstances it seems likely that both guessing behavior and selective patterns of retained information would serve to reveal related attitudes.

Examples of items measuring attitudes toward "labor-management" by forcing the respondent to choose between two alternatives which are equally incorrect but in opposite directions are: "The average weekly wage of the war worker in 1945 was (a) $37.00; (b) $57.00." "Financial reports show that out of every dollar (a) 16¢; (b) 3½¢ is profit" (3). Although several attempts were made to develop similar items regarding the exceptional child, none of these proved satisfactory and the instrument was eventually abandoned as impracticable. Such questions as: "A reasonable estimate of the percentage of emotionally disturbed children in the public schools would be (a) 5%; (b) 25%," or "Most teachers are inclined to feel that the socially maladjusted child (a) needs discipline; (b) will respond to affection and understanding," only underscore the fact that lack of information may frequently depend on a lack of common definitions of terms, e.g., "emotional disturbance," rather than absence of knowledge.

Furthermore, the minimal ego-involvement of the majority of the teachers with respect to the exceptional child seemed likely to produce random rather than systematic response "errors." A person's choice of "the most outstanding brand" from among Buick, Cadillac, or Lincoln motor cars is more susceptible to interpretation than a similar choice among Savastamp, Peluze, or Triner letter scales. However, posing questions regarding etiology and prognosis for various types of deviates, i.e., predisposing factors and eventual outcomes associated with epilepsy or cerebral palsy, for example, suggests a possibility which may prove more successful than the one attempted here.

However, the obvious need for some measure of factual information regarding exceptionality in children led to the development of a *General Information Inventory* which will be described below.

2. A number of researchers (4) have explored the use of a quasi-projective test in which subjects are asked to "tell what people are like by looking at their faces." In the present instance it was proposed to vary sets of photographs systematically in terms of (a) sex; (b) color; (c) eth-

nic; (d) socioeconomic; and (e) physical disability factors, requiring the subject to select the child in each set who appears "most adaptable," "lazy," "persevering," "a good sport," etc. Systematic organization of these sets would permit an evaluation of the relative importance of each of the five factors in determining the subject's response. This test seems useful and feasible, but would require an extensive photographic source and considerable time before a workable pilot form could be developed. No further work along these lines was attempted.

3. Previous research (5) has demonstrated the usefulness of a psychodynamically-oriented interest inventory in identifying patterns of personality needs characteristic of various professional fields. Eight psychologists independently attempted to code over 1,000 items describing commonplace daily activities in terms of a modified version of thirty-six of Murray's "needs" (6). Some 400 of these items were unanimously considered to be diagnostic of one or another of the elements of this personality taxonomy, and these were assembled into an Activities Index to which subjects could respond by indicating their like, dislike, or indifference for each activity.

This early form was given to groups of graduate students in physics, theology, and teacher training (5). Systematic differences were found in the needs pattern characterizing each of these groups, and between successful and unsuccessful students within each field. A modified version of this test was included in the present battery in order to throw light on personality characteristics associated with differences in performance on some of the other measures employed in the study. Specifically, it could be expected to yield information concerning personality differences between teachers who indicate initial acceptance and those who indicate initial rejection of the exceptional child, as well as differences between those who show considerable gain in modifying attitudes toward the exceptional child in contrast to those who show little change in attitude. Ultimately, these and related data could be employed in the derivation of a criterion measure for discriminating those teachers whose relations with exceptional children are extremely unlikely to prove adequate. Pre-test results with the *Activities Index* are described in the section which follows.

4. An experimental version of the *Activities Index* has been developed by the Board of Examinations of The University of Chicago in which each item has been reduced from a need-related *activity* to a need-related *adjective*. The ease of administration for this modified adjective check-list form suggested the possibility of requesting four sets of responses from each participating teacher: (a) self; (b) normal

child; (c) exceptional child; and (d) the effective teacher. Intercorrelating these various needs configurations would permit comparisons between the self-evaluation and the remaining three, contributing to our knowledge concerning the content of stereotyped projections of the normal and exceptional child, and the effective teacher.

Both the *Activities Index* and the *Adjective Checklist* were given to a group of fifty-three summer session students in Special Education. Although the two forms were found to be significantly related, beyond the .01 level, peculiar behavior for several of the adjective subscales indicated a need for substantial revision. No attempt to accomplish this was made at the time, although further work would seem to be clearly justified.

5. The previous discussion of needs configurations and patterns among teachers as revealed by the Activities Index implies a tacit recognition of discriminable teacher personality types. Several tentative models of such basic reaction types were elaborated during preliminary discussions. The motivational structures suggested here carry no implications concerning mental health or adjustment, or adequacy in fulfilling teaching commitments. They are intended to reflect only the dominant trend or intent, under which a wide range of other behaviors for each individual might be subsumed, including those of differential significance regarding probable relationships with exceptional children.

(a) The *security-minded teacher,* whose major concerns center around maintaining social status and financial security. Such individuals are likely to come from marginal lower-middle class backgrounds, seeing in teaching the opportunity to maintain status which had previously been in jeopardy.

(b) The *achievement-oriented teacher,* from an upwardly mobile background rather than one of downward mobility. In this case anxiety centers around acquiring new successes and wider recognition, and the risks taken will be commensurately greater than for the cautious and conservative security-minded teacher.

(c) The *narcissistic teacher* who sees in teaching an opportunity to give to children the affection and love which she considers to have been denied herself as a child. Thus, "giving children the breaks they deserve" involves seeing herself and her own problems in each of the children with whom she interacts. The narcissist may be predominantly nurturant in her orientation toward the child, giving support and affection freely to each projection of herself she teaches, regardless of their response. An alternative, however, may involve essential dependence upon the children themselves for a return in kind, giving only for the sake of receiving, and accordingly utilizing her pupils in an attempt to find personal gratifications which have not been obtained from other sources.

(d) The *dominant teacher* who establishes her own sense of value by achieving ascendant relationships over others. This may be reflected in persistent forays against superiors and authority figures, in attempts to dominate her peers, or in a close and exacting control over her pupils.

(e) The *technique-oriented teacher* who has sought refuge in technical skills or bureaucratic detail as a haven against the uncertainties and trauma of interpersonal relationships. The essential motive here is to erect and maintain an impersonal barrier of "know-how" behind which the teacher may legitimately function in isolation without being drawn into personal interactions.

Through the use of Q-sorting procedures (7) it is possible to construct a direct test of the tenability and significance of such types among a given sample of teachers. A lack of sufficient interview material prevented the development of such an instrument for these in the present study, but a pilot test along these lines is now being proposed.

Disguised — Nonstructured Devices. The instruments described above have developed roughly along a continuum of unconscious motivation, ranging from the highly cognitive and self-validating *Classroom Integration Inventory* to the more devious and less obvious devices intended to assess personality trends. Further extension of this development leads to the consideration of ambiguous, nonstructured materials which the respondent may organize spontaneously in accordance with his own needs.

The first projective device considered here was the Thematic Apperception Test (6), consisting of provocative pictures of adults and children in a variety of relationships which the subject is asked to describe and elaborate in the form of a story. Eight of the original TAT series were selected as being particularly relevant for the exploration of role and personality among teachers, and five additional pictures were developed which bear more directly upon orientation toward the exceptional child. In the section which follows, the individual pictures and the results of a pre-test of the Picture Judgment Test are described more fully.

Earlier studies of differences between representatives of various professional fields (5) have indicated that spontaneous drawings of the relevant work situation, *e.g.*, "a physicist at work in the laboratory," "a minister at work in the church," "a teacher at work in the classroom," etc., are of considerable importance in isolating the unique perceptions which each individual has of his role. This procedure, a modification of the Machover draw-a-person technique (8), was reluctantly abandoned in the present project in consideration of the demands already being made of the participating teachers.

PRE-TESTING PROCEDURES AND RESULTS

Several of the instruments described above were administered to a group of summer school students in Special Education. As a result of this pre-test, three were selected for inclusion in the battery to be used in measuring attitude change among the experimental groups of teachers participating in the workshop sessions. These three were (a) the Classroom Integration Inventory; (b) the Activities Index; and (c) the Picture Judgment Test.

The Classroom Integration Inventory was completed by 53 subjects, 71 returned the Activities Index (45 completed both tests), and ten students volunteered for one-hour individual sessions at which the projective pictures were administered. The results of the pre-test for each of the three instruments are described below.

It may prove helpful, in evaluating the results of the pre-tests, to keep certain characteristics of this student sample in mind. A brief open-end questionnaire was distributed among the group, consisting of five questions:

1. Describe your present position.
2. What kind of preparation did you have for it?
3. What got you started in this work?
4. Why did you enroll for summer session classes in Special Education?
5. Given unlimited opportunity, what would you like to achieve in the next ten years?

Approximately 49 per cent of the respondents proved to be already employed as special education teachers, working primarily with mentally retarded, orthopedic, or speech cases, although many other areas were also represented. Another 17 per cent were teaching normal children in elementary school classes, and 9 per cent claimed supervisory positions in public education. Thus, three-fourths of the group were already engaged in teaching activities, ranging in experience from one to twenty-seven years. The remaining 25 per cent consisted predominantly of full-time undergraduate students, with a small number of graduate students and nurses.

Although 50 per cent of the group had some normal school, teachers college, or liberal arts training, less than 10 per cent had a Master of

Arts degree, and only one individual in the group had the degree of Doctor of Education. Most of them reported that they were led to the field because of a personal interest in the handicapped, largely as a result of contact with a few isolated cases in the course of routine teaching. Roughly 25 per cent of the group, however, cited such pragmatic considerations as the fact that they needed a job, or were advised by a superintendent or principal to turn to their present assignment.

The utilitarian quality of this reply becomes clearer in the responses to the last two questions. The major reasons given for summer session enrollment involves obtaining credits for learning techniques; less than 4 per cent indicated that they considered it an opportunity to further more general educational objectives or as an enjoyable experience in itself. Their ultimate goals were similarly concrete, 60 per cent clearly specifying practical professional objectives such as developing their own programs, becoming a recognized consultant and specialist, or assuming administrative responsibilities. Thirty per cent specified educational achievement in obtaining their degree within the next ten years; the remaining 10 per cent cited marriage as their major objective for the decade.

The Classroom Integration Inventory (CII). In its original form the CII consisted of thirty items, each describing a deviate child in behavioral terms. An attempt was made to present a variety of problem cases involving emotional, intellectual, visual, auditory, and speech deficits. The fifty-three students drawn from the summer session in Special Education as respondents to the CII, nearly all of them teaching elementary school classes of their own during the balance of the year, were asked to mark each item in accordance with the following key:

A. If you feel you could handle such a student in your regular classroom without any *fundamental* change in your present procedures.
B. If you feel you could handle such a student in your regular classroom provided that advice from a specialist or consultant were occasionally made available to you whenever you felt a need for such aid in dealing with some particular problem.
C. If you feel you could handle such a student in your regular classroom provided that a full-time specialist were available at your school who could provide supplementary training for the student and frequent consultation with you.
D. If you feel that such a student would benefit most by being assigned to a special class or school.
E. If you feel that such a child cannot be handled profitably within the context of regular or special public education.

By assigning numerical weights to each alternative, varying from 5 for an A response to 1 for E, a score could be computed for the thirty items with a maximum of 150. These scores ranged from 72 to 136, and yielded a split-half reliability of .61, corrected. The highest scoring respondent accepted each item on the average at approximately level A (regular class) of the key above, the lowest respondent at level D (special class). The median respondent for this group accepted items on the average at level C (full-time assistance).

The individual items appear to fall into ten clusters, each of which is distributed among the five levels of the key in a peculiarly unique fashion. Table 1 indicates the distribution of choices for the items comprising each cluster.

Cluster 1. As indicated in Table 1, only two of the thirty deviate children described in the CII were considered immediately acceptable in the regular classroom (level A) by a significant proportion of respondents. These two were:

11. Alan wears a leg brace and walks with the aid of crutches; he gets along quite well by himself though, and ordinarily needs no help from anyone. ($M_e = 1.18$, $Q = .385$)

16. Betty is only a little over seven but she can read the fifth grade reader very well; however, her handwriting is poor and she is about average in most other things. ($M_e = 1.24$, $Q = .535$)

TABLE 1

Percentage of Respondents Selecting Each Category for the Ten Discriminable Clusters of Items on the Classroom Integration Inventory (N=53)

Cluster	No. of Items	Percentage in Each Category					Average Median[a]	Average Q[a]
		A	B	C	D	E		
1	2	70[b]	15	5	10	0	1.21	.460
2	4	53	18	6	21	1	1.48	.955
3	4	45	39	10	5	1	1.64	.604
4	1	19	68	13	0	0	1.96	.370
5	6	17	39	32	13	0	2.36	.688
6	3	29	18	15	36	1	2.52	1.242
7	4	7	30	19	44	1	3.16	.876
8	1	4	21	27	23	25	3.43	1.250
9	3	9	6	9	73	3	3.84	.548
10	2	5	10	6	49	31	4.15	.558

[a]In computing the medians (M_e) and interquartile range (Q), the following class intervals were employed: A = .5 ↔ 1.5, B = 1.5 ↔ 2.5, C = 2.5 ↔ 3.5, D = 3.5 ↔ 4.5, E = 4.5 ↔ 5.5.

[b]Cells containing high percentages in each cluster have been put in *italic type* for additional emphasis.

Cluster 2. Close behind these are four items which over half the group categorizes in A, but about which there is some ambivalence. A number of respondents held out for level D, the special class or building, as is reflected in the larger values of Q. In this group of items, it will be noted, appear the first signs of clear-cut physical involvement severe enough to affect the teacher as well as the pupil.

25. Generally speaking, Everett can control his bladder or bowel, although he is likely to have an occasional accident. ($M_e = 1.46$, $Q = .760$)

23. Chuck doesn't seem to catch on to things as quickly as most, and needs to have things explained over and over again; eventually, though, he appears to learn everything the others do even though it has taken longer. ($M_e = 1.68$, $Q = 1.020$)

8. Ben is unable to walk and has been confined to a wheelchair; he manages this very skillfully and needs very little help. ($M_e = 1.34$, $Q = .735$)

14. Debby cannot use bathroom facilities unless someone is there to help her; she is perfectly capable of making her needs known in ample time to avoid accidents. ($M_e = 1.43$, $Q = 1.305$)

Cluster 3. The four items appearing next are selected almost as frequently at level A as they are at level B. Although fewer respondents were ready to accept them without qualification in their present classrooms, many of these summer session students were willing to consider such pupils appropriate if part-time aid from a consultant was made available. Judging by the content of three of these items it seems likely that a number of the respondents were trying to say that they would really appreciate any part-time assistance they could get in such cases.

13. Cora is supposed to have a hearing loss, but she seems to hear all right when she sits at the right end of the front row of seats. ($M_e = 1.33$, $Q = .510$)

12. Bernard is a bully, given to teasing other children and provoking fights with them. ($M_e = 1.55$, $Q = .560$)

1. Alfred is defiant and stubborn, likely to argue with the teacher, be willfully disobedient, and otherwise interfere with normal classroom discipline. ($M_e = 1.81$, $Q = .625$)

6. Florence is a persistent talker and whisperer; she bursts into tears whenever she is reprimanded, however, and is immature and oversensitive in many other ways. ($M_e = 1.87$, $Q = .720$)

Cluster 4. The following item is analagous to the two cited in Cluster 1 with respect to the unanimity of response accorded to it. In this case, however, over two-thirds of the group concurred in considering it a problem which clearly requires part-time aid as specified under category B.

15. Albert does not pronounce all of his speech sounds correctly, but can be understood. ($M_e = 1.96$, $Q = .370$)

Cluster 5. The next six items were distributed somewhat uniformly between the B and C categories of the key. Almost three-fourths were ready to accept such children in their classrooms provided outside assistance was made available; they disagreed, however, on the amount of assistance considered necessary or desirable. The remaining four speech items are in this group (the only other item dealing with speech pathology was No. 15, just cited), as well as two behavior problems slightly more severe than items 12, 1 and 6 given previously in Cluster 3.

19. Occasionally Edward will repeat a sound 2 or 3 times before he seems able to go on; he speaks when called on, but does not volunteer much. ($M_e = 2.07$, $Q = .625$)

24. Doris is slow, absent-minded, and a daydreamer; she seems unusually quiet and withdrawn, avoids others, and is inhibited and restrained in her behavior. ($M_e = 2.21$, $Q = .780$)

17. Chester is deceitful, tells lies, and cheats in school and at play; he has been involved in several thefts, and is a persistent truant. ($M_e = 2.41$, $Q = .646$)

9. Clara has a noticeable scar on her upper lip; her speech seems to be coming through her nose, and she is hard to understand. ($M_e = 2.47$, $Q = .685$)

4. Donald is six years old and does not speak very much; what he does say is indistinct and childish, with many missing or incorrect sounds. ($M_e = 2.45$, $Q = .700$)

22. Bill has difficulty in starting to talk, grimaces and strains, and repeats sounds on about half the words he says in class. ($M_e = 2.58$, $Q = .690$)

Cluster 6. Following these in Table 1 are three items similar to the second cluster cited. Again the group splits between categories A and D, but this time the number of respondents willing to accept such pupils in their present classrooms has diminished considerably. Item 5 in this group has a somewhat higher median value than the other two; apparently this attempted description of a mentally-retarded child needs further revision.

5. Earl is eight and wears cowboy boots to class because he hasn't learned to tie his own shoe-laces; he hardly ever talks in class and doesn't really participate in anything except when he can paint or color things. ($M_e = 1.83$, $Q = 1.190$)

21. Arnold is an extremely bright nine year old who is far ahead of the rest of his class in most subjects; he spends a good deal of his time working on a mathematical system he calls "kinestatics." ($M_e = 2.79$, $Q = 1.265$)

28. Harold is a capable student but he has a physical defect which appears to evoke laughter, ridicule, avoidance and rejection from the other children. ($M_e = 2.94$, $Q = 1.272$)

Cluster 7. The respondents also disagree on the next four items. Although in these cases there is no longer much question that the children described are in need of assistance, the group polarizes between categories B and D. Roughly two-fifths of the respondents consider such pupils acceptable in their regular classroom providing some part-time assistance is available; an equal number of respondents consider the special classroom or school to be the only appropriate answer.

18. David squints through his eye-glasses, even when he sits at the front of the room. ($M_e = 2.72$, $Q = .950$)

7. Alice does not hear everything that is said in class, even though she wears a hearing aid; her voice sounds flat and hollow. ($M_e = 3.00$, $Q = .915$)

10. Dotty is eight; she has difficulty following the class, and doesn't seem able to learn to read at all. ($M_e = 3.32$, $Q = .815$)

2. Barbara wears thick glasses, and her eye-balls jerk spasmodically from side to side; she can't see the blackboard very well, and reads poorly. ($M_e = 3.61$, $Q = .825$)

Cluster 8. Item 29 stands alone among the entire group of 30 in showing such an extreme spread among the five placement alternatives that it was assigned to a cluster of its own. Equal numbers of respondents considered this one appropriate for levels B through E, from "part-time aid" to "keep out of public education." The one thing practically everyone agreed upon was that he couldn't be handled in a regular classroom unless some fundamental changes were made. Only two other items had Q values higher than this: items 14 (needs toilet help) and 21 (genius). In both these cases, however, the group was split between "no special aid required" and "special class only" (levels A and D) unlike the following item which the group seemed totally unprepared to categorize in any uniform fashion.

29. Irv is sexually precocious; masturbates in class, uses obscene language, and has made advances to several girls in his class. ($M_e = 3.43$, $Q = 1.250$)

Cluster 9. The following three items are uniformly coded by nearly three-fourths of the respondents for the special classroom or school. All three describe fairly severe organic involvements.

27. Greg tires easily and needs frequent opportunities to rest; excessive stimulation or excitement must also be avoided. ($M_e = 3.73$, $Q = 1.005$)

30. Jane can tell the direction from which the sunshine enters her classroom; she cannot read the letters in an ordinary book. ($M_e = 3.87$, $Q = .315$)

26. Fred can feel the vibrations of loud music from a radio or phonograph, knows when a door has been slammed, but does not hear speech unless it is shouted. ($M_e = 3.92$, $Q = .325$)

Cluster 10. Unlike the previous items in Cluster 9, the two which follow were coded on level E by a significant number of respondents. These both represent the borderline of acceptability in the public schools for this group, particularly item 20. It will be noted that these two describe cases which not only involve extensive physical damage, but also require some degree of active response from the teacher in connection with the disability. Nevertheless, almost half the group considered the special class or school capable of coping with such problems.

> 3. Chuck can get about only in a wheelchair; someone must move it for him, or carry him in their arms, because he is unable to control any of his limbs. ($M_e = 3.98$, $Q = .695$)
>
> 20. Flora has neither bladder nor bowl control and must be taken to the bathroom at frequent intervals. ($M_e = 4.32$, $Q = .695$)

To summarize these findings briefly, it might be noted that the most highly acceptable cases for the group of summer session students in Special Education were represented by items 11 (the boy on crutches) and 16 (the bright normal); the least acceptable were items 20 (the incontinent child) and 3 (cerebral palsy); the most variable response was given to item 29 (the sexual deviate).

Table 2 provides another viewpoint in considering these data by grouping the items in terms of the area of involvement suggested by the item content. Eight areas were covered in the original development of items. Four of the eight areas had at least one item with a median value placing it in the range of level A, indicating that over one-half the group had considered such a student to be integrable in a conventional class without entailing any change in basic procedures. No item in any area was considered to be unacceptable for public education by more than one-half of the respondents, although five of the eight areas had one or more items with median values in the range of level D, restricting such cases to the special class or school.

The most acceptable areas involved mental deviates and orthopedic problems; the least acceptable were concerned with sensory deficit, particularly visual, as well as two miscellaneous items describing a cardiac case and a child of markedly grotesque appearance. These latter two items were also the most widely dispersed among the five levels of the key ($\overline{Q} = 1.138$), apparently involving problems for which this group of respondents had no ready solution. The orthopedic cases, on the other hand, were rated quite consistently by all respondents ($\overline{Q} = .513$), suggesting this to be an area well covered in their training and experience. A similar degree of agreement exists in the case of the hearing problems ($\overline{Q} = .583$), and to only a slightly lesser degree in speech ($\overline{Q} = .614$.)

The relative lack of agreement concerning the mental deviates ($\overline{Q} = .965$) seems to raise a special problem. It will be noted that the five items attempted to describe behavior characteristic of children with approximate I.Q.'s of 40, 60, 80, 120, and 160, respectively. As

Table 2 indicates, the bright normal was considered more immediately acceptable than the moron, who was in turn considered to require less assistance than either the genius or the imbecile. The rating of the supposed idiot is misplaced, however, being grouped with the moron under part-time aid whereas the genius and the imbecile drop down to full-time assistance. Apparently, as was noted before, item 5 describing an idiot was somewhat misleading. The respondents appear to have had some difficulty in scaling the mentally retarded children solely on the basis of behavioral cues.

As a result of these findings, several items were revised and the test doubled in length. The final form adopted for the study (see Appendix A) covers ten areas of exceptionality, each composed of six items representing two slight, two moderate, and two severe examples of impairment in the area. The ten areas are (a) Behavior Disorders, (b) Emotional Disturbances, (c) Impaired Hearing, (d) Impaired Speech, (e) Retarded and Superior Intellectual Ability, (f) Orthopedic and Cardiac Disorders, (g) Physical Attractiveness, (h) Seizures, (i) Bowel and Bladder Incontinence, and (j) Visual Handicaps.

An example of items for each level of impairment in the area of visual handicaps would be:

2. Barbara wears thick glasses, and her eye-balls jerk spasmodically from side to side; she can't see the blackboard very well, and reads poorly.

36. Virginia rubs and blinks her eyes occasionally when reading, and seems to find it difficult to distinguish between certain letters of the alphabet.

51. John has no difficulty on the playground or at the blackboard but he gets quite uncomfortable when he has to use his eyes at close range for any length of time.

Two methods of scoring the CII were employed. The *acceptance* score was found by weighting response alternative *A* as *4*, *B* as *3*, *C* as *2*, *D* as *1* and *E* as *0*, giving a maximum possible range of scores from 0 to 240. Thus, *A* (if you feel you could handle such a student in your regular classroom without any fundamental change in your present procedures) was considered to be the most accepting response irrespective of the nature of the handicaps, and *E* (if you feel that such a child cannot be handled profitably within the context of regular or special public education) was considered the least accepting. This procedure yielded a split half-reliability of .84 (corrected), as compared with .61 for the original pilot version.

In computing the *realism score*, five specialists in the area of exceptional children were asked to judge each item with reference to the most *realistic placement* of the case described in the item. The judges

TABLE 2

Distribution of Items Within Each Area of Pathological Involvement Among the Categorical Levels of Acceptance

Scale Category	Area of Involvement							
	Intelligence	Orthopedic	Behavior	Speech	Sphincter Control	Audition	Miscellaneous	Vision
A ($M_e = .5 – 1.5$) "Regular Classroom"	16—IQ 120	11—Crutches 8—Wheelchair, Self-Propelled			25—Occasional Accident 14—Limited Control	13—Seating Correction		
B ($M_e = 1.5 – 2.5$) "Part-time Aid"	23—IQ 80 5—IQ 40		12—Bully 1—Disobedient 6—Tearful 24—Schizoid 17—Delinquent	15—Articulation, Mild 19—Mild Stutter 9—Cleft Palate 4—Articulation, Severe				

TABLE 2 (*continued*)

Scale Category	Area of Involvement							
	Intelligence	Orthopedic	Behavior	Speech	Sphincter Control	Audition	Miscellaneous	Vision
C ($M_e = 2.5 - 3.5$) "Full-time Aid"	21—IQ 160 10—IQ 60		29—Sex Deviate	22—Severe Stuttering		7—Limited Correction	28—Grotesque Appearance	18—Squint
D ($M_e = 2.5 - 3.5$) "Special Class"		3—Cerebral palsy			20—Incontinent	26—Deaf	27—Cardiac	2—Nystagmus 30—Blind
No. Items	5	3	6	5	3	3	2	3
Av. Item M_e	2.17	2.17	2.21	2.31	2.40	2.75	3.34	3.40
Av. Item Q	.965	.513	.763	.614	.920	.583	1.138	.697

were asked to rank their five choices of placement giving their first, second, third, fourth, and fifth choices on each of the 60 items. The five specialists judged all of the items independently and their percentage of agreement was computed. Among the judges' choices for placement, 71 percent agreement was found. The judges were then asked to meet together and reach common agreement on the five choices of placement of the 60 items. The teachers' *realism scores* were then found by assigning the values of 4 if their choice on the item was the same as the judges' first choice, a value of 3, if their choice was the same as the judges' second choice, a value of 2, if their choice was the same as the judges' third choice, and so forth. As an example, if a teacher chose B and the judges selected B as their second choice the teacher would receive 3 points for that item.

The Activities Index (AI). The Activities Index is a disguised-structured technique for personality evaluation consisting of 300 commonplace activities. The subject is requested to respond to each item as to whether he likes or dislikes the activity mentioned. The activities included in the AI are based upon a modified version of Murray's "needs" (6).

The activities are divided into thirty-two subscales. Nine of the subscales involve interpersonal relationships. Three of these describe the direction of interaction with others, *i.e.,* affiliation, rejection, or narcissim. Six involve characteristic mechanisms employed in coping with this interaction, such as succorance, nurturance, dominance, deference, abasement, etc. Twenty-three subscales are concerned with measures of an intrapersonal nature. Seven of these describe inner state characteristics, *i.e.,* energy level, achievement, ego ideal, sex, sentience, etc. Nine measure the sources of control utilized in inhibiting, denying or sublimating such impulses, and the remaining seven involve cathective processes.

There are ten items or activities for each of thirty dimensions, the remaining two being composites of other subscales. Definitions of the thirty-two dimensions are:[1]

1. *Reactions to Others.* Direction of process of interaction with others.
    1.1 Affiliation
        Positive association with other persons, either peers or authority figures, valued as an activity involving friendly recip-

---

[1]Adapted with permission of the copyright owners, from Stern, G. G., Stein, M. I., and Bloom, B. S. *Methods in Personality Assessment,* Glencoe, Ill.: Free Press, 1956, pp. 70-73.

rocal interaction with others. Ex. Going on a vacation to a place where there are lots of people.

1.2 Rejection

Disassociation from other persons, either specifically or in general, limiting opportunities for interaction with others. Computed: $20 - \dfrac{(affiliation + nurturance)}{2}$

1.3 Narcissism

Preoccupation with self. Ex. Having people ask me about myself.

2. *Coping Mechanisms.* Characteristics of process of interaction with others.

2.1 Nurturance

Supporting others by providing love, assistance, and protection. Ex. Giving my time and energy to someone who's in need of help.

2.2 Succorance-Autonomy

(Suc) — Helplessness; infantile dependence upon others for love, assistance, and protection. Ex. Knowing an older person to whom I can go for sympathy and guidance.

(Aut) — Self-sustained; independent and unfettered. Ex. living on my own away from home.

2.3 Dominance

Achieving assertive, autocratic ascendency over others. Ex. Winning out over someone else in a competition.

2.4 Deference

Sycophantic submission to the opinion or preference of another; emphasis on the glorification of another who is perceived as superior. Ex. Being useful to someone I admire and respect.

2.5 Abasement

Self-depreciation; mortifying, mutilating, or otherwise devaluing the self. Ex. Suffering for a good cause or for someone I love.

2.6 Aggression-Blamavoidance

(Agg) — Hostility toward others, overt or covert, in fact or in fantasy. Ex. Picking a fight when I'm in the mood.

(Bla) — Denial of feelings of hostility in order to avoid criticism or disapproval. Ex. Being a model of restraint, patience and self control.

3. *Inner States.* Characteristic drives, feelings, and sensations.
    3.1 Energy-Psychasthenia
        (Eny) — Liberation of affective or effective tension; sustained effort. Ex. Staying up all night if necessary to work at something which interests me.
        (Psy) — Inability to liberate affective or effective tension; lack of sustained effort. Ex. Getting to bed early in order to have lots of sleep and rest.
    3.2 Achievement
        The drive for success, accomplishment and recognition; surmounting obstacles (physical, personal, and interpersonal) in order to achieve success. Ex. Setting difficult goals for myself.
    3.3 Ego Ideal
        Fantasied achievement. Ex. Reading about the lives of great people.
    3.4 Sex-Superego Conflict
        (Sex) — Erotic interest or expression. Ex. Learning more about sex.
        (SC) — Rejection of erotic interest or expression. Ex. (Dislike) Being with girls who are dressed in revealing or provocative clothes.
    3.5 Sentience
        Sensuous or voluptuous self-gratification. Ex. Running something very soft against my skin.
    3.6 Exhibition
        Self-display. Ex. Being the center of attention at a party.
    3.7 Play
        Valuing of amusement and entertainment. Ex. Getting as much fun as I can out of life even if it means sometimes neglecting more serious things.

4. *Impulse Control.* Regulatory processes controlling inner states.
    4.1 Harmavoidance
        Avoidance, withdrawal, or protection from situations which might result in physical pain, injury, illness or death. Ex. Selecting foods carefully for their health-giving, nutritive qualities.
    4.2 Infavoidance
        Avoidance, withdrawal, or protection from situations which might result in frustration, failure, humiliation, or embarrassment. Computed: $20 - \dfrac{(exhibition + counteraction)}{2}$

4.3 Adaptiveness
Acceptance of criticism, control, frustration, or humiliation.
Ex. Admitting when I'm in the wrong.

4.4 Counteraction
Restriving in order to overcome experienced frustration,
failure, or humiliation. Ex. Working twice as hard to make
up for a failure.

4.5 Order
Organization of immediate environment; preoccupation with
cleanliness, neatness, orderliness, arrangement, collecting, detailed precision. Ex. Keeping my bureau drawers and desk in
perfect order.

4.6 Conjunctivity-Disjunctivity
(Cnj) — Purposeful coordination, organization and integration of specific activities as well as broader goals. Ex. Planning my reading and outlining a reading program for myself.
(Dsj) — Confused, uncoordinated, disorganized, diffuse, or
conflicted activity. Ex. Going from one activity to another
according to my mood, without bothering to organize or plan
things.

4.7 Change-Sameness
(Cha) — Plastic, unroutinized, labile, changeable behavior.
Ex. Being quite changeable in my likes and dislikes.
(Sam) — Fixated, repetitive, perseverative behavior. Ex. Being
generally consistent and unchanging in my behavior.

4.8 Impulsion-Deliberation
(Imp) — Impulsive, spontaneous, unreflected behavior. Ex.
Acting impulsively just to blow off steam.
(Del) — Hesitant, cautious, deliberative behavior. Ex. Think-
ing carefully before speaking.

4.9 Emotionality-Placidity
(Emo) — Mobile, active, expressive, intense emotional responsiveness. Ex. Being unrestrained and open about my
feelings and emotions.
(Pla) — Passive, phlegmatic, restrained emotional responsiveness. Ex. Doing things leisurely without excitement or tension.

5. *Cathective Processes.* Fundamental orientation; life style; intellectual and cognitive processes.
  5.1 Exocathection-Extraception
  The manipulation of external objects (physical or interpersonal) through practical, concrete, physical or social action;

adaptation to reality "as given" for more-or-less immediately tangible ends. Ex. Achieving wealth and social prestige through success in practical affairs.

5.2 Exocathection-Intraception

Dramatic, idealistic social action; active modification of reality to conform to private value system; expression of ideals in concrete action. Ex. Taking an active part in social or political reform.

5.3 Endocathection-Extraception: Natural Sciences

The manipulation of external objects through speculative abstract thought or discussion, relative to the area of the natural sciences; reflection and discussion about events or systems; data collection and empirical analysis. Ex. Reading scientific theories about the origin of the earth and other planets.

5.4 Endocathection-Extraception: Social Sciences

The manipulation of external objects through speculative abstract thought or discussion, relative to the area of the social sciences; reflection and discussion about events or systems; data collection and empirical analysis. Ex. Hearing lectures or radio talks on political and social problems.

5.5 Endocathection-Intraception

Preoccupation with private experience; psychological, spiritual, esthetic, or metaphysical truth; introspection and logical synthesis. Ex. Seeking solutions to inner conflicts, moral problems and spiritual dilemmas.

5.6 Understanding

Disinterested intellectualization; analysis, abstraction, synthesis for the sake of conceptualization rather than action. Ex. Living a life of contemplation and study.

5.7 Objectivity

Rejection of autistic fantasy and egocentric perception; absence of animistic, anthropomorphic, mystical, or superstitious thought. Ex. (Dislike) Making up little games or schemes that will bring luck if they come out right.

Previous administrations of earlier forms of the Activities Index to graduate students in physics, teacher-training, and a liberal Protestant theological school, yielded a number of interesting findings (5). All three of these groups at the University of Chicago were found to have common interests in activities involving coordinated, organized, or integrated action on specific problems as well as long-term goals. They were also alike in their concern for theoretical speculation involving both abstract psychological, spiritual, esthetic, or metaphysical truth, and more concrete reflection and discussion related to contemporary social events and systems.

These common attributes of the three groups of Chicago graduate students did not obscure further differentiation more closely related to their specific professional fields of training. Teachers and theologians, in marked contrast to the physicists, emphasized activities involving mature interrelationships with other people. For the teachers this concern with interpersonal activities was coupled with an interest in providing nurturant support for others. The theologians, however, seemed more dependent or succorant on a personal level; their interest in others was also organized in terms of idealistic social action, involving more impersonal attempts to instill a private value-system or ethic in the lives of others.

The physicists resemble neither of these groups in this matter, being concerned predominantly with intellectual activities rather than with relations to people. A high degree of energy is indicated, expended in connection with analytic and inductive interests involving physical (and social) phenomena. In some respects the theologians share this interest in abstract and theoretical matters, although this is restricted to social and cultural issues in their case. The physicists also share some of the theologians' personal introspectiveness, a characteristic not present in the teachers to the same degree.

The sample of summer session students in Special Education at Syracuse University proved most like the teacher-trainees studied previously, in their performance on the AI. The most extreme scores center in interpersonal relations. They appear to be an especially warm and friendly group, eager to interact with others, particularly in relationships which afford them opportunities to provide love, assistance, support, or protection for others. They also seek to receive such succor in return, although to a somewhat lesser degree, suggesting a fairly literal acceptance of the implications of the Golden Rule.

In order to maintain such relationships they exercise close control over the expression of hostility or aggression, being concerned lest they incur the criticism or disapproval of others. Anxieties concerning the avoidance of blame extend to their relationships with superiors, toward whom they are deferent and humble. They are not excessive in their self-depreciation, however, and are comfortably acceptant of impulses involving erotic interest or self-gratification.

Unlike their Chicago counterparts there are apparently no strong needs for achievement or mastery, nor are there signs of any particularly cohesive value-orientation characteristic of the group as a whole. Although the Syracuse students lack markedly intellectual or abstractive interests, they strive for coordinated and purposeful behavior, organizing and integrating specific activities as well as broader goals. Like graduate students elsewhere, they are oriented toward the counteracting of failure, and will persist in their attempts to overcome experienced frustrations by frontal assault rather than by concealment, avoidance, or withdrawal. Of particular interest is the relatively high score on harmavoidance for the Special Education students, verging on statistical significance. A high group score in this area is unusual, and reveals a preoccupation with threats of physical pain, injury, illness or death.

These generalizations are based on inferences from the pattern of the subscales on which each group had achieved statistically significant scores. Subjective analyses of Rorschach and TAT protocols for the Chicago subjects paralleled the findings of the AI. Furthermore, analyses of items in the relevant keys of the Strong Vocational Interest Inventory reveal configurations which are closely related to those described above. In an unpublished study by Lane, the AI patterns obtained from teacher-trainees, physics, and theological students were found to parallel in their most important aspects the elements isolated empirically by Strong. The Strong does not appear to cover the full range of needs adequately, however, having an overabundance of items of equivalent diagnostic significance and being completely deficient in the representation of other needs areas. A more systematic coverage, such as is offered by the AI, seems likely to prove of even greater diagnostic and predictive value than has been achieved heretofore.

The version of the Activities Index adopted for use with the workshop was the first of two revisions designed to facilitate quantitative analysis. An unpublished cluster analysis by Van Buskirk, necessarily crude because of the limitations of the early Index form on which it was based, revealed nine interrelated clusters. These may be seen as the segments labeled 1A, 1B . . . 4A, going counterclockwise in the next to outermost ring of the circle in Figure 1. The needs subscales represented in each cluster are shown as wedges written on each of these segments. It will be noted that, in each case, there are two subscales which correlate with their own cluster as well as with the respective adjacent clusters. Thus, the nine clusters can only be laid out in the continuous circular fashion shown in Figure 1 since the overlap be-

FIG. I

ACTIVITIES INDEX
FORM 156

DIAGNOSTIC SUMMARY

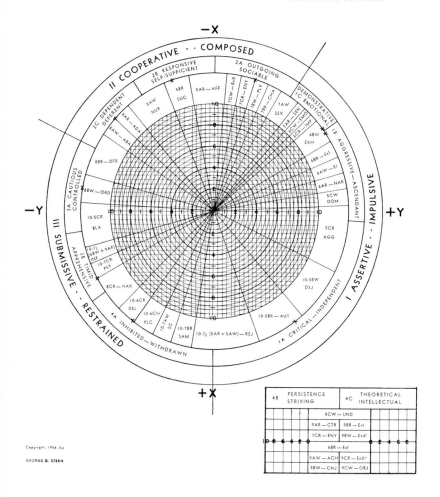

4B	PERSISTENCE STRIVING		4C	THEORETICAL INTELLECTUAL	
		8CW — UND			
		9AR — CTR	9BR — EnI		
		7CR — ENY	9BW — EnX·		
		6BR — ExI			
		9AW — ACH	9CR — EnX·		
		5BW — CNJ	9CW — OBJ		

tween them permits no other arrangement. This appears to represent a unique empirical demonstration of the hypothetical circumplex suggested by Guttman (9).

The psychological significance of these empirical clusters will become apparent if the circle is examined in detail, starting at the bottom with *REJ* (Rejection) and moving in a counterclockwise direction. Cluster 1A will be seen to consist of four needs subscales: rejection, autonomy, disjunctivity, and aggression. The overlap of rejection with cluster 4A, and of aggression with 1B should be noted. This first group of needs seems to refer to a hostile, critical, independent mode of behavior, and is thus labeled 1A Critical-Independent. The next cluster, 1B, contains needs subscales aggression, dominance, narcissism, ego ideal, exocathection-intraception, and exhibition, the latter overlapping with cluster 1C. The 1B cluster is labeled Aggressive-Ascendant, insofar as it appears to reflect a highly self-centered, domineering mode of behavior which is less isolated and less critical than 1A. Cluster 1C continues with exhibitionism, impulsion, emotionality, sentience and sex — self-centered by implication, but less concerned with ascendance than with personal impulse-expression.

These appear to be the first three steps of an interpersonal continuum which proceeds through the next three clusters, identifiable as outgoing and deferent variants on the social prototype found in 2B at the top of the circle, and culminates with three increasingly submissive and restrained patterns. The last of these, 4A, appears to represent a withdrawn isolate at the opposite extreme from the aggressive isolate with which we began in 1A. These two clusters share the rejection subscale, thus closing the circle. The Index has seemingly yielded a continuous interpersonal space, reflecting personality trends in terms of a continuum ranging from extreme inhibition and withdrawal through increasing degrees of socially responsive behavior, terminating in uncontrolled aggression against others.

The three broader categories implied here have no statistical justification but do provide an interesting correspondence between this descriptive continuum and Horney's theorizing regarding directional characteristics of personality: movements against, toward, or away from interpersonal contacts.

All of the clusters within the circle are co-planar, which means that cluster scores may be combined, averaged and represented by vectors on polar coordinates. An over-all resultant for the entire 360° profile may be readily calculated, and group comparisons can be made for such vectors by means of Hotelling's t (10, 11) or Tukey's generalization of the analysis of variance (12, 13). Although such single resultants are of little descriptive value, as contrasted with the wealth of diagnostic material which may be derived from a qualitative analysis of the subscale configuration, they do provide a quantitative summary of the subjective pattern which is susceptible to statistical analysis.

The current form may be scored by either hand or machine. Besides being more accessible to quantitative manipulation than such tests as the Strong or the Kuder, the Activities Index provides a more immediately meaningful over-all pattern and a highly detailed elaboration of that pattern when broken down into its individual needs components. Reliabilities of the thirty-two subscales, based on the tetrachoric correlation between the pre-scores and post-scores for the teachers over the thirty-week workshop period, ranged from .47 to .93 with a median of .70. This is surprisingly high, considering the brevity of the scales (10 items each), the length of time intervening, and the nature of the interspersed workshop experience.

The Picture Judgment Test (PJT). Two interests were paramount behind the development of a set of projective pictures. On the one hand, the pictures were to evoke responses relevant to role and personality among teachers in general. At the same time, however, it was considered desirable to elicit responses which would be more specifically related to the subject's feelings about exceptional children.

Unfortunately, available pictures of exceptional children seemed restricted to a portrayal of the mere *fact* of handicap alone. The types of response elicited by such materials are analogous to the reactions one might obtain by asking for free associations to the sight of a crutch, artificial leg, or hearing aid. The limitations of such an approach have been amply demonstrated by Cruickshank and his associates (14, 15, 16). Although determining the feelings of an exceptional child, or those of his parents, toward the disabling condition in the abstract may be useful for certain purposes, in the case of the teachers who may be called upon to deal with exceptional children the important issue would appear to lie in their reactions to the deviate *within a social and interpersonal context,* rather than in isolation. In order to properly assess these feelings an adequate projective picture must present several competing stimuli, physical disability as such being only one of several factors requiring resolution on the part of the respondent. Such pictures would permit the subject to demonstrate the extent to which he is specifically sensitive to the exceptional child, whether this dominates his reaction to the situation, is subordinated to other interests, or is completely withheld from the thematic content.

Five pictures were developed to meet these requirements, four of them reflecting these criteria implicitly, and the fifth deliberately negating them. Professor Carl G. Roters, School of Art, Syracuse University, is to be credited for the skill and artistry with which he transformed crude verbal specifications into the graphic portrayals which have been reproduced in Appendix A.

Card 1 shows a heterogeneous group of children arranged about a young woman playing the piano. One of the children has been drawn so as to suggest a working-class background, another is a negro, the third is apparently middle class, and the fourth represents a case of divergent strabismus. Three of the children are evidently enjoying themselves, while the middle-class girl and the adult have pensive expressions.

Card 2 shows a woman in the foreground, holding a broom and gazing thoughtfully into space. Behind her a young girl with a brace on one leg stands at the foot of a flight of stairs, one hand on the newel post, her head inclined upwards.

Card 3 shows a boy and girl engaged in conflict. The boy holds a crutch in the air, and one leg is deformed; the girl is seated behind a worktable with no apparent disability. An overturned chair, and their expressions and posture, suggest tension. In the background stands an adult, looking back at the children as she leaves the room.

Card 4 portrays a severely crippled girl standing with the aid of two crutches and with braces on both legs, one of which is markedly shorter than the other. The child's expression makes an explicit appeal for sympathy.

Card 5 is a picture of a young boy pulling a cat by the tail and apparently enjoying the cat's discomfiture. He wears an unobtrusive hearing aid. In the room behind him stands a woman with her arm around a young girl, both with their backs to the boy in the foreground. Next to him, on a table, are a man's hat and gloves.

The preliminary work-sketches of these situations were administered to ten summer session subjects, along with the following eight standard TAT pictures:

2   Country scene: in the foreground is a young woman with books in her hand; in the background a man is working in the fields and an older woman is looking on.

6GF   A young woman sitting on the edge of a sofa looks back over her shoulder at an older man with a pipe in his mouth who seems to be addressing her.

9GF   A young woman with a magazine and a purse in her hand looks from behind a tree at another young woman in a party dress running along the beach.

3GF   A young woman is standing with downcast head, her face covered with her right hand. Her left arm is stretched forward against a wooden door.

5   A middle-aged woman is standing on the threshold of a half-opened door looking into a room.

13MF A young man is standing with his head buried in his arms. Behind him is a figure of a half-nude woman lying in bed.

8GF   A young woman sits with her chin in her hand, looking off into space.

7GF   An older woman is sitting on a sofa close beside a girl, speaking or reading to her. The girl, who holds a doll in her lap, is looking away.

The ten subjects who contributed fantasy materials in response to this series yielded an encouraging range of themas related to empathy, understanding, emotional acceptance, overidentification, and stereotyping of the exceptional child, as well as with respect to achievement, autonomy, anxiety, guilt, dependence, nurturance, defensiveness, sex role, etc. All ten showed a marked concern with interpersonal relations, and are sensitive to social approval or criticism. The ten differ markedly, however, in their orientation to a number of things, including nurturant relationships with others. Contraindications concerning potentiality for graduate school performance are marked in two cases characterized by passivity, low energy, and lack of motivation for achievement. The remaining eight show varying capacities for nurturance, based on a variety of emotional complexes. Three are involved in oedipal relationships which appear to place them in league with children against parents!

Inasmuch as no other information was obtained for these ten subjects, a more extensive analysis of their records would be of little value. The major purpose of the present administration of the TAT material was to obtain a measure of the variability of responses to the selected stimulus materials.

The results of this pre-testing suggested a number of minor modifications in each of the five experimental pictures. The five pictures of handicapped children and the eight TAT cards were made up into slides which were presented to the teachers by projection onto a screen. The subjects were asked to tell a story about each picture. They were instructed to write about what is happening in the picture, what has happened and what will probably happen in the future. It was suggested that they allow their minds to wander freely and write anything that came to them. A five-minute time limit was allowed on each card.

The resulting Picture Judgment protocols were scored on a five-point scale, sentence by sentence, on the basis of the following criteria:

$N = -1$ if it is probably more negative than the structure of the card would indicate, *e.g.* "This gal has given up and is completely defeated which is caused by a failure in herself."

$Dn = -\frac{1}{2}$ if it is descriptive with a negative judgment, *e.g.*, "The girl has done something which she appears to be scared about." Or, "The lady has a very worried and serious expression on her face."

$D = 0$ if it is purely descriptive without evidence of judgment, *e.g.*, "The lady is sitting in a chair looking into space." Or, "The boy is pulling the cat's tail."

$Dp = \frac{1}{2}$ if it is descriptive with a positive judgment, *e.g.*, "The colored boy appears to be the happiest." "The children are being entertained as well as learning from the music teacher."

$P = 1$ if it is decidedly positive regardless of the structure of the card, *e.g.,* "She has a happy outlook on life and a great deal of determination." "He will win approval from his mother and friends."

The scale values were weighted as follows:
$N = -1, Dn = -\frac{1}{2}, D = O, Dp = \frac{1}{2}, P = 1.$

There were some sentences in which both positive and negative attitudes were expressed. In this case, if the overtones of the total sentence seemed to be more negative than positive, it was scored *Dn, e.g.,* "She is depressed and the outlook is not bright unless the wrong done at this time can be righted." If the overtones of the sentence seemed to be more positive than negative it was scored *Dp, e.g.,* "The situation will turn out happily for all concerned unless something unforeseen happens." Or, "She will lead a productive, happy life, unless something occurs to prevent it."

A good many general attitudes were expressed by the teachers toward their role and toward the role of handicapped children. These were categorized as positive and negative by utilizing the following criteria:

POSITIVE	NEGATIVE
Attitude of adult to child	
acceptance	rejection
empathy	pity
effective guidance	extreme punitiveness
approval	disapproval
development of healthy independence	overprotection
giving pleasure	preventing pleasure ·
understanding	resentment
Attitude of child to adult	
self-sufficiency	extreme dependency
healthy acceptance of authority and adjustment to authority	undue rebellion against authority
Reaction to frustration	
constructive planning	withdrawal
effective action	hostile aggression
Solution to conflict or reaction to unfavorable environment	
counteraction	flight or perseveration
Treatment of sexual thema	
love	guilt
tenderness	hostile aggressiveness
General	
active participation in activities with enjoyment	lack of enjoyment in activities
self-actualization	self-destruction

The responses on the "normal" (TAT) cards and the "handicapped" (Picture) cards were totaled separately and the total score was found by summing the responses on the "normal" and the "handicapped" cards. Because some of the teachers were more verbal than others a ratio had to be found so that the number of positive and negative scores would be meaningful. This ratio was found by subtracting the negative responses (N and Dn) from the positive responses (P and Dp) and dividing by the number of responses given on the respective "normal" or "handicapped" cards. The total ratio of responses was found similarly by subtracting the total number of negative responses from the total number of positive responses and dividing by the total number of responses.

In order to determine reliability of these scores, three trained judges were asked to rate ten of the protocols from the Picture Judgment Test. The percentage of agreement with the one scorer who examined all of the protocols was determined by pooling Dn and N responses and Dp and P responses, leaving the final ratings to consist of a three-point scale which were N, D, and P. As an example, if a judge rated a sentence as Dn and the scorer rated the sentence as N, this was not considered to be a disagreement; however, if a judge rated a sentence as D and the scorer rated it as Dn, this was considered a disagreement. In this manner the number of agreements between each judge and the scorer on each of the ten protocols was converted into a percentage of total responses per protocol; the average agreement between the three judges and the scorer was found to be 76 per cent. The Ohlsen and Schulz study (17) reported 80 per cent agreement between judges in rating TAT responses. The 76 per cent agreement in the present study seemed sufficiently high to justify accepting the remaining protocols prepared by the one scorer alone.

The agreement in scoring the same Picture Judgment Test protocols by the same judge was computed eight months after the original scoring. Ten protocols were selected randomly from the total number of tests and rescored eight months later without the judge having any knowledge of the first scores. The average agreement between the second and first rating of ten protocols was 92.7 per cent. The average disagreement was only 7.3 per cent.

In addition, matched-pair t tests were performed to determine whether there were significant differences between the normal, handicapped and total scores of the first rating and the second rating. None of the t's was found to be significant.

EVALUATION INSTRUMENTS: FINAL CONSIDERATIONS

The three pre-tested instruments described in the preceding section, the Classroom Integration Inventory, the Activities Index, and the Picture Judgment Test, were given to the teachers in the first and last sessions of the workshop experience. A fourth instrument, the General Information Inventory, was also included with these three, while the Critical Incident Test was given in the last session only. Throughout the testing process the teacher's anonymity was preserved through the use of a code name employed on both the pre-tests and post-tests, and known only to the individual teacher.

The General Information Inventory (GII). Insofar as accurate information would appear basic to understanding and acceptance of the exceptional child, it was believed necessary that an assessment be made to determine any increase in information gained by the teachers as a result of the workshop. The General Information Inventory (see Appendix A) was constructed to measure specific information concerning the exceptional child in the following areas of handicap:

1. Mental Retardation
2. Speech Impairment
3. Acoustical Handicap
4. Visual Handicap
5. Orthopedic Handicap
6. Emotional Disturbance
7. Intellectual Exceptionality

The General Information Inventory contains 100 items covering these seven areas of deviation. The first 97 items are multiple choice and the last three items are essay type questions. One point is scored for each correct response, giving a range of possible scores from 0 to 100. The questions include many of the popular misconceptions of the intellectual, physical, emotional and social nature of exceptional children. Two examples of the items follow:

79. The blind (a) have superior sensory acuity, (b) pay attention to auditory cues more than do seeing peoples, (c) develop a sixth sense, (d) have markedly superior musical ability.

87. From personality studies of the gifted, we find (a) they are better adjusted than most children, (b) they have an abnormally large number of fears, (c) they are more apt to become psychotic, (d) they adjust poorly to social conditions.

The Critical Incident Test. The four instruments thus far described make it possible to measure objectively changes in information, acceptance, attitudes and personality which presumably occurred as a result of the workshop experience in which the teachers participated. To determine whether or not the teachers actually used the information, understanding and insights about exceptional children which they gained from the workshop is another problem. Since continuous access to the classrooms was not possible, the Critical Incident technique seemed to be among the few methods which could be used to validate the findings on the General Information Inventory and the Classroom Integration Inventory. The Critical Incident is a straight-forward technique which asked the subject to cite any way in which a certain experience had influenced his behavior. Specifically, the teachers were asked to describe in detail the things they did differently as a result of the understanding they had gained from the workshop.

The treatment of this data once it had been collected was somewhat more complex. In this instance the responses of the teachers were divided into the kinds of exceptional children mentioned, *i.e.*, critical incidents reported in connection with children with speech and hearing disorders, gifted children, emotionally disturbed children, and so forth. The critical incidents were then divided into two kinds of response categories under each main area of deviation. These two categories were:

1. general attitudes and behavior, and
2. specific attitudes and behavior.

A response such as "recognize children's difficulty more readily" would be classified under general attitudes, whereas "remembered such little things as 'wait for the stutterer to finish,'" was considered an example of specific attitude. One additional area was set up to handle general responses which could not be categorized in any of the areas of deviation, such as "I feel that certain attitudes and techniques on my part have changed which could be noted if I were presented with further opportunity to put the attitude into practice."

Having categorized the responses in this manner, the frequency of the type of responses for each division of exceptional children was totaled. The total number, then, was the frequency of instances of change rather than the length of the reports or the quality of the incident.

An example of how this was done is as follows:

As a result of Dr. Amster's lectures on those with speech and hearing difficulties, I was more acutely conscious of my method, manner, and functioning in both areas. I also recognized children's difficulties more readily and remembered such little things as "wait for the stutterer to finish" or "not to put words in a child's mouth," etc. Those with emotional disturbances revealed memories of working with such a group and the techniques I used, and I've found certain attitudes and techniques would be changed now if I were ever presented a further opportunity. With respect to the gifted child, I've realized that I haven't used their full potential in giving them leadership responsibilities or in recognition of their needs and I'm attempting to change that.

This response may be divided into three main areas of deviation *i.e.*, speech and hearing, emotional disturbances, and gifted. Under speech and hearing, there are two general incidents and two specific incidents, *i.e.*, "I was more acutely conscious of my method, manner, and functioning in both areas," and "I also recognized children's difficulties more readily . . ." The two specific responses are: "remembered such little things as 'wait for the stutterer to finish' and 'not to put the words in a child's mouth.'" One general incident is given in the area of emotional disturbances, *i.e.*, "I've found that certain attitudes and techniques would be changed now if I were ever presented a further opportunity." In the area of the gifted child, one general incident may be found, *i.e.*, "I've realized that I haven't used their full potential in giving them leadership responsibilities or in recognition of their needs and I'm attempting to change that." In this example, then, there are four general incidents and two specific incidents.

SUMMARY

This chapter has described the experimental design and procedures utilized in the study of teachers' attitudes toward exceptional children and their modifications. The characteristics of the participating schools, the organization of the workshop, and the development of the battery of instruments for measuring change, have been discussed in detail. Copies of the five tests are to be found in Appendix A.

REFERENCES

1. Campbell, D. T., "The Indirect Assessment of Social Attitudes," *Psychological Bulletin*, XLVII (1950), 1, 15-38.
2. Likert, Rennis, "A Technique for the Measurement of Attitudes," *Archives of Psychology*, XXII (1932), 5-43.
3. Hammond, K. R., "Measuring Attitudes by Error-choices and Indirect Method," *Journal of Abnormal and Social Psychology*, XLIII (1948), 38-48.
4. Rose, A., *Studies in Reduction of Prejudice*, Chicago: American Council on Race Relations, 1948.

5. Stern, G. G., Stein, M. I., and Bloom, B. S., *Methods in Personality Assessment*, Glencoe, Illinois: The Free Press, 1956.

6. Murray, H. A., *Explorations in Personality*, New York: Oxford University Press, 1938.

7. Stephenson, W., *The Study of Behavior*, Chicago: University of Chicago Press, 1953.

8. Machover, K., *Personality Projection in the Drawing of the Human Figure*, Springfield: C. C. Thomas Company, 1948.

9. Guttman, L., "A New Approach to Factor Analysis: The Radex," in P. F. Lazarfeld (ed) *Mathematical Thinking in the Social Sciences*, Glencoe: The Free Press, 1954, pp. 258-348.

10. Hotelling, H. "The Generalization of Student's Ratio." *Annals of Mathematical Statistics*," II (1931), 360-78.

11. Hicks, C. R. "A Study of Hotelling's t Statistic and its Application to Problems in Psychology, Education, and Industrial Research." Unpublished doctor's dissertation, Syracuse University, 1953.

12. Tukey, J. W. "Dyadic Anova, An Analysis of Variance for Vectors." *Human Biology*, XXI (1949), 65-110.

13. Tukey, J. W. "Components in Regression." *Biometrics*, VII (1951), 33-69.

14. Broida, D. C., Izard, C. E., and Cruickshank, W. M., "Thematic Apperception Reactions of Crippled Children," *Journal of Clinical Psychology*, VI (1950), 243-48.

15. Cruickshank, W. M., "The Relation of Physical Disability to Personal Aspiration," *Quarterly Journal of Child Behavior*, III (1951), 323-33.

16. Greenbaum, M., Qualtere, T., Carruth, B., and Cruickshank, W. M., "Evaluation of a Modification of the Thematic Apperception Test for Use with Physically Handicapped Children," *Journal of Clinical Psychology*, IX (1953), 40-44.

17. Ohlsen, M. M., and Schulz, R. E., "Projective Test Response Patterns for Best and Poorest Student Teachers." *Educational and Psychological Measurement*, XV (1955), 18-27.

CHAPTER FOUR

RESULTS

THE DATA COLLECTED FROM THE PRE-TEST AND POST-test administration of the General Information Inventory, the Classroom Integration Inventory, the Activities Index and the Picture Judgment Test were used to test the following specific hypotheses:

1. There will be a significant gain in the information concerning exceptional children as a result of the workshop.

2. There will be a significant gain in a positive direction in teachers' attitudes toward exceptional children resulting from the additional experiences given through the workshop.

3. There will be a significant gain in the abilities of teachers to judge the most realistic educational placement for exceptional children.

4. Changes in attitudes of teachers toward exceptional children will involve basic changes in their personality structure.

5. There will be significant differences in the amount of increase in acceptance demonstrated by the teachers throughout the areas of exceptionality, *e.g.*, teachers will gain significantly more in acceptance toward children with certain exceptionalities.

6. There will be significant differences in the amount of gain in acceptance demonstrated by the teachers from the four schools used in the study.

GENERAL INFORMATION INVENTORY (GII)

The first analysis was done on the General Information Inventory. This test was designed to measure the amount of information that the teachers had at the beginning of the workshop. The test was readministered at the final meeting, thirty weeks later, to determine the gains in information that were made by the teachers as a result of the experiences they had from the workshop.

ANALYSIS

The analysis of the differences between the scores of the pre-test and the post-test on the GII was performed with the matched-pair t test. From Table 3, it is obvious that each of the four schools as well as the four schools considered as a total group made highly significant gains in information. School I[1] (City) showed a significant increase in information at the .01 level. Schools II (Suburban), III (Rural), and IV (Parochial) showed an increase which was found to be significant at the .001 level. For all four schools as a group, the increase was also found to be significant at the .001 level.

TABLE 3

Matched-Pair t Test for Difference Between the Mean Scores of the Pre-Test and the Post-Test on the General Information Inventory for Each of the Four Schools and for the Total Group

	Schools				
	I	II	III	IV	Total
	City	Suburban	Rural	Parochial	
Mean Gain	6.1111	4.94	9.0192	19.5714	8.6525
N	19	34	52	15	120
t	3.439	3.912	8.2217	8.244	10.5802
P	.01	.001	.001	.001	.001

The amount of gain demonstrated by each of the schools varies considerably. School IV (Parochial) showed the highest mean increase. School III (Rural) had the next highest mean improvement with Schools I (City) and II (Suburban) following in the order stated. An analysis of variance was carried out on the difference in scores of the pre-test and post-test between schools and yielded a significant F at the .001 level (see Table 4). This indicated that there was a significant difference between means, *i.e.*, that some schools improved significantly more than others on the post-test.

---

[1]When reference is made to Schools I, II, III or IV, the authors intend the reader to understand that they are referring to the participating teachers and administrators in that school.

TABLE 4

Analysis of Variance of the Difference Between Mean Improvement for the Four Schools on the General Information Inventory

Source of Variation	Sum of Squares	df	Mean Square	F	P
Between schools	2,260.685	3	753.5617	12.3214	.001
Within groups	6,972.070	114	61.1585		
Total	9,232.755	117			

The Bartlett test for homogeneity of variance was performed in conjunction with the analysis of variance and was found not to be significant. The increase in mean gain does not appear to be consistently related to the mean scores on the pre-test.

Through an inspection of the pre-test means for the schools, it can be seen that their initial scores on the GII were different (see Table 5). School I (City) had the highest mean score on the pre-test, but ranked third in gain. It is interesting to note that School IV (Parochial) had the lowest mean score on the pre-test but made the highest gain.

TABLE 5

Pre-Test and Post-Test Means for the General Information Inventory for the Four Schools

Schools	Pre-test Means	Post-test Means	Difference between Pre-test and Post-test Means
I (City)	61.17	67.28	6.11
II (Suburban)	56.29	61.24	4.94
III (Rural)	55.76	64.79	9.02
IV (Parochial)	50.71	70.29	19.57

DISCUSSION

Each of the four schools made a highly significant improvement in information about exceptional children. Even though the mean differences were larger in some schools than in others and the analysis of variance between schools was significant, it can be concluded that there was a substantial gain in information which occurred throughout the total group. The fairly wide difference in initial information possessed by the teachers in each of the four schools may account, in some measure, for the differences in improvement. It might also be helpful at this point to restress the fact that the teachers from Schools I (City) and III (Rural) had greater experiences with exceptional children than did the teachers from Schools II (Suburban) and IV (Parochial). School IV (Parochial) had only a few exceptional children enrolled in it during the time of the workshop yet the teachers from this school made the greatest increase in information. On the other hand, School III (Rural) carried a rather substantial number of exceptional children on its registers and the teachers there made next to the highest increase. Apparently having experiences with exceptional children does not have a systematic influence upon the amount of increase that the teachers can show on the information level.

THE CLASSROOM INTEGRATION INVENTORY (CII) – TEACHER ACCEPTANCE

This test has been designed to reveal the degree of acceptance characterizing the teacher's relationship to exceptional children. Acceptance was measured on a 240 point scale based on the teacher's selection of an educational placement for various kinds of exceptionalities ranging from regular classroom assignment without special assistance to complete exclusion from the public school system.

ANALYSIS BY TOTAL GROUP

Difference scores for each subject were found by subtracting the pretest score from the post-test score. The matched-pair t test was applied to each of the ten areas for the total group and for the four schools.

As a total group (N = 120), the teachers showed significant increases in acceptance on seven of the ten areas. The increase in acceptance was significant at the .001 level for children with hearing handicaps, children with seizures, children with speech handicaps, and children with visual handicaps. The teachers demonstrated an increase in their attitudes of acceptance toward children with orthopedic and cardiac disorders at the .01 level; children with emotional disturbances and physical unattractiveness, at the .02 level. There was no significant change shown by the teachers' acceptance scores for children who were mentally retarded or gifted, children with behavior disorders, or children who required special toilet handling (see Table 6).

TABLE 6

Matched-Pair t Test on the Classroom Integration Inventory for the Total Group

Area of Deviation	Mean Gain[a]	σ_D	t	P
Behavior disorders	.425	.2657	1.599	—
Emotionally disturbed	.658	.2757	2.387	.02
Hearing handicapped	1.167	.2823	4.134	.001
Intelligence (gifted and retarded)	.050	.3392	.147	—
Orthopedic and cardiac disorders	1.008	.3733	2.700	.01
Physical attractiveness	.692	.2917	2.372	.02
Seizures	2.675	.3670	7.289	.001
Special toilet handling	−.500	.4413	1.133	—
Speech	1.100	.2841	3.872	.001
Vision	1.192	.3204	3.720	.001

Further information on this same problem can be obtained by examining separately the scores of the teachers in the four participating schools. By an inspection of the pre-test and post-test mean scores for the four schools it can be seen that the mean scores varied widely on both administrations.

Personnel in Schools II (Suburban) and III (Rural) had equally high mean scores on the pre-test. Whereas personnel in School III (Rural) made a substantial gain on the post-test, teachers in School II (Suburban) made virtually no gain. School I (City) had the lowest mean on the pre-test but made greatest gain on the post-test. School IV (Parochial) teachers had next to the lowest mean on the pre-test and showed a slight loss on the post-test. Apparently the differences in gain in acceptance scores were not a function of the schools' initial standings on this measure (see Table 7). The initial degree of acceptance also appears to be independent of the amount of actual experience with exceptional children.

It is obvious that some schools became more accepting of exceptional children than others; *i.e.*, some showed significant increases in more areas of deviation than others. To test whether these were significant differences, the analysis of variance was performed on the acceptance scores between the four schools, yielding an F of 4.276 significant at the .01 level (see Table 8). The Bartlett test for homogeneity of variance was performed and was not significant (corrected $x^2 = 6.2838$).

---

[a]Minus sign indicates a decrease in acceptance.

TABLE 7

Pre-Test and Post-Test Means for Areas of Deviation on Acceptance Scores for the Four Schools and Total Group

Area of Deviation		School I City	School II Suburban	School III Rural	School IV Parochial	Total Group
Behavior disorders	Pre-test Mean	17.15	18.36	17.35	14.49	17.24
	Post-test Mean	18.04	18.28	18.28	13.85	17.66
Emotionally disturbed	Pre-test Mean	17.98	20.25	20.68	19.99	19.99
	Post-test Mean	19.65	21.14	21.10	19.63	20.65
Hearing handicapped	Pre-test Mean	13.71	16.36	17.00	14.14	15.92
	Post-test Mean	16.37	16.92	18.03	15.42	17.08
Intelligence (gifted and retarded)	Pre-test Mean	16.93	19.87	19.36	20.13	19.18
	Post-test Mean	17.70	19.06	20.11	18.99	19.23
Orthopedic and cardiac disorders	Pre-test Mean	11.04	14.85	15.39	11.78	14.10
	Post-test Mean	13.32	15.42	16.56	11.70	15.10
Physical attractiveness	Pre-test Mean	17.48	21.03	20.46	21.85	20.28
	Post-test Mean	18.81	21.06	21.36	22.70	20.97
Seizures	Pre-test Mean	10.77	13.01	12.76	11.49	12.35
	Post-test Mean	14.60	14.55	16.07	13.35	15.14

TABLE 7 — *Continued*

Speech handicapped	Pre-test Mean	13.93	16.17	16.46	15.14	15.79
	Post-test Mean	16.00	16.44	17.93	15.85	16.88
Special toilet handling	Pre-test Mean	12.15	14.27	14.60	13.42	14.10
	Post-test Mean	13.71	13.93	14.90	8.28	13.60
Visually handicapped	Pre-test Mean	13.99	15.85	16.21	13.35	15.38
	Post-test Mean	16.70	16.66	17.54	12.92	16.57
Total	Pre-test Mean	145.28	170.46	170.46	155.86	164.65
	Post-test Mean	165.17	173.64	181.94	152.79	173.29

TABLE 8

Analysis of Variance of Acceptance Scores Between Schools

Sources of Deviation	Sum of Squares	df	Mean Square	F	P
Between schools	5,690.97	3	1,896.99	4.276	.01
Within schools	51,464.90	114	451.45		
Total	57,155.87	117			

In order that a statement might be made concerning which of the schools made the greatest increase in acceptance, the Tukey test (1) was applied to the mean acceptance scores for the four schools (see Table 9).

The four schools were found to reduce into two groups. Schools I (City) and III (Rural) (Group A) made a significantly greater change than did Schools II (Suburban) and IV (Parochial) (Group B). Unlike the results on the General Information Inventory, there appears to be a definite and systematic relationship between the number of handicapped children enrolled in the school and the teachers' ability to show increased acceptance toward these children.

TABLE 9

Tukey Test for Comparing School Means in the Analysis of Variance on Acceptance Scores

School	n	$\overline{D}$	Group
I (City School)	18	19.89	
III (Rural School)	51	11.43	A
II (Suburban School)	33	3.19	
IV (Parochial School)	14	−3.07	B

Apparently the impact of the workshop differed from school to school. The evidence gained from the results of the acceptance scores suggests that when teachers have an opportunity for actual teaching experiences with exceptional children, a workshop in this area can be quite effective in inducing greater acceptance toward these children. On the other hand, a workshop of this nature seems to be rather ineffectual in modifying the attitudes of teachers toward increased acceptance where they have little opportunity for experiences with exceptional children.

ANALYSIS OF THE FOUR SCHOOLS INDIVIDUALLY

An analysis of the acceptance scores by the four schools separately was done to achieve a better understanding of the particular areas of exceptionality toward which the teachers demonstrated significantly greater acceptance. As in the case of the analysis of the total group, the analysis for each school was done by performing the match-pair t test on the difference score for each of the ten areas of deviation. Because Schools I (City) and III (Rural) grouped together in showing the greatest increase in acceptance and Schools II (Suburban) and IV (Parochial) were in second place, the schools were analyzed in that order.

School I (City) demonstrated a significant increase in acceptance on six of the ten areas. The increase was found to be significant at the .001 level for children with hearing handicaps, at the .01 level for children with seizures and visual handicaps, and at the .05 level for children with emotional disturbances, orthopedic and cardiac disorders, and speech handicaps (see Table 10). Although School I (City) was next to last among the schools in gain on the General Information Inventory the teachers from this school were able to increase in their acceptance for a substantial number of areas. From this it might be suggested that there is little direct relationship between the amount of gain the teachers show in information and their ability to become more accepting of exceptional children.

TABLE 10

Matched-Pair t Test on the Classroom Integration Inventory School I
(City Public School)

Area of Deviation	Mean Gain	σ_D	t	P
Behavior disorders	.889	.4829	1.279	——
Emotionally disturbed	1.667	.6543	2.548	.05
Hearing	2.667	.8966	2.975	.001
Intelligence	.778	.8614	.903	——
Orthopedic and cardiac disorders	2.278	1.0990	2.073	.05
Physical attractiveness	1.333	1.0180	1.309	——
Seizures	3.833	1.0550	3.633	.01
Speech	2.056	.8892	2.312	.05
Special toilet handling	1.556	.8827	1.763	——
Vision	2.833	.8373	3.383	.01

TABLE 11

Matched-Pair t Test on the Classroom Integration Inventory School III
(Rural School)

Area of Deviation	Mean Gain	σ_D	t	P
Behavior disorders	.922	.3240	.846	.01
Emotionally disturbed	.412	.3653	1.128	——
Hearing	1.039	.3531	2.943	.01
Intelligence	.745	.5028	1.482	——
Orthopedic and cardiac disorders	1.176	.4779	2.461	.02
Physical attractiveness	.902	.4340	2.078	.05
Seizures	3.314	.5263	6.297	.001
Speech	1.471	.4099	3.589	.001
Special toilet handling	.118	.5805	.203	——
Vision	1.333	.4960	2.688	.01

School III (Rural) showed, as noted in Table 11, a significant increase in acceptance in seven of the ten areas of exceptionality. The teachers showed an increase in acceptance which was found to be significant at the .01 level for children with behavior disorders, hearing handicaps, and visual handicaps. The teachers improved significantly at the .02 level for children with orthopedic or cardiac disorders. The increased acceptance for children who deviated in physical attractiveness was found to be significant at the .05 level. The teachers from School III (Rural) showed the greatest amount of gain in acceptance as compared with the other schools. School III (Rural) is a centralized school located in a rural area which has no special classes. As a result, children with exceptionality in each of the ten areas can be found within the regular classroom. The teachers in this school consequently have had considerable experience with exceptional children. The fact that the workshop was effective in bringing about increased acceptance among these teachers, and the fact that these teachers had actual contact with exceptional children, lends support to the interpretation that having actual experiences with exceptional children plays an important role in the subsequent modification of attitudes through a workshop.

School II (Suburban) showed an increase in acceptance in only one area. The teachers became more accepting of children with seizures, significant at the .05 level (see Table 12). Their mean increase in acceptance of children with emotional disturbances, hearing handicaps, intellectual deviations and visual handicaps approached significance ($P = .1$). This is also consistent with the observation of an apparently direct relationship between the experiences teachers have with exceptional children and their ability to increase in acceptance toward these children as a result of a workshop. The teachers for School II (Subur-

TABLE 12

Matched-Pair t Test on the Classroom Integration Inventory School II (Suburban District)

Area of Deviation	Mean Gain[a]	σ_D	t	P
Behavior disorders	−.081	.5830	.139	——
Emotionally disturbed	.892	.5790	1.541	.1
Hearing	.568	.4368	1.300	.1
Intelligence	−.811	.5699	1.423	.1
Orthopedic and cardiac disorders	.568	.8025	.708	——
Physical attractiveness	.027	.4863	.056	——
Seizures	1.541	.6971	2.211	.05
Speech	.270	.4172	.647	——
Special toilet handling	−.340	.8773	.678	——
Vision	.810	.5553	1.460	.1

[a]Minus sign indicates a decrease in acceptance.

ban) had relatively few opportunities for contact with exceptional children. With the exception of a considerable number of gifted children and a few children with speech handicaps, no other exceptional children were enrolled in this school.

The teachers from School IV (Parochial) showed a significant increase in acceptance at the .05 level for children with seizures. It is interesting to note that these teachers showed a significant decrease (P = .001) in acceptance of children who required special handling with respect to toilet care (see Table 13). This was the only school that showed a significant decrease in any of the areas.

It is important to note here again, as in the case of the teachers from School II (Suburban), that not having actual experiences with exceptional children seems to limit the effectiveness of a workshop to induce greater acceptance of these children.

TABLE 13

Matched-Pair t Test on the Classroom Integration Inventory School IV (Parochial School)

Area of Deviation	Mean Gain[a]	σ_D	t	P
Behavior disorders	−.500	.7346	.681	——
Emotionally disturbed	−.350	.8426	.424	——
Hearing	1.286	1.2080	1.065	——
Intelligence	−1.143	1.1960	.956	——
Orthopedic and cardiac disorders	−.071	.8349	.085	——
Physical attractiveness	.857	.6450	1.329	——
Seizures	1.857	.8377	2.217	.05
Speech	.714	1.0440	.683	——
Special toilet handling	−5.143	1.1950	4.304	.001[b]
Vision	− .429	.8136	.527	——

ANALYSIS BETWEEN AREAS OF EXCEPTIONALITY

Referring back to the increase in acceptance demonstrated by the total group for the ten areas of exceptionality, it can be seen that there are fairly wide differences in the mean gain for these areas (see Table 6). In order to determine if this difference was significant, the analysis of variance was applied to the difference scores for the ten areas. The Bartlett test for homogeneity of variance was performed and found to be not significant.

The difference in mean gain made by the teachers for the ten areas

---

[a]Minus sign indicates a decrease in acceptance.
[b]Significant decrease.

was found to be significant at the .001 level (see Table 14). This means that the teachers showed a greater increase in acceptance in some areas than in others.

TABLE 14

Analysis of Variance of Acceptance Scores Between Areas on the Classroom Integration Inventory

Sources of Variation	Sum of Squares	df	Mean Square	F	P
Between areas	760.81	9	84.534	6.530	.001
Within groups	15,404.97	1,190	12.945		
Total	16,165.78	1,199			

In order to determine which of the areas elicited the most gain by the teachers, the Tukey test was used for comparing the area means (1).

From Table 15, it can be seen that children with seizures received the most gain. Children with vision, hearing, and speech handicaps fell in the next group. Children who deviated intellectually and children who required special toilet handling, each grouping separately, made the least gain in acceptance as expressed by the teachers.

TABLE 15

Tukey Test for Comparing Area Means in Analysis of Variance for Acceptance Scores

Area of Deviation	N	$\overline{D}$	Groups
Seizures	120	2.675	A
Vision	120	1.192	
Hearing	120	1.167	B
Speech	120	1.100	
Orthopedic and cardiac disorders	120	1.008	C
Physical attractiveness	120	.692	
Emotional disturbances	120	.658	D
Behavior disorders	120	.425	
Intelligence	120	.050	E
Special toilet handling	120	−.500	F

It is understandable that children with seizures might show the greatest increase in acceptance by the teachers because, unless the seizures are quite severe, this child requires no special educational planning. Some children with seizures can be placed in the regular classroom and gain from this placement. In addition, it may be noted in Table 7 that the teachers had a low pre-test mean score in this area, indicating initial feelings of fear or rejection. Apparently the consultant and/or the discussion in this area was quite effective in inducing increased acceptance among the teachers for children with seizures. Children with vision, hearing and speech handicaps of a slight or moderate degree are usually placed in the regular classroom. Consequently the teachers have had at least some experiences with this group of children. It is very possible that having taught these children at one time or another influenced their ability to become more accepting of these handicaps.

It is also logical that children who are either mentally retarded or gifted would *not* show an increase in acceptance using the regular classroom as a frame of reference. By and large, children with mental retardation are placed in special classes in urban and suburban areas. The consultant in this area supported special classroom placement for mentally handicapped children and expressed that philosophy to the teachers. By examining the pre-test and post-test scores in the area of the gifted it was found that the teachers were high in acceptance for these children on both administrations and as a consequence they could not have shown a marked increase. Children who required special toilet handling showed a slight decrease in mean acceptance. School IV (Parochial) was the only school that decreased in acceptance toward this handicap, causing this area to receive the lowest mean increase as compared with other areas.

ANALYSIS BETWEEN DEGREES OF IMPAIRMENT

While the mean gains in each of the areas seemed to be consistent for the three degrees of severity of impairment incorporated in the test for each area, an analysis of variance was applied to the acceptance scores to determine if there were significant differences between these degrees of impairment (see Table 16).

TABLE 16

Analysis of Variance of Differences in Acceptance Based on Severity of Impairment

Sources of Variation	Sum of Squares	df	Mean Square	F
Between degrees	197.41	2	98.71	1.403
Within groups	25,117.21	357	70.36	
Total	25,314.62	359		

The differences between degrees of impairment was found to be not significant. This indicated that the teachers did not increase in acceptance more in one degree of severity than in another degree; consequently the increase in acceptance was a function of the areas of exceptionality rather than the degree of severity of impairment.

DISCUSSION

To summarize the results of the analysis on the acceptance scores, the four schools as a total group showed significant increases in their attitudes of acceptance toward exceptional children in seven areas as assessed by the Classroom Integration Inventory. These areas were:

1. emotionally disturbed
2. hearing
3. orthopedic and cardiac disorders
4. physical attractiveness
5. seizures
6. speech
7. vision.

Through an analysis of the four schools individually, it was found that School III (Rural) demonstrated the greatest gain in terms of the number of areas. These teachers increased in the following seven areas of exceptionality:

1. behavior disorders
2. hearing
3. orthopedic and cardiac disorders
4. physical attractiveness
5. seizures
6. speech
7. vision.

The teachers from school I (City), falling in second place, demonstrated an increase in the following areas of deviation:

1. emotionally disturbed
2. hearing
3. orthopedic and cardiac disorders
4. seizures
5. speech
6. vision.

School II (Suburban) gained significantly in only one area. That area was children with seizures. School IV (Parochial) showed a significant increase in acceptance for children with seizures; however, this increase was offset by a significant decrease for children who required special toilet handling.

The teachers were able to modify their attitudes more readily for some areas of deviation than for others. The area concerned with seizures was isolated by the Tukey test as showing the largest extent of increase. The areas of vision, hearing and speech handicaps grouped together in second place. The areas of deviation seemed to group in a fairly logical fashion which was related to the experiences teachers might have had with the particular area of deviation and the influence they gained from the consultant in that particular area.

There was no significant difference found between the amount of increase for the three degrees of deviation. Apparently the teachers did not discriminate in their acceptance of any particular area of deviation in terms of the degree of impairment.

It seemed obvious throughout the analysis of the acceptance scores that the schools which enrolled the greatest number of exceptional children were affected to a far greater extent by the workshop. The two schools, School II (Suburban) and IV (Parochial), which had but a few exceptional children, gained little if any in acceptance as a result of the workshop.

THE CLASSROOM INTEGRATION INVENTORY (CII) — REALISTIC PLACEMENT

Continued use of the Classroom Integration Inventory revealed that the scale had some deeper meanings and implications for assessment of change than were being considered by scoring for acceptance alone. The direction taken by the lectures and the discussion groups aimed toward the realistic placement of exceptional children rather than the indiscriminate placement of exceptional children in the regular classroom, irrespective of the area of deviation and the degree of involvement. As a result of this, it was believed desirable to assess the increase in the ability of teachers to be realistic about the placement of exceptional children, as measured by the correspondence between their responses and those of established specialists.

Analysis by Total Group

Difference scores were used in the analysis, as found by subtracting the pre-test scores from the post-test scores. The matched-pair t test was performed on each area by four schools individually and for the total group.

Analyzed as a total group the teachers showed a significant increase at the .001 level in their ability to be realistic about the placement of children with seizures. By referring to Table 6 it can be seen that the teachers increased in acceptance toward these children. In this case the increased acceptance was consistent with the judges' opinion of the most accurate placement of children with seizures. On the other hand, they showed a decrease in their judgment of the most realistic placement for children with behavior disorders which was found to be significant at the .001 level. For this area, the teachers showed a significant increase in acceptance which was inconsistent with the judges' opinion of a realistic placement. Apparently the teachers became more accepting for children with behavior disorders than the judges would advocate. They also decreased significantly at the .02 level in placing children who require special toilet handling. The teachers became less realistic concerning the placing of these children. Judging from their decrease in acceptance toward these children, the teachers were less accepting than the judges in this area (see Table 17).

TABLE 17

Matched-Pair t Test on Realism Scores on the Classroom Integration Inventory (The Total Group)

Area of Deviation	Mean Gain[a]	σ_D	t	P
Behavior disorders	− .909	.2445	3.7180	.001[b]
Emotionally disturbed	− .017	.4517	.0376	——
Hearing	.132	.2612	.5054	——
Intelligence	− .198	.4909	.4033	——
Orthopedic and cardiac disorders	.380	.3479	1.0920	——
Physical attractiveness	.339	.2435	1.3920	——
Seizures	1.802	.3405	5.2920	.001
Speech	− .083	.4347	.1909	——
Special toilet handling	−1.116	.4339	2.5720	.02[b]
Vision	.025	.2339	.1069	——

Although the teachers as a total group did not show any marked increase in their ability to be realistic about the placement of exceptional children, it was believed that somewhat more meaningful evidence could be presented with regard to the changes on this dimension through a subsequent analysis of the individual schools.

ANALYSIS BY INDIVIDUAL SCHOOLS

The first analysis was performed for School I (City). The teachers from this school did not show a significant increase in their ability to

---

[a]Minus sign indicates a decrease in realism.
[b]Significant decrease.

select realistic placements for the children in any of the ten areas. The greatest mean increase was in the area of hearing handicaps, which approached significance (P = .1).

Although the teachers from School I (City) showed no increase in their ability to make realistic placements for exceptional children, they increased in acceptance of these children in six areas of deviation. This would indicate they became more accepting of exceptional children irrespective of the judges' opinion of the most accurate or realistic placement (see Table 18).

TABLE 18

Matched-Pair t Test on Realism Scores on the Classroom Integration Inventory School I (City School)

Area of Deviation	Mean Gain	σ_D	t	P
Behavior disorders	.1579	.5030	.3140	——
Emotionally disturbed	1.0526	.7778	1.3530	——
Hearing	1.5263	.8497	1.7960	.1
Intelligence	− .1052	.3912	.1680	——
Orthopedic and cardiac disorders	.5789	.9561	.6050	——
Physical attractiveness	.7368	.5663	.9790	——
Seizures	1.2632	.9108	1.3870	——
Speech	.7874	.6202	.3158	——
Special toilet handling	− .2632	.6958	.3783	——
Vision	− .1052	.6752	.1558	——

The teachers from School III (Rural) showed a significant increase at the .001 level in the realistic placement of children with seizures. Their choice of placement for children with orthopedic and cardiac disorders became significantly more realistic at the .05 level. These teachers showed significantly less realism in their placement of children with behavior disorders at the .01 level (see Table 19).

In Table 11 it was seen that these teachers increased in acceptance as well as their judgment of realistic placement of children with seizures. The increase in acceptance in this area was consistent with the judges' opinion.

The increased acceptance of children with orthopedic and cardiac disorders expressed by the teachers from School III (Rural) was consistent with their increase in the realistic placement of these children. This indicated that on both the acceptance and realism scores the teachers moved in a direction which was in agreement with the specialist. Their increased acceptance of children with behavior disorders was reflected in a decrease in their realism score. In going back to the raw

TABLE 19

Matched-Pair t Test on Realism Scores on the Classroom Integration Inventory
School III (Rural School)

Area of Deviation	Mean Gain[a]	σ_D	t	P
Behavior disorders	−1.204	.3714	3.2420	.01[b]
Emotionally disturbed	− .296	.9038	.3275	——
Hearing	− .259	.3325	.7789	——
Intelligence	− .222	1.0010	.2218	——
Orthopedic and cardiac disorders	.981	.4529	2.1660	.05
Physical attractiveness	.296	.3240	.9136	——
Seizures	2.074	.5256	3.9460	.001
Speech	− .574	.8118	.7071	——
Special toilet handling	− .648	.5438	1.1920	——
Vision	− .444	.3271	1.3570	——

scores it was observed that the majority of these teachers accepted children with behavior disorders in their regular classrooms without assistance, whereas the judges felt that the most realistic placement of these children would require at least part-time assistance. The teachers' increase in acceptance in this area was at the expense of realistic placement as viewed by the specialists.

The teachers from School II (Suburban) also showed a significant increase in their ability to judge the most realistic educational placement for children with seizures at (P = .02). These teachers increased in the realistic placement of children with visual handicaps at the .05 level (see Table 20).

TABLE 20

Matched-Pair t Test on Realism Scores on the Classroom Integration Inventory
School II (Suburban District)

Area of Deviation	Mean Gain[a]	σ_D	t	P
Behavior disorders	− .529	.4268	1.2390	——
Emotionally disturbed	− .529	.4687	1.1290	——
Hearing	.3529	.4604	.7665	——
Intelligence	− .029	.4539	.0639	——
Orthopedic and cardiac disorders	.794	.6358	1.2490	——
Physical attractiveness	.176	.4669	.3770	——
Seizures	1.618	.6291	2.5720	.02
Speech	.176	.5718	.3078	——
Special toilet handling	− .412	.9648	.4270	——
Vision	.971	.4438	2.1880	.05

[a]Minus sign indicates a decrease in realism.
[b]Significant decrease.

It can be seen by referring to Table 12 that the teachers from School II (Suburban) made a significant increase in acceptance of children with seizures at the .05 level. The increased acceptance of children with seizures was in a direction consistent with that of the specialist. The increase in realistic placement of children with visual handicaps expressed by these teachers was not matched, however, by a significant increase in acceptance. Although the teachers became more realistic concerning the placement of visually handicapped children, they did not increase their acceptance toward these children.

School IV (Parochial) approached significance in their increase in selecting a more realistic placement for children with seizures (P = .06). These teachers decreased significantly in three areas. They were significantly less realistic in placing children who require special toilet handling (P = .001). They decreased significantly at the .01 level in the placement of children with orthopedic and cardiac disorders. Their decrease in realistic placement for children with behavior disorders was significant at the .05 level (see Table 21).

TABLE 21

Matched-Pair t Test on Realism Scores on the Classroom Integration Inventory School IV (Parochial School)

Area of Deviation	Mean Gain[a]	σ_D	t	P
Behavior disorders	−2.143	.8443	2.5380	.05[b]
Emotionally disturbed	.857	.8311	1.0310	——
Hearing	− .786	.8462	.9289	——
Intelligence	− .643	1.068	.6195	——
Orthopedic and cardiac disorders	−3.214	1.049	3.0630	.01[b]
Physical attractiveness	.357	.8025	.4449	——
Seizures	1.929	.9167	2.1040	.06
Speech	1.500	1.118	1.3420	——
Special toilet handling	−5.786	1.347	4.2950	.001[b]
Vision	− .286	.6107	.4683	——

The teachers from School IV (Parochial) decreased in acceptance toward children who required special toilet handling and also showed a significant decrease in the realistic placement of these children (see Table 13). Apparently these teachers could not accept children who required this special kind of care or be realistic concerning their educational placement.

---

[a]Minus sign indicates a decrease in realism.
[b]Significant decrease.

School IV (Parochial) demonstrated a slight but not significant decrease on their mean acceptance scores toward children with orthopedic and cardiac disorders and those having behavior disorders. This, in addition to the fact that they decreased in their ability to be realistic concerning the educational placement in these areas, indicated that they changed in a direction which was less accepting than the specialist would advocate.

DIFFERENCES BETWEEN SCHOOLS

Although the analysis throughout the four schools revealed a significant increase for realistic placement in only a few areas, there were some indications that the schools differed in the amount of change that had been made on this dimension. As an example, School III (Rural) demonstrated an increase in realistic placement for two areas of deviation whereas School IV (Parochial) showed a decrease for three areas.

To determine if there are real differences in the changes shown by the teachers in the four schools with regard to their ability to select the most realistic placement, the analysis of variance was performed for the schools. A significant difference at the .05 level was found to exist between the schools (see Table 22). The Bartlett test for homogeneity of variance was applied and found to be not significant.

TABLE 22

Analysis of Variance of Realism Scores for Differences in Change Between the Four Schools

Source of Variation	Sum of Squares	df	Mean Square	F	P
Between schools	1,551.12	3	517.04	2.978	.05
Within schools	20,314.60	114	178.20		
Total	21,865.72	117			

The Tukey test was again used to determine which school or schools demonstrated the greatest change in realistic judgment concerning the classroom placement of exceptional children. The mean differences between Schools I (City), II (Suburban), and III (Rural) were not enough to afford separate grouping for these schools. School IV (Parochial), however, differed significantly at the .05 level and afforded a separate group (see Table 23).

The mean differences among Schools I (City), II (Suburban), and III (Rural) were not significant; consequently no statements can be made with regard to their relative positions. These teachers from School IV (Parochial), as compared with the other three schools, became the least

TABLE 23

Tukey Test for Comparing the Means of the Four Schools in the Analysis of Variance for the Realism Scores

Schools	N	$\bar{D}$	Group
I City School	19	4.50	
II Common School District	34	2.59	A
III Centralized School	52	− .30	
IV Parochial School	15	−8.21	B

realistic in selecting classroom placement for exceptional children as based upon the opinions of the specialists.

ANALYSIS BY AREAS OF EXCEPTIONALITY AND DEGREE OF IMPAIRMENT

It was believed that summing the three degrees of deviation within each area masked some of the increases that might have occurred by degree. To determine whether or not this suspicion was valid, the matched-pair t test was applied to the realism scores by degree. This brought to light two signifiant t's. School I (City) made a significant increase at the .01 level for children with a moderate degree of hearing handicaps and School II (Suburban) made a significant increase at the .05 level for children with a moderate degree of visual handicap. These differences were not considered enough to validate the suspicion that real differences were being covered by treating the three degrees of deviation together in each area.

To determine if there was a significant difference among the areas of deviation as shown by the teachers in their selection of realistic placement, the analysis of variance technique was contemplated for analyzing the ten areas and the three degrees of deviation. The Bartlett test for homogeneity of variance was applied and found to be significant at the .01 level. Obviously a fairly marked degree of heterogeneity of variance exists in this situation. Lindquist (2) points out that the form of the sampling distribution of the mean square ratios is not very markedly affected by moderate degrees of heterogeneity of variance. Therefore, the F test may still be performed in many experimental situations. This was supported further in a study conducted by Norton (3) to investigate the effects of nonnormality and of heterogeneity of variance upon the F-distribution. Although there are many more ramifications to his study than are stated here, he found that marked heterogeneity of variances has a small effect on the form of the F-distribution. Norton suggests that when marked heterogeneity of variance is expected it is desirable to allow for this discrepancy by selecting a higher level of significance than would normally be employed.

The subsequent analysis was performed with a full awareness that rejecting the hypothesis, even though highly significant differences are found between the means, may be hazardous because of the influence the lack of homogeneity of variance might have upon the means. With this understanding, the analysis of variance was performed on the ten areas by the three degrees of deviation.

With the knowledge that heterogeneity of variance does exist, to reject the hypothesis that the means are different at the .01 level would be erroneous because of the significant difference in the variances. It is unlikely, however, that this difference in variance would account for a difference as great as that between the means. Rejecting the hypothesis that the means came from the same population might be tenable at the .001 level (3). In spite of this significant difference in variances, it is reasonable to say that there are significant differences between the areas.

The difference between the three degrees was not significant, indicating that the teachers did not increase any more in one degree of deviation than another with respect to realistic placement. The interaction between areas and degree, however, was found to be significant at the .001 level (see Table 24). This is interpreted to mean that in spite of the fact that the difference between degrees was not significant, the nature of the modification of the ability of teachers to be realistic about the placement of exceptional children in the ten areas was dependent not only upon the areas presented, but also upon the degree of deviation involved.

TABLE 24

Analysis of Variance of Realism Scores for Differences in Change Between Areas and Degrees

Source of Variation	Sum of Squares	df	Mean Square	F	P
Between areas	188.453	9	20.939	6.827	.001
Between degrees	1.272	2	.636		
Interaction: area x degrees	178.618	18	9.923	3.235	.001
Within groups	11,040.78	3,600	3.067		
Total	11,409.12	3,629			

Making the assumption that significant differences do exist between the areas, the Tukey method was employed to determine in which areas the teachers showed the most gain. It was found that out of the ten areas the greatest modification in the teachers' ability to be realistic occurred with children who have seizures. In second place, as grouped by the differences between the means were children with orthopedic and cardiac disorders. Next, also forming a separate group, were children who are physically less attractive. The six areas of hearing, vision, emotional disturbances, behavior disorders, speech, and intelligence, grouped together. The difference between the mean for children who required special toilet handling was significant and afforded separate grouping in last place (see Table 25).

TABLE 25

Tukey Test for Comparing Area Means in the Analysis of Variance for the Realism Scores

Area of Deviation	N	$\overline{D}$	Group
Seizures	120	.601	A
Orthopedic and cardiac disorders	120	.127	B
Physical attractiveness	120	.113	C
Hearing	120	.044	
Vision	120	.008	
Emotional disturbances	120	−.006	D
Behavior disorders	120	−.019	
Speech	120	−.028	
Intelligence	120	−.066	
Special toilet handling	120	−.372	E

In interpreting the results of the grouping yielded by the Tukey test, it can be stated that children with seizures (Group A) showed the greatest gain with respect to the teachers' ability to agree with the opinions of the specialists. The fact that the pre-test scores of the teachers in this area were particularly low would indicate that the teachers' initial status in this area was quite unrealistic. Apparently the effect of the consultant and/or the discussion influenced the teachers toward a more realistic judgment of these children.

Not a great deal can be said for the areas that fell in the middle groups, B, C, or D. Although some increase in the teachers' ability to become more realistic in placing children with orthopedic and cardiac disorders may be noted, it would be misleading to suggest that significant increases among the four schools were demonstrated in this area.

On the other hand, it is fairly obvious that children who required special toilet handling (Group E) received the least amount of increase in realistic placement as far as the teachers' judgments were concerned. In fact all evidence points to a substantial decrease in becoming realistic toward the classroom placement of these children.

DISCUSSION

By and large, the teachers did not show marked increases in their ability to become more realistic concerning the accurate placement of exceptional children. Considering the four schools as a total group, it was found that the teachers became more realistic in selecting placement for children with seizures; however, they became less realistic about children with behavior disorders and children who require special toilet handling.

The increase in realistic judgment demonstrated by the teachers in the area of seizures was matched by a significant increase in acceptance for this area. In this case the increased acceptance shown by the teachers was consistent with the specialists' opinion of the most accurate placement of children with seizures. In the area of behavior disorders, the teachers' increase in acceptance was inconsistent with that of the specialists. On the post-test for the acceptance scores, the teachers showed a trend toward the placement of children with behavior disorders into the regular classroom without specialized assistance. The specialists believed that the regular classroom teacher should have at least part-time assistance; consequently their increased acceptance was greater than the specialist felt was realistic in terms of more adequate educational advantages for children with this handicap.

The significant decrease in selecting the most realistic placement for children who required special toilet handling on the part of the teachers was paralleled by a significant decrease in acceptance for children with this handicap. For these children the teachers became less accepting than the specialists would advocate.

The analysis for the four schools individually revealed significant increases in only a few areas of exceptionality with respect to the teachers' ability to select realistic placements. These increases, however, were offset by significant decreases in other areas. School I (City) made no significant change in either direction on the realism scores. The acceptance scores of these teachers were significantly greater in six areas. Apparently they became more accepting without increasing in their realistic judgment concerning placement.

The teachers from School III (Rural) increased significantly in the realistic placement of children with seizures and for children with orthopedic and cardiac disorders. Their increases in both of these areas were paralleled by significant increases in acceptance. These teachers showed significantly less realism in their placement of children with behavior disorders. Although the teachers showed a significant increase in their acceptance in this area, their realism toward placement was reduced. This indicated that these teachers were willing to accept children with behavior disorders to a greater extent than the specialist would suggest.

As was the case with School III (Rural), the teachers from School II (Suburban) increased significantly in their mean realism scores for children with seizures. These teachers also became more accepting in this area. Their increased acceptance was in a direction consistent with the opinion of the specialists. The teachers' significant change toward more realistic placement of children with visual handicaps was not matched with a significant increase in acceptance.

The teachers from School IV (Parochial) decreased significantly for selecting realistic placement in three areas. Those were: behavior disorders, orthopedic and cardiac disorders, and special toilet handling. In each case they became less accepting than the specialists would suggest in selecting an accurate placement for these children.

Compared with the other three schools, School IV (Parochial) demonstrated the least increase in being realistic concerning the placement of exceptional children. Actually it is misleading to refer to the change shown by these teachers in positive terms because they became substantially less realistic toward exceptional children. The workshop obviously effected a negative change for these teachers with regard to their capacity to be accepting as well as realistic toward children with some handicaps.

There were highly significant differences in the amount of change that was evidenced by the teachers toward the ten areas of deviation. Children with seizures showed the greatest increase as far as teachers' selection of realistic placement was concerned. The increase of realism in this area was toward greater acceptance. Children who require special toilet handling showed the greatest decrease in realistic placement as a result of the teachers becoming less accepting in this area.

ACTIVITIES INDEX

The effect of the workshop upon the teachers has been seen with relation to their changes in information, acceptance, and realistic placement of exceptional children. The following analysis will be concerned with the changes that were brought about by the workshop on the personality structure of the teachers.

The teachers in the four schools were given the Activities Index before and after the workshop. A resultant vector, summarizing the overall position of each school on the pre-test and post-test, was computed and analyzed by means of of Hotelling's t. Difference scores were also obtained for each of the thirty-two dimensions by subtracting post-test from pre-test scores. A matched-pair t test was carried out for the total group and for each of the four schools individually.

Vector Analysis

Figures 2 and 3 show the total group patterns on the pre-tests and post-tests, together with the resultant vectors for each of the four schools. While these are fairly stable, the underlying areas of change being apparently minimal, it will be noted that the schools are lying somewhat closer together after the workshop than they were before. The difference between pre-test and pro-test vectors for the total group yields an F of 8.87, significant at the .01 level, attributable entirely to the School II (Suburban) shift downward toward the submissive-restrained area.

It will also be noted that School IV (Parochial) lies closest to the submissive-restrained area, and is furthest from the other three schools. Schools I (City), II (Suburban), and III (Rural) are not significantly different from one another on either the pre-testing or the post-testing, but School IV (Parochial) is significantly different from these others beyond the .01 level on both occasions. Apparently the parochial school staff must be regarded as differing significantly in personality structure from the teachers in the other three schools.

The clarification of these differences will require a more detailed examination of the individual needs subscales.

Subscale Analysis for the Total Group

The results of the t tests for the total group demonstrated significant changes on three dimensions. On dimension 16 (Exocathection-Extraception), the post-test scores were significantly lower than the pre-test scores (P = .05). This indicated a decrease on the part of the teachers as a total group in their expression of interest for this dimension which is defined as, "The manipulation of external objects (physical or interpersonal) through practical, concrete, physical or social action; adaptation to reality 'as given' for more-or-less immediately tangible ends."

On dimension 19 (Endocathection-Extraception, social), the post-test

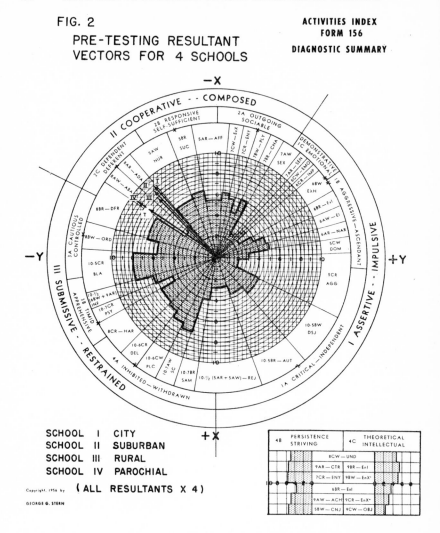

FIG. 2

PRE-TESTING RESULTANT
VECTORS FOR 4 SCHOOLS

ACTIVITIES INDEX
FORM 156

DIAGNOSTIC SUMMARY

SCHOOL I CITY
SCHOOL II SUBURBAN
SCHOOL III RURAL
SCHOOL IV PAROCHIAL

(ALL RESULTANTS X 4)

Copyright, 1956 by

GEORGE G. STERN

scores were also lower than the pre-test scores (P = .05). This indicates a decrease in the teachers' expression of desire to participate in activities concerned with "the manipulation of external objects through speculative abstract thought or discussion relative to the area of the social sciences; reflection or discussion about social events or systems; data collection and inductive reasoning."

The teachers' post-test scores were significantly higher than their pre-

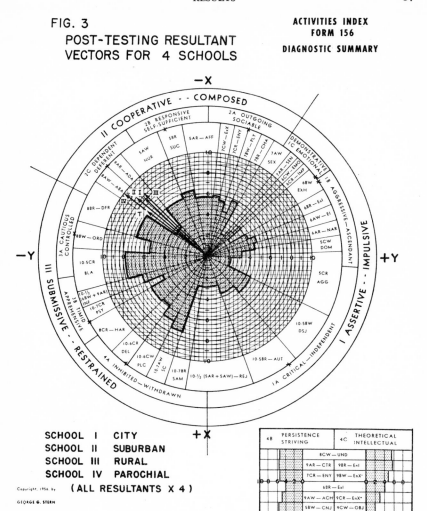

FIG. 3

POST-TESTING RESULTANT
VECTORS FOR 4 SCHOOLS

ACTIVITIES INDEX
FORM 156
DIAGNOSTIC SUMMARY

SCHOOL I   CITY
SCHOOL II   SUBURBAN
SCHOOL III RURAL
SCHOOL IV   PAROCHIAL

(ALL RESULTANTS X 4)

Copyright, 1956 by
GEORGE G. STERN

test scores on dimension 29 (Impulsion-Deliberation) which was significant at the .01 level. This was interpreted to mean that on the post-test,
the teachers expressed a reduction in preference for deliberative,
planned activity (see Table 26).

Based upon the kinds of activities which make up these three dimensions, the teachers as a total group evidenced the following significant
trends:

TABLE 26

Matched-Pair t Test on Thirty-Two Dimensions on the Activities Index
(Total Group)

Dimension	Mean Difference[a]	σ_D	t	P
1. Affiliation	.1885	.1536	1.227	——
2. Nurturance	.1475	.1196	1.233	——
3. Narcissism	−.0246	.1530	.161	——
4. Succorance-Autonomy	.0738	.1575	.469	——
5. Dominance	.0410	.1345	.305	——
6. Deference	.0738	.1353	.545	——
7. Abasement	.0082	.1249	.066	——
8. Aggression-Blamavoidance	.1393	.1288	1.082	——
9. Sex-Superego Conflict	−.1885	.1469	1.283	——
10. Sentience	.1721	.1127	1.527	——
11. Exhibition	−.0820	.1342	.611	——
12. Play	.0656	.1425	.460	——
13. Energy-Psychasthenia	−.0984	.1634	.602	——
14. Achievement	−.0492	.1411	.349	——
15. Ego Ideal	−.0492	.1622	.303	——
16. Exocathection-Extraception	−.3115	.1546	2.015	.05[b]
17. Exocathection-Intraception	.2459	.1446	1.701	——
18. Endocathection-Extraception (Physical)	.0082	.1723	.048	——
19. Endocathection-Extraception (Social)	−.3934	.1828	2.152	.05[b]
20. Endocathection-Intraception	.0328	.1425	.230	——
21. Understanding	.2541	.1543	1.647	——
22. Projectivity-Objectivity	−.1721	.1389	1.239	——
23. Harmavoidance	−.2787	.1550	1.798	——
24. Defensiveness	.1066	.1565	.681	——
25. Counteraction	−.0328	.1841	.178	——
26. Order	−.2131	.1449	1.471	——
27. Conjunctivity-Disjunctivity	−.0082	.1389	.059	——
28. Sameness-Change	.1066	.1327	.803	——
29. Impulsion-Deliberation	.4754	.1652	2.878	.01
30. Emotionality-Placidity	.1475	.1396	1.057	——
31. Rejection	.0656	.1149	.571	——
32. Infavoidance	.0820	.1127	.728	——

1. a reduction in concrete action
2. a decreased interest in the analysis of material relating to social behavior

---

[a]Minus sign indicates a decrease in score.
[b]Significant decrease.

3. less deliberative or planful action.

Although the significant differences noted between the pre-testing and post-testing indicated only slight changes resulting from the workshop, the differences that did occur suggest a resistance to the workshop material. This is consistent with the shift in the direction of withdrawal already noted in the vector analysis.

The apparent resistance expressed by the teachers toward the workshop motivated an interest into the initial characteristics of the teachers. To gain this information the pre-test means for each school and the total group were computed for the thirty-two dimensions. From an inspection of these pre-test means, a consistent pattern can be detected. The teachers from all four schools showed a significant lack of expression on four dimensions. Those dimensions were: aggression, sentience, exhibition and projectivity-objectivity. The teachers from Schools I (City), II (Suburban), and III (Rural) expressed significantly low needs on dimension 31 (rejection). Schools II (Suburban), III (Rural), and IV (Parochial) were significantly low in their expression of sex needs. Schools I (City) and IV (Parochial) were significantly low in expressing activities on six dimensions. Those dimensions were: aggression, sex, sentience, exhibition, projectivity-objectivity and rejection (see Table 27). This pattern suggests considerable restraint on the part of the teachers in impulse expression.

It can be seen from the post-test means that the teachers from the four schools remained significantly low in their expression of activities on the following dimensions: aggression, sex, exhibition, projectivity-objectivity and rejection. Schools I (City) and IV (Parochial) remained significantly low in their expression of dominance (see Table 28).

The characteristic pattern shown by the teachers was that of extreme personal reserve. It was desired that the workshop would have affected the personality structure of the teachers toward a greater expression of personal feelings. Unfortunately, however, the teachers as a total group moved in just the reverse direction. The changes that did occur seemed to be very superficially related to the workshop experience and imply a rejection of the workshop itself.

It is entirely possible that within the total group one or two schools did show a significantly greater release through the expression of personal feelings. Since the four schools have shown differences on the previously discussed measures, it was believed necessary to do an analysis on the results shown by the schools individually.

TABLE 27

Pre-Test Means for the Four Schools and Total Group on the Thirty-Two Dimensions of the Activities Index

Dimension	School I (City)	School II (Suburban)	School III (Rural)	School IV (Parochial)	Total Group
1. Affiliation	5.89	5.74	5.31	5.07	5.50
2. Nurturance	4.42	5.77	6.67	5.64	5.94
3. Narcissism	4.05	4.97	4.43	4.43	4.52
4. Succorance-Autonomy	6.16	6.74	6.35	6.43	6.44
5. Dominance	2.89a	3.40	3.37	1.93a	3.14
6. Deference	6.21	7.06	6.93	6.64	6.82
7. Abasement	3.32	3.69	3.46	4.29	3.60
8. Aggression-Blamavoidance	2.21a	1.80a	2.35a	1.29a	2.05a
9. Sex-Superego Conflict	3.11	2.94a	2.44a	1.29a	2.56a
10. Sentience	2.84a	2.83a	2.87a	2.29a	2.79a
11. Exhibition	2.58a	2.69a	2.56a	1.86a	2.52a
12. Play	5.00	4.26	4.65	3.57	4.47
13. Energy-Psychasthenia	6.21	5.54	5.52	4.93	5.57
14. Achievement	4.84	5.09	4.74	5.43	4.93
15. Ego Ideal	4.21	5.14	4.69	5.00	4.78
16. Exocathection-Extraception	7.00	6.11	6.20	5.07	6.17
17. Exocathection-Intraception	4.00	3.74	3.72	4.07	3.81
18. Endocathection-Extraception (Phys.)	3.79	3.09	3.37	3.00	3.31
19. Endocathection-Extraception (Soc.)	5.47	4.83	5.54	5.71	5.34

TABLE 27—*Continued*

Dimension	School I (City)	School II (Suburban)	School III (Rural)	School IV (Parochial)	Total Group
20. Endocathection-Intraception	6.37	5.71	5.28	5.36	5.58
21. Understanding	5.68	4.57	4.87	5.57	4.99
22. Projectivity-Objectivity	2.47a	2.06a	2.41a	1.21a	2.18a
23. Harmavoidance	5.95	6.63	6.19	6.57	6.32
24. Defensiveness	6.37	6.29	6.02	6.43	6.20
25. Counteraction	5.21	5.89	5.48	4.93	5.49
26. Order	5.11	5.51	5.72	6.14	5.61
27. Conjunctivity-Disjunctivity	4.63	5.69	5.57	6.57	5.57
28. Sameness-Change	3.16	3.89	3.87	5.71	3.98
29. Impulsion-Deliberation	4.11	3.80	3.93	1.86a	3.68
30. Emotionality-Placidity	3.21	3.54	3.31	2.14a	3.23
31. Rejection	2.11a	2.43a	2.93a	3.14	2.68a
32. Infavoidance	6.37	5.98	6.15	6.71	6.20

aLack of expression at the .05 level of significance.

TABLE 28

Post-Test Means for the Four Schools and Total Group on the Thirty-Two Dimensions of the Activities Index

Dimension	School I (City)	School II (Suburban)	School III (Rural)	School IV (Parochial)	Total Group
1. Affiliation	5.74	5.14	6.02	5.71	5.69
2. Nurturance	5.16	6.54	6.35	5.21	6.09
3. Narcissism	3.89	4.60	4.85	3.71	4.50
4. Succorance-Autonomy	6.11	6.40	6.76	6.43	6.52
5. Dominance	2.79[a]	3.11	3.44	2.86[a]	3.18
6. Deference	6.79	6.83	7.02	6.71	6.89
7. Abasement	3.21	3.91	3.39	4.21	3.61
8. Aggression-Blamavoidance	2.47[a]	1.74[a]	2.46[a]	1.81[a]	2.19[a]
9. Sex-Superego Conflict	2.74[a]	2.49[a]	2.57[a]	.79[a]	2.37[a]
10. Sentience	3.05	3.06	3.09	2.07[a]	2.96[a]
11. Exhibition	2.53[a]	2.40[a]	2.69[a]	1.43[a]	2.43[a]
12. Play	4.95	3.94	5.04	3.50	4.53
13. Energy-Psychasthenia	5.79	5.49	5.44	5.07	5.47
14. Achievement	4.21	5.34	4.78	5.07	4.89
15. Ego Ideal	4.26	4.71	5.00	4.36	4.73
16. Exocathection-Extraception	6.00	5.60	6.09	5.43	5.86
17. Exocathection-Intraception	4.37	4.00	4.02	3.93	4.06
18. Endocathection-Extraception (Phys.)	3.58	2.80[a]	3.46	3.71	3.32

TABLE 28—*Continued*

Dimension	School I (City)	School II (Suburban)	School III (Rural)	School IV (Parochial)	Total Group
19. Endocathection-Extraception (Soc.)	5.21	4.74	5.07	4.64	4.95
20. Endocathection-Intraception	6.37	5.54	5.52	5.14	5.61
21. Understanding	5.84	4.63	5.48	5.07	5.25
22. Projectivity-Objectivity	2.00[a]	1.63[a]	2.52[a]	1.00[a]	2.01[a]
23. Harmavoidance	5.79	6.23	6.33	4.79	6.04
24. Defensiveness	6.37	5.94	6.44	6.57	6.30
25. Counteraction	5.58	5.17	5.57	5.57	5.46
26. Order	4.95	5.11	5.35	6.93	5.40
27. Conjunctivity-Disjunctivity	4.21	5.89	5.65	6.29	5.57
28. Sameness-Change	3.53	3.97	3.91	5.79	4.08
29. Impulsion-Deliberation	4.68	4.00	4.48	2.57	4.16
30. Emotionality-Placidity	3.26	3.26	3.17	2.07[a]	3.08
31. Rejection	2.95[a]	2.34[a]	2.89[a]	2.93[a]	2.75[a]
32. Infavoidance	6.21	6.31	6.13	6.86	6.28

———

[a]Lack of expression at the .05 level of significance.

ANALYSIS FOR THE FOUR SCHOOLS

To retain the pattern utilized for the analysis on the previous instruments, Schools I (City) and III (Rural) which had regular contacts with exceptional children, and Schools II (Suburban) and IV (Parochial) will be discussed in that order. School I (City) made significant changes on two dimensions. The teachers' post-test scores were significantly higher on dimension 2 (Nurturance) than their pre-test scores, at the .05 level. This indicates that the teachers made a significant increase in the selection of nurturant activities revealing a higher need to support others by providing love, assistance, and protection.

These teachers became significantly lower on dimension 16 (Exocathection-Extraception) at the .01 level. This indicates a decreased desire on the part of the teachers to participate in activities which require action either practical, concrete, physical, or social. The overall changes evidenced from the results of these teachers reveal somewhat limited reflection of the desire for participation in nurturant behavior. They became less interested in bringing about changes which would require them to take definite action of almost any nature (See Table 29).

The results from School III (Rural) indicate greater expression in several areas. These teachers demonstrated significant changes toward greater expression of activities on five dimensions. On dimension 1 (Affiliation), the post-test scores were significantly higher than the pre-test scores at the .01 level, indicating that these teachers expressed a greater desire for participation in social activities. On dimension 3 (Narcissism), the post-test scores were significantly higher than the pre-test scores (P = .05), which indicates an increase in self-preoccupation. On dimension 12 (Play), the post-test scores were significantly higher than the pre-test scores at the .05 level which indicates that this group of teachers increased in their expression of activities involving amusement. On dimension 21 (Understanding), the post-test scores were significantly higher than the pre-test scores (P = .01). This indicates that this group increased in their selection of intellectual activities regardless of any interest or practical application that this intellectualization might hold for them. On dimension 29 (Impulsion-Deliberation), the post-test scores were significantly higher than the pre-test scores (P = .05). This indicates that these teachers increased in the expression of need for impulsive spontaneous behavior (see Table 29).

The teachers from School III (Rural) evidenced a pattern which was contradictory to that shown by the teachers' analysis as a total group. As a total group, the teachers became somewhat less expressive and more resistive to change. School III (Rural), however, became notice-

TABLE 29

Matched-Pair t Test on Thirty-Two Dimensions on the Activities Index for Schools I (City) and III (Rural)

Dimension	School I (City) Mean Difference	σ_D	t	School III (Rural) Mean Difference	σ_D	t
1. Affiliation	− .1579	.3270	.483	.7037	.2008	3.504c
2. Nurturance	.7368	.3140	2.346a	−.3148	.1625	1.937
3. Narcissism	− .1579	.3770	.419	.4259	.2025	2.103a
4. Succorance-Autonomy	− .0526	.3710	.142	.4074	.2091	1.948
5. Dominance	− .1053	.3143	.335	.0741	.2210	.335
6. Deference	.5789	.3270	1.770	.0926	.2000	.463
7. Abasement	− .1053	.2520	.418	−.0741	.2130	.348
8. Aggression-Blamavoidance	.2632	.3320	.793	.1111	.2240	.496
9. Sex-Superego Conflict	− .3684	.4730	.779	.1269	.2320	.559
10. Sentience	.2105	.2240	.940	.2222	.1845	1.204
11. Exhibition	− .0526	.3705	.142	.1296	.2305	.562
12. Play	− .0526	.4080	.129	.3889	.1894	2.053a
13. Energy-Psychasthenia	− .4211	.3183	1.323	−.0741	.2602	.285
14. Achievement	− .6316	.3351	1.885	.0370	.2180	.170
15. Ego Ideal	.0526	.3625	.145	.3148	.2449	1.285
16. Exocathection-Extraception	−1.0000	.2862	3.494c	−.1111	.2742	.405
17. Exocathection-Intraception	.3684	.3350	1.010	.2963	.2344	1.264
18. Endocathection-Extraception (Physical)	− .2105	.5545	.380	.0926	.2325	.398
19. Endocathection-Extraception (Social)	− .2632	.349	.754	−.4630	.2975	1.556
20. Endocathection-Intraception	.0000	.3000	.000	.2407	.232	1.038
21. Understanding	.1579	.4735	.334	.6111	.2155	2.836c
22. Projectivity-Objectivity	− .4737	.3366	1.407	.1111	.2314	.480
23. Harmavoidance	− .1579	.3355	.471	.1481	.1967	.753
24. Defensiveness	.0000	.3000	.000	.4259	.2328	1.829
25. Counteraction	.3684	.3760	.980	.0926	.2875	.322
26. Order	− .1579	.3688	.428	−.3704	.2035	1.820
27. Conjunctivity-Disjunctivity	− .4211	.3090	1.363	.0741	.2257	.328

TABLE 29 — *Continued*

Dimension	School I (City)			School III (Rural)		
	Mean Difference	σ_{D}	t	Mean Difference	σ_{D}	t
28. Sameness-Change	.3684	.2780	1.325	.0370	.2195	.169
29. Impulsion-Deliberation	.5789	.4140	1.398	.5556	.236	2.354a
30. Emotionality-Placidity	.0526	.3710	.142	−.1481	.2297	.645
31. Rejection	.8421	.2786	3.023b	−.0370	.1563	.237
32. Infavoidance	.1579	.2450	.6445	−.0185	.1915	.091

ably more expressive concerning both personal and professional activities (see Table 29).

The teachers for School II (Suburban), on the other hand, proved to be consistent with the pattern shown by the total group. These teachers decreased on three dimensions and increased on only one. On dimension 1 (Affiliation) their post-test scores were significantly lower at the .05 level. This indicates that these teachers decreased significantly in their selection of activities which required them to participate in social activities. Their post-test scores were significantly lower on dimension 16 (Exocathection-Extraception) at the .05 level indicating a resistance for action either practical, physical, concrete or social. On dimension 25 (Counteraction), the post-test scores were significantly lower than the pre-test scores (P = .05), indicating that these teachers decreased in their expression of a desire to take positive action in solving problems, or overcoming obstacles.

School II (Suburban) showed a significant increase at the .01 level for the selection of activities which support others by providing love, assistance, and protection. The increase on this dimension (Nurturance) could possibly mean that the content of the workshop effected a change among these teachers toward giving greater support and assistance to other individuals, presumably exceptional children. However, there has been no other evidence which would support this hypothesis (see Table 34 for a similar inconsistency for this school).

---

a.05 level of significance
b.02 level of significance
c.01 level of significance

TABLE 30

Matched-Pair t Test on Thirty-Two Dimensions on the Activities Index for Schools II (Suburban) and IV (Parochial)

Dimension	School II (Suburban) Mean Difference	σ_D	t	School IV (Parochial) Mean Difference	σ_D	t
1. Affiliation	−.6000	.2816	2.131[a]	.6429	.5800	1.108
2. Nurturance	.7714	.2172	3.552[b]	− .4286	.2276	1.883
3. Narcissism	−.3714	.3097	1.199	− .7143	.4853	1.472
4. Succorance-Autonomy	−.3429	.2492	1.376	.0000	.7703	.000
5. Dominance	−.2857	.2153	1.327	.9286	.3550	2.616[a]
6. Deference	−.2286	.2250	1.016	.0714	.5290	.135
7. Abasement	.2286	.2357	1.012	− .0714	.2452	.291
8. Aggression-Blamavoidance	−.0571	.1877	.304	.5714	.3095	1.846
9. Sex-Superego Conflict	−.4571	.2333	1.959	− .5000	.2724	1.836
10. Sentience	.2286	.2055	1.112	− .2143	.3344	.641
11. Exhibition	−.2857	.1668	1.713	− .4286	.3882	1.104
12. Play	−.3143	.2682	1.172	− .0714	.4857	.147
13. Energy-Psychasthenia	−.0571	.3250	.176	.1429	.4552	.314
14. Achievement	.2571	.2700	.952	− .3571	.3412	1.047
15. Ego Ideal	−.4286	.3210	1.335	− .6429	.4141	1.553
16. Exocathection-Extraception	−.5143	.2333	2.204[a]	.3571	.3720	.960
17. Exocathection-Intraception	.2571	.2570	1.000	− .1429	.4173	.342
18. Endocathection-Extraception (Physical)	−.2857	.3320	.861	.7143	.4500	1.587
19. Endocathection-Extraception (Social)	−.0857	.3240	.265	−1.0714	.5881	1.822
20. Endocathection-Intraception	−.1714	.2510	.683	− .2143	.3805	.563
21. Understanding	.0571	.2560	.223	− .5000	.5110	.978
22. Projectivity-Objectivity	−.4286	.2256	1.900	− .2143	.3657	.586
23. Harmavoidance	−.4000	.2466	1.622			
24. Defensiveness	−.3429	.2926	1.172	.1429	.4430	.323
25. Counteraction	−.7143	.3493	2.045[a]	.6429	.4879	1.320
26. Order	−.4000	.3155	1.268	.7857	.2385	3.294[c]
27. Conjunctivity-Disjunctivity	.2000	.2835	.705	− .2857	.1634	1.748

TABLE 30 — *Continued*

Dimension	School II (Suburban) Mean			School IV (Parochial) Mean		
	Difference	σ_D	t	Difference	σ_D	t
28. Sameness-Change	.0857	.2105	.407	.0714	.4742	.151
29. Impulsion-Deliberation	.2000	.3300	.606	.7143	.5287	1.351
30. Emotionality-Placidity	−.2857	.2410	1.185	− .0714	.3225	.221
31. Rejection	−.0857	.2224	.385	− .2143	.3805	.563
32. Infavoidance	.3429	.2005	1.710	.1429	.2310	.619

By and large, the little change that did take place among the teachers from School II (Suburban) indicated a resistance to or even a rejection of the workshop experience. The evidence for the statement is based upon the significant decrease in expression of action, counteraction and affiliation on the part of these teachers. The over-all pattern shown by School II (Suburban) suggests a subject matter orientation and a desire to remain within that type of structure. The teachers might be expected to show signs of defensiveness when asked to participate in group or individual activity.

School IV (Parochial) showed a rather unique change as compared with the other three schools. These teachers increase significantly in their preference for activities on two dimensions: dominance (P = .05) and order (P = .01) (see Table 30). Their increase in expression for participating in dominant behavior may be interpreted to mean that these teachers were resistant to the workshop experience. Their increased preference for activities related to orderliness indicated rather markedly the obsessive-compulsive characteristics of these teachers. It can be seen from Table 25 that their initial score was relatively high on this dimension. They became even higher in their needs for detailed precision and orderliness on the post-test administration. From this information, the reaction of these teachers toward special toilet handling comes into clearer focus. It may be recalled that on the Classroom Integration Inventory School IV (Parochial) decreased significantly in acceptance of children who required special toilet handling. In addition,

---

a.05 level of significance

b.02 level of significance

c.01 level of significance

they decreased in their ability to be realistic in the educational placement of these children.

DISCUSSION

The changes of personality characteristic shown by the teachers as a
total group which could be attributed to the workshop were very minor.
What evidence of change that was revealed through the analysis indicated a resistance on the part of the teachers to the workshop experiences.

In general, the teachers as a total group remained relatively stable in
their expression of needs from the pre-test to the post-test. On the basis
of the contrast between the scales on which they were relatively high, as
compared with those on which their scores were low, it might be said
that the teachers characteristically expressed a need to provide love,
assistance, and protection for others and they were dependent upon
others for returning this support. They showed a tendency to emphasize
and glorify those whom they perceive as being superior. They were
somewhat defensive and attempted to justify their feelings of failure
and humiliation.

The teachers were unusually restricted in their expression of hostility
toward others, either overt or covert. They seemed to have very little
erotic interest. Their need for voluptuous self-gratification was either
restrained or almost nonexistent. In general, they withdrew from any
activity in which they would stand out from others. The teachers seem
opposed to superstitious, mystic, or anthropomorphic ideology, indicating a tendency toward realistic objectivity.

On the Activities Index, as on the previously discussed measures, the
teachers from each of the schools responded in their own characteristic
fashion. The most impressive change favorable to the goal intended for
the workshop was that demonstrated by the teachers from School III
(Rural). These teachers became more expressive on both a personal and
a professional level. They seemed to feel that they could open up and
express themselves without being defensive of what they might say.

Schools I (City) and II (Suburban) showed somewhat similar patterns
of change. In both cases there was an increased preference for activities
through which they could provide love, support, and assistance for
other individuals. School II (Suburban) expressed considerably more
resistance to the workshop itself, decreasing in action, counteraction
and affiliation.

School IV (Parochial) revealed changes different from those found in
any of the other schools. These teachers, who were originally high in
obsessive-compulsive characteristics, became even more so throughout

the workshop. This finding was supported by their attitudes of rejection toward children who required special toilet handling, as assessed by the Classroom Integration Inventory. In this area these teachers became significantly less accepting even to the point of being unrealistic toward this handicap.

Some subjective evidence to validate the changes observed through the analysis of the results on the Activities Index will be reported subsequently in this chapter.

THE PICTURE JUDGMENT TEST

Although the Activities Index failed to show changes in personality structure of the teachers which had specific relevance to exceptional children, data from another test are also available for this purpose. This test, The Picture Judgment Test, includes thirteen pictures. Eight picture cards were selected from the Thematic Apperception Test and five were specifically developed for this study. The five new pictures portrayed handicapped children in varying social situations. (See Appendix.) The handicapped pictures were designed to elicit feelings, attitudes, and reactions of teachers toward handicapped children.

The scoring of the protocols was accomplished by judging each complete thought of the story on the basis of one dimension, negativism-positivism. The negativity-positivity scale was assigned five points based on the following criteria:

1. If the sentence or thought was more negative than the structure of the picture would indicate, it was scored a minus one.
2. If the sentence or thought was descriptive with a negative judgment, it was scored a minus one-half.
3. If the sentence or thought was purely descriptive, it was scored zero.
4. If the sentence or thought was descriptive with a positive judgment, it was scored plus one-half.
5. If the sentence or thought was positive regardless of the structure of the picture, it was scored a plus one.

Wassertheil (4) found this method of scoring to be effective in discriminating between a negative and a positive group of individuals. She compared the personality needs, as assessed by the Activities Index, of two such groups and found significant differences on several dimensions of personality. Wassertheil concluded that positive individuals have more satisfactory relationships, and are more secure and less rigid. Negative individuals, on the other hand, are significantly more rigid, less secure in their interpersonal relationships, and attempt to gain social acceptance through self-sacrifice and self-devaluation. Increases in positivity would seem relevant evidence, therefore, in assessing the contribution of the workshop experiences.

The structure of the Picture Judgment Test is such that it elicits a preponderance of negative responses. Although many of the cards presented negative stimuli even to the most positive of people, it was thought that since all subjects were accorded the same stimuli, the objectivity negative aspects of the cards would provide a constant factor in all the protocols and would not affect the relative position of individuals on the negativity-positivity dimension.

This instrument was also administered before and after the workshop and the difference scores were found by subtracting the pre-test from the post-test. The matched-pair t test was applied to the teachers' scores for the handicapped pictures, the TAT cards, and the handicapped pictures plus the TAT cards. This analysis was carried out for the total group and the four schools individually.

ANALYSIS

For the total group, the teachers showed a significant increase between the pre-test and the post-test which indicates that they responded more positively toward the handicapped children portrayed in the pictures. There was no significant gain in positiveness revealed on the TAT cards and the increase for the total scale for all of the teachers was not significant (see Table 31).

From the results on the previous measures it has been seen that the analysis of the total group can mask important patterns of change which come to light only through the analysis of the four schools individually. In keeping with the system of analysis already established, the four schools will be examined separately in this order. Schools I (City), III (Rural), II (Suburban) and IV (Parochial).

TABLE 31

Matched-Pair t Test on the Picture Judgment Test on the Handicapped Pictures—TAT Cards—Total Scale Total Group

	Handicapped	TAT	Total Scale
Pre-test mean	− 92.13	−294.05	−213.96
Post-test mean	− 45.68	−287.79	−195.12
Mean gain	46.45	6.26	18.84
N	121	121	121
t	1.9119	.3532	1.1649
P	.05	.4	.2

In School I (City), the teachers showed a considerable increase on the post-test scores for the handicapped pictures; however, this increase was not found to be significant, using the .05 level of confidence. Being unable to reject the hypothesis was partly due to a very large variance on the pre-test. The variance was considerably reduced on the post-test. This might be interpreted to mean that the effect of the workshop reduced extreme scores and produced a more homogeneous response to the handicapped pictures. On the TAT cards, the teachers modified their responses in a positive direction, but this was not found to be significant. The mean difference between the pre-test and the post-test on the total scale showed a slight increase in positivity but this too was not significant (see Table 32).

TABLE 32

Matched-Pair t Test on the Picture Judgment Test on the Handicapped Pictures—TAT Cards—Total Scale School I (City)

	Handicapped	TAT	Total Scale
Pre-test mean	−101.06	−262.95	−206.83
Post-test mean	− 39.83	−230.44	−158.61
Mean gain	61.23	32.51	48.22
N	19	19	19
t	.90162	.8166	1.2255
P	.4	.3	.2

The teachers at School III (Rural) showed an increase in positiveness on the handicapped pictures, but this was not found to be significant. There was no increase shown on the TAT cards or the total scale (see Table 33).

TABLE 33

Matched-Pair t Test on the Picture Judgment Test on the Handicapped Pictures—TAT Cards—Total Scale School III (Rural)

	Handicapped	TAT	Total Scale
Pre-test mean	−66.42	−279.60	−191.96
Post-test mean	−36.25	−288.21	−198.35
Mean gain	30.17	− 8.61	− 6.39
N	54	54	54
t	.8132	.30258	.2583
P	.3	——	——

School II (Suburban) showed a sizeable increase in mean differences in a positive direction on the handicapped pictures. This increase approached significance; however, the null hypothesis could not be rejected at the .05 level. These teachers were significantly more positive on the eight TAT cards at the .01 level. On the total scale, the teachers showed an increase in positivity which was significant at the .05 level (see Table 34).

TABLE 34

Matched-Pair t Test on the Picture Judgment Test on the Handicapped Pictures—TAT Cards—Total Scale School II (Suburban)

	Handicapped	TAT	Total Scale
Pre-test mean	−116.74	−325.59	−245.12
Post-test mean	− 46.74	−298.53	−192.35
Mean gain	70.00	27.06	52.77
N	34	34	34
t	1.566	2.5419	1.714
P	.1	.01	.05

The teachers at School IV (Parochial) showed an increase in mean differences between the post-test and pre-test. These differences, however, were not significant. The teachers showed no increase on the TAT cards or the total scale (see Table 35).

TABLE 35

Matched-Pair t Test on the Picture Judgment Test on the Handicapped Pictures—TAT Cards—Total Scale School IV (Parochial)

	Handicapped	TAT	Total Scale
Pre-test mean	−118.23	−312.46	−230.31
Post-test mean	− 88.77	−337.38	−240.0
Mean gain	− 29.46	− 24.92	− 9.69
N	14	1.066	14
t	.448	.5564	.2234
P	.4	.3	.5

DISCUSSION

There was no significant difference between the pre-test and the post-test handicapped means for any one of the four schools. Each school, however, did demonstrate a mean increase in positive scores ranging from 29 to 70. Although the increase was not significant, there was a tendency for the teachers in each school to respond more positively toward the handicapped children. Analyzing the four schools as a group, the additional degrees of freedom which were afforded made it possible to reject the hypothesis at the .05 level. This indicated that for the total group the teachers were significantly more positive toward handicapped children.

On the TAT pictures, School II (Suburban) was the only school which showed a significant gain in positive responses (P = .01). Schools III (Rural) and IV (Parochial) showed a slight decrease in mean scores between the post-test and the pre-test although this decrease was not significant. School II (Suburban) showed a significant improvement between the post-test and the pre-test on the total scale at the .05 level. None of the other three schools demonstrated an improvement for the total scale.

Generally speaking, the thematic protocols failed to show interpretable gains on the part of the teachers. The increases were greatest, although not statistically significant, for the handicapped pictures. This is reasonable because the experience gained from the workshop was, of course, more specific in that area. As with the Activities Index, however, these results suggest relatively little change in basic personality organization as a result of the workshop.

VALIDATION OF INSTRUMENT FINDINGS

The results from the General Information Inventory, and the Classroom Integration Inventory revealed significant gains in information, attitudes of acceptance and realistic judgment of the educational placement for exceptional children. In addition, the results on the Activities Index and the Picture Judgment Test indicated that the teachers showed slight changes in their personality characteristics and their feelings toward handicapped children and other individuals. These changes, however, have little meaning unless the teachers actually modified their behavior in some way as a result. The continuous observation of all of the teachers in their classrooms obviously was impossible. In place of direct observation for the validation of the reported changes on the General Information Inventory and the Classroom Integration Inventory, the Critical Incident technique was employed. To substantiate the changes in personality structure of the teachers and of their feelings toward handicapped children and other persons, a subjective analysis of the tape recordings of each discussion group was performed.

CRITICAL INCIDENT TECHNIQUE

This technique is a straightforward one which asks the teachers to describe in detail the things that they did differently as a result of the information of increased acceptance they experienced from the workshop. It was suggested that they think first of the most impressive experiences they could remember from the workshop and see if they could recall any way in which these experiences influenced them. The teachers were instructed to be objective in answering the questions and to cite only those incidents where they felt they had used something from the workshop.

In scoring, the teachers' responses were divided into three categories: specific, general, and unclassifiable. Incidents in which specific techniques, materials, or methods were used were classified as specific incidents. Those in which, as a result of a change in attitude or philosophy, their responses to exceptional children were more accepting, but mentioned no specific action, were classified as general incidents. Incidents where changes had occurred in either a specific or a general way, but did not occur in a particular area of deviation, were categorized as unclassifiable. The incidents were tallied in this manner and summed by area of deviation for the total group and for each of the four schools individually.

Analysis for total group. The greatest incidence of change in classroom procedure, teaching methods, or philosophy for the total group occurred in the areas of the gifted, speech and hearing handicaps, mental retardation, emotionally disturbed and educationally retarded. This, of course, is reasonable because each of the four schools had at least a few children in each of these areas of exceptionality within the classrooms. The teachers cited the least changes in actual teaching practices for these two areas:
1. children with physical handicaps which included cerebral palsy, orthopedic and cardiac disorders and seizures
2. children with visual handicaps or blindness.

Again this is logical because only a few of the teachers had actual experiences with these children. Throughout the four schools there was only one cerebral palsied child, two children with orthopedic or cardiac disorders, three children with epilepsy. There were no blind children in any of the schools. All of the children with the above-mentioned handicaps were in either Schools I (City) or III (Rural). No references involving change were made with regard to behavior disorders, physical attractiveness, or special toilet handling.

The mean number of incidents, as cited by the teachers, was 2.60. There were a total of 122 general incidents and 169 specific changes of attitude, instruction, or behavior mentioned by the teachers (see Table 36). The extensive change in actual practices mentioned by the teachers would suggest that the gain in information and acceptance revealed by the General Information Inventory and the Classroom Integration Inventory were incorporated into the behavior of the teachers.

TABLE 36

Incidents Involving Change in Teaching Practices Reported by Teachers in Relation to Exceptional Children for the Total Group

Area of Deviation	General	Categories Specific	Unclassified	Total
Mental retardation	31	37		68
Speech and hearing	19	38		57
Gifted	23	46		69
Visually handicapped (blind)	17	0		17
Emotionally disturbed	15	19		34
Educationally retarded	12	21		33
Cerebral palsy, Orthopedic and Cardiac disorders	5	8		13
Total incidents	122	169	36	327
N = 130 $\overline{X}$ = 2.60				

Schools I (City) and III (Rural) had considerably more exceptional children enrolled at the time of the workshop than did Schools II (Suburban) and IV (Parochial). Because of this, plus the wide variation of change demonstrated by the schools when analyzed separately on other measures, the incidents describing change from each of the schools were summed individually. In addition to summing the general and specific incidents involving change, two responses, selected randomly, from each school will be quoted in order to give the reader some idea of the quality of the teachers' responses.

Analysis for each of the four schools. The teachers at School I (City) cited a total of 56 incidents in six areas of deviation. Out of the 56 incidents, 29 were general and 13 were specific. The largest number of incidents in which the teachers cited changes were in the area of mental retardation. The fact that the teachers reported the most change in this area is consistent with what would be expected. School I (City) has three special classes for mentally retarded children (see Table 37).

TABLE 37

*Incidents Involving Change in Teaching Practices Reported by Teachers
from School I (City) in Relation to Exceptional Children*

Area of Deviation	Categories General	Specific	Unclassified	Total
Mental retardation	8	3		11
Speech	5	4		9
Gifted	3	4		7
Visually handicapped (blind)	7	0		7
Emotionally disturbed	3	2		5
Educationally retarded	3	0		3
Total incidents	29	13	14	56
$N = 21$ $\bar{X} = 2.66$				

From the 21 responses at School I (City), two incidents were selected
at random to give as typical examples of the types of modifications the
teachers at that school made in their teaching relationships with exceptional children.

School I (City) — Teacher 14: "It is difficult to say what things I have done
differently as a result of the understanding I gained during the workshop. I
doubt that my particular classroom methods have changed to any extent. My
relationships with youngsters have always been good and we have had mutual
understanding. I do feel, however, that I have developed a tolerance for other
teachers in our school and elsewhere. Through hearing analytical discussions of
their problems without the undertones of complaint, I have begun to realize
that perhaps teachers are individuals too, as well as our youngsters, and that
their behavior indicates underlying factors in the way they respond to certain
situations. I believe that I have always been rather one-sided in my feelings
toward education and I have never really understood teachers as a group. Now
I realize that I was wrong in grouping teachers."

Although this teacher mentioned no particular changes with respect
to exceptional children, it is believed that she might be able to achieve
better relationships with the other teachers in her school building
which in turn may be reflected in her relationship with the children.

School I (City) — Teacher 16: "I think my most impressive incidents were some
of the group discussions. The teachers were allowed to speak freely, and you
felt that you were not the only one with similar problems. Specifically I recall
one teacher asking how to handle tensions in the room. Since then I have tried
to use the ideas we discussed in that meeting. I have tried to minimize tense
situations by seeing the funny side, and having a good laugh if possible, or
leave the room for a moment to get a drink of water so that I might come back
and handle the situation a little less emotionally. Frequently, I change the
procedure by interrupting the tenseness with a period of freedom such as game

time, a song, or playtime activity. I have tried a recreation period in the gym, or clay activity.

One concrete action which I have taken as a result of the workshop is to order a portable punching bag for next term. I work with mentally retarded children, some of whom are very disturbed."

School III (Rural) had more than twice as many specific incidents than general incidents, *i.e.*, 46 general and 104 specific. The incidents of change in teaching cited most frequently were in the area of the gifted, and the least number of incidents occurred in the area of visually handicapped and cerebral palsy, each having three. The mean number of incidents cited at School III (Rural) was 2.90, a slight increase over the other three schools. The fact that School III (Rural) has a larger number of exceptional children might account for this (see Table 38).

TABLE 38

Incidents Involving Change in Teaching Practices Reported by Teachers from School III (Rural) in Relation to Exceptional Children

Area of Deviation	Categories			
	General	Specific	Unclassified	Total
Mental retardation	13	24		37
Speech and hearing	6	15		21
Gifted	10	28		38
Visually handicapped (blind)	3			3
Emotionally disturbed	6	14		20
Educationally retarded	5	18		23
Cerebral palsy, Orthopedic and				
Cardiac disorders	3	5		8
Total incidents	46	104	10	160
N = 58 $\overline{X}$ = 2.90				

The first example for School III (Rural) gave a good over-all picture of the modification that has taken place in that school. All of the incidents mentioned were concerned with curriculum reorganization and changes in philosophy.

School III (Rural) — Teacher 92: "The workshop taught our group how to work cooperatively on a common project through group discussions and it gave the opportunity to practice group dynamics in the solution of a problem our school faces.

The workshop made us realize that there are exceptional children in our school and that we have an obligation to do our best to plan for their needs. For instance, we have put into action a program for slow learners in the junior high.

Through the workshop the teachers were given the opportunity to see what the other person is doing and to learn why he is doing as he is. The heterogeneous discussion groups not only helped fix the theory we heard in the lectures, but gave us the opportunity to find out what other teachers are doing in their classrooms.

As a result of the workshop the group was stimulated to do professional study beyond that involved in the immediate classroom situation. For instance, twelve teaching and administrative persons have been taking a course in mental health which supplements the work of the workshop. In addition, the workshop gave us personal contacts with specialists which most of the group would never have made otherwise."

The major points made were the increased working relations of the teachers, some special consideration of a program for slow learners, and additional professional study over and above that required for the workshop or teaching.

The second example cited several specific incidents through which this teacher made changes in classroom procedure and organization.

School III (Rural) — Teacher 119: "As a result of the workshop, I have endeavored to make the learning experiences for the gifted more practical to them. I gave them outside work to do in related subject matter areas. I assigned group projects, library research in their area of interest, and group discussions.

In using insights I gained from Dr. Johnson, I changed the curriculum for the slow learners in my class, giving them work that they could do in the area of their interest. As a result they were able to find success. This seemed to lessen the discipline problems in my classroom considerably.

In general, I feel that the workshop increased my effectiveness as a teacher because it made me realize that the needs of all children differ in one respect or another."

At School II (Suburban) the teachers gave a total of 65 incidences in which they used insights gained from the workshop in their teaching experiences. In contrast with School I (City), these teachers cited more specific incidents than general incidents, i. e., 38 specific and 27 general. School I (City) had substantially more exceptional children enrolled than did School II (Suburban). School II (Suburban), being located in a higher socioeconomic area, had a considerable number of gifted children enrolled. It can be seen from Table 38 that a large number of the specific incidents which were reported from School II (Suburban) were in the area of the gifted. The teachers from School II (Suburban) reported the lowest mean number of incidents of change ($\overline{X} = 1.97$) (see Table 39).

The two samples selected at random from School II (Suburban) give adequate examples of specific and concrete action in the area of emotional disturbances, speech and mental retardation.

TABLE 39

Incidents Involving Change in Teaching Practices Reported by Teachers from School II (Suburban) in Relation to Exceptional Children

Area of Deviation	Categories			
	General	Specific	Unclassified	Total
Mental retardation	7	5		12
Speech and hearing	4	17		21
Gifted	8	10		18
Visually handicapped (blind)	1			1
Emotionally disturbed	4	1		5
Educationally retarded	2	2		4
Orthopedic and cardiac	1	3		4
Total incidents	27	38	8	73
N = 38 X̄ = 1.97				

School II (Suburban) — Teacher 34: "I had a better understanding of the two boys in my class who are retarded. I stopped pushing them to cover material, gave more thought to their happiness in the group. After hearing Dr. Sheldon I felt some of their reading habits which were depressing me most weren't faults at all but a normal thing to expect of a slow learning child.

I was very much impressed by Dr. Amster. I had been guilty of doing the wrong thing with a child who was a stutterer. I have always said, 'Stop now, and think what you want to say.' Now I try to provide a more relaxed atmosphere for him when he is speaking, by giving him plenty of time to say what he has to say."

This teacher has cited several very positive changes which may have an important influence upon the development of the exceptional children she has mentioned. Her realization that the slow learner cannot compete with the other children in the classroom is the first step in this teacher's reorganization of the curriculum to meet the needs of the slow learner with materials that the child can do. Judging from the examples she gave, it seems that she has become less anxious about these children. Her attitude has become more positive toward the stutterer she has mentioned. Through the insights she has gained with respect to dealing with this child's speech, it is entirely possible that she will be able to give the other children in the room better understanding of this child and consequently help them to accept his speech.

The second teacher sighted concrete action in terms of the referral of a child with an emotional disturbance which led to a speech problem.

School II (Suburban) — Teacher 59: "In my room I have an emotionally disturbed child. He began to have difficulty with speech which resulted from nervousness and tension. He is a poor reader and is not up to grade level. I have worked with him hour upon hour attempting to increase his academic and social adjustment, but could not stop the growing speech difficulty which eventually led into stuttering especially after a bad time at home. After hearing Dr. Amster, I immediately got to work and met with our speech therapist. The boy is now attending speech classes. He loves it, gets a great deal of satisfaction and we have arranged it so that he feels he gains status in the group through attending the classes. Also, the special attention which he craves so much has been received."

This is an excellent example of how a greater understanding of the causes of speech problems may stimulate the teacher to get help from a specialist. Obviously, she did a very good job in supporting the work done by the therapist in the techniques she used to give the child the feeling that the special classes were a source of status.

At School IV (Parochial), the teachers cited 38 incidents in which they made some changes in their teaching as a result of the workshop. The area in which the greatest number of incidents were cited was mental retardation and the least incidents were cited in the area of orthopedic and cardiac disorders. The mean number of incidents of change at School IV (Parochial) was 2.91 (see Table 40).

TABLE 40

Incidents Involving Change in Teaching Practices Reported by Teachers from School IV (Parochial) in Relation to Exceptional Children

Area of Deviation	Categories			
	General	Specific	Unclassified	Total
Mental retardation	3	5		8
Speech and hearing	4	2		6
Gifted	2	4		6
Visually handicapped (blind)	6			6
Emotionally disturbed	2	2		4
Educationally retarded	2	1		3
Orthopedic and cardiac disorders	1			1
Total incidents	20	14	4	38
$N = 13$ $\overline{X} = 2.91$				

As in the other three schools two samples were selected at random to use as examples of incidents of change expressed by the teachers at School IV (Parochial).

School IV (Parochial) — Teacher 116: "Because of the workshop I feel I have tried to help my pupils who were very slow in reading. The classes have given me good, concrete suggestions which were very helpful. Before the workshop began I had almost given some of them up as hopeless. Now, after trying the ideas suggested in the lectures and the discussions, I find they really can read and are very happy about it.

The lecture we had on speech problems was most interesting. I have become much more accepting of imperfect speech in my classroom and have tried to provide an opportunity for one child who is nonfluent to speak freely.

Dr. Strang's class was most interesting. She helped me to realize that I have some very gifted children in my classroom. The next day I found myself noticing the work of these children with an entirely different idea. I tried several new techniques with them to increase their interest and effort."

If the realization that this teacher mentioned with regard to both the "slow readers" and the "gifted children" has influenced her teaching as she feels it has, obviously she will be a more effective teacher. Her reference to the speech area was interesting; however, the changes cited were quite general.

In this next example only one incident was mentioned, but this one has broad implications.

School IV (Parochial) — Teacher 119: "The greatest influence upon me, that I gained from the workshop, was the understanding that the most important thing in the education of the slow learning child, in fact any child, is providing an opportunity for them to be a useful, happy, self-supporting citizen of the community. I have already started an experiment with one slow learning child to develop a certain skill that he had. It gained new impetus after Dr. Johnson's lecture on the slow learner. This individual has gained new and stronger self-confidence in himself and his fellow classmates realize that he has potentialities that they didn't know about. He is now looked up to and his opinions are respected."

Discussion. The Critical Incident technique was used to validate the results on the General Information Inventory and the Classroom Integration Inventory. The teachers as a total group cited 327 general and specific incidents involving change which resulted from their workshop experiences. Many of these changes in teaching practice appear to depend on the development of attitudes of increased acceptance and understanding, suggesting that the gains measured by the General Information Inventory and the Classroom Integration Inventory are an accurate reflection of attitude development among the teachers engendered by the workshop.

The number of incidents involving change reported by the teachers from each of the schools was related to the number of exceptional children enrolled in the school. The teachers from School IV (Parochial), however, did report a relatively high mean number of incidents and had relatively few exceptional children. The majority of the changes cited by these teachers in the actual teaching relationships or practices were with slow learners and speech-handicapped children. School IV

(Parochial) did have several children with speech handicaps and a number of children with slow learning mental ability.

The specific kinds of changes reported were directly dependent upon the number and types of exceptional children enrolled in each of the schools. The teachers, of course, cannot modify their practices or relationships with exceptional children who were not in their classrooms. Furthermore, it is less likely that teachers will demonstrate any real changes in their attitudes of acceptance toward exceptional children unless they can have actual experiences with these children.

TAPE RECORDINGS

To serve in some measure as validation for the results of the teachers on the Activities Index and the Picture Judgment Test, an independent, subjective analysis of the tape recordings for each of the groups was performed. The tape recordings were analyzed in terms of the nature and quality of the discussion, the underlying dynamics of the groups and the over-all attitudes of the groups toward the workshop experiences. Any other information which might help the reader gain a clearer understanding of the nature of the discussion groups will also be reported.

School I. School I is a city school located in a lower socioeconomic neighborhood. There were a substantial number of exceptional children enrolled there at the time of the workshop. The teaching staff was completely female, ranging in age from approximately 24 to 65 years of age, with a predominant number over 45.

By way of recapitulation, it was found through the analysis of the Activities Index that these teachers were somewhat restrained, particularly in the area of personal expression. On the post-test, an increased need for the expression of nurturant behavior, *i. e.*, supporting others by providing love, assistance or protection, was revealed from the results of these teachers. They decreased in their preference for activities involving action of any nature. There were no significant increases shown in this group as assessed by the Picture Judgment Test.

The discussion throughout the first half of the workshop was tense and restricted with some expression of pity for children in some areas of exceptionality. During this period the discussion consisted predominantly of direct questions to the discussion leader. Beginning with the tenth discussion meeting, a few of the teachers expressed personal feeling toward blind children. From that point the discussions became somewhat less restricted. The interaction between the teachers became more relaxed which resulted in greater group participation. However, several of the teachers remained passive toward any group participation throughout the workshop.

The tape recordings revealed considerably greater expression of realistic acceptance toward exceptional children during the last quarter of the workshop. The teachers revealed more understanding for children with crippling conditions and children with blindness. These two areas elicited a fairly large amount of pity content from the teachers. Four teachers expressed less hostility for the emotionally disturbed children in their classrooms.

Although there were no indications from the recordings that the workshop effected any changes in the personality structure of the teachers in either group, there were signs of modifications in attitudes and understandings of exceptional children. Several steps requiring action on the part of the teachers and the administrator were taken which indicated a greater interest in the integration of exceptional children. A kindergarten teacher and the administrator demonstrated considerable planning of materials and classroom organization for a blind child who was to be integrated in the kindergarten class the following year. Several other teachers expressed a desire to cooperate in the planning for this child. This action on the part of the teachers occurred after they had learned that a blind child was to be placed in that school.

The somewhat restrained nature of this group of teachers as observed from the recordings support the results found on the Activities Index. What was not revealed in the group analysis based on this instrument was that a number of these teachers became eager in later discussion sessions to gain additional understandings from the workshop to help them in the resolution of the problems of the handicapped children who were in their classrooms. Whether these particular individuals showed comparable shifts in the Index cannot be determined, unfortunately, since there is no way of identifying individual test protocols.

School III. School III is a centralized school located in a rural area. The teachers there ranged in age from approximately 27 to 55 with the majority ranging in age from 30 to 45 years of age. Twenty of the 56 teachers and administrators were males.

In review of the findings on the Activities Index the teachers from School III demonstrated increased expressions of needs on five dimensions. These were: affiliation, narcissism, understanding, play and impulsiveness. The over-all pattern on the Activities Index revealed increased freedom of expression on both a personal and professional level. No significant changes were found on the Picture Judgment Test.

The analysis of the recordings from the three discussion groups gives considerable support to the results from the Activities Index. The discussions throughout the workshop were free and spontaneous. There appeared to be very little defensiveness on the part of a majority of the teachers, and they were able to express personal feelings and attitudes freely. Good interaction was observed among the discussion groups. The teachers seemed eager to gain more information concerning exceptional children and ardent in discussing their own problems with exceptional children.

It was believed that some, although perhaps temporary, changes in personality structure occurred as a result of the workshop. The pattern revealed from the Activities Index suggests that an increase in the abilities of these teachers to express needs of a personal nature occurred as a result of the workshop. This seemed apparent throughout the discussion groups. On a few occasions problems of a personal nature, not related to exceptional children, were expressed and discussed by the groups. Although the discussion leaders did not attempt to play a therapeutic role, it is believed that some release of personal tensions was provided the teachers from time to time.

School II. School II is a common school district located in a higher socioeconomic suburban area. The teachers employed there ranged in age from approximately 25 to 50 years of age with a predominant number between 30 and 40 years of age. A considerably greater number of gifted children were enrolled in School II than in any of the other three schools. With the exception of the gifted children and several children with speech and hearing handicaps, only two or three children in all other areas of deviation attended that school.

In referring back to the results on the Activities Index, this was the group which showed the significant shift toward withdrawal on the over-all resultant vector analysis. These teachers showed a decrease in their expression of needs on three dimensions. Those were: affiliation, exocathection-extraception, and counteraction. They increased in their preference for activities involving nurturant behavior. This suggests that the teacher became *less* willing to participate in activities requiring them:

1. to have associations with other persons
2. to take positive action of a practical, concrete, physical or social nature

3. to take constructive action leading to the solution of frustration. They did, however, express a greater preference for activities through which they could provide love, assistance and protection for others. Despite this apparently superficial reflection of the workshop content, in general, the results on the Activities Index indicated a pattern of resistance to the workshop material, and to any additional work that this experience might cause them.

The initial atmosphere in the discussion groups seemed restricted and tense. There were indications of underlying hostility, defensiveness and suspicion among the teachers. These attitudes that several of the teachers had were not disclosed during the discussions, but came out in personal interviews with the discussion leader after the meetings.

The discussion groups remained continuously tense and restrained throughout the workshop. Almost all of the discussion consisted of questions directed to the group leaders. The atmosphere of the discussion groups suggested considerable defensiveness and some hostility toward the workshop itself. Very little change was noted from the recordings either with regard to attitudes toward exceptional children or in the personality structure of the teachers involved.

All of the evidence disclosed from the recordings supports the findings on the Activities Index. The teachers seemed to have a strict subject matter philosophy which resulted in a reluctance to enter into group participation.

The results from the Picture Judgment Test showed a significant increase in expression of positiveness toward themselves and toward other individuals. There was no evidence throughout the analysis of the tape recordings or any of the instruments to support this finding.

School IV. School IV is a parochial school located in an average socio-economic neighborhood. The teachers and administrators were Catholic sisters. Three other teachers who were not sisters participated in the discussion group. The teachers ranged in age from approximately 25 to 55 years of age. Relatively few exceptional children attended School IV. There were several speech-handicapped children and a number of educationally retarded children enrolled there.

The results on the Activities Index disclosed an increase in the preference of these teachers for activities involving dominant behavior and orderliness. Because of their high initial scores on orderliness, the personality structure of these teachers was interpreted as being somewhat obsessive-compulsive. The findings on the Activities Index with regard to the compulsive characteristics of these teachers was supported by the decrease revealed in acceptance for children who required special toilet handling, as assessed by the Classroom Integration Inventory.

The original plan for the discussion at this school was to divide into two groups; however, after the first meeting the sisters asked to remain in one group, and the idea for two groups was abandoned. The content of the discussion consisted entirely of questions from the sisters directed to the discussion leader. At no time was there a personal opinion or attitude expressed from the group. The group remained quite tense throughout the workshop and seemed uneasy when they were asked to contribute.

SUMMARY

1. The teachers from all four schools increased significantly in information about exceptional children as a result of the workshop. Having experiences with exceptional children does not have a systematic influence upon the amount of increase that the teachers show on the information level.

2. As a total group, the teachers demonstrated significant increases in acceptance of exceptional children for seven areas of exceptionality. The teachers from the two schools having relatively large numbers of exceptional children increased in acceptance for a substantial number of areas of deviation. The two schools with few exceptional children showed very slight increases in acceptance.

3. The teachers were able to modify their attitudes for some areas of exceptionality more readily than for others. The significant differences between the areas of deviation were a function of the teachers' initial acceptance in the area, and the number of experiences with exceptional children in the area. There were no significant differences between the three degrees of involvement within the areas of deviation.

4. The teachers did not show marked increases in their ability to become more realistic concerning the accurate placement of exceptional children. The significant increases that were demonstrated in realistic placement for some areas were offset by significant decreases in others.

5. The personality structure of the teachers as a total group did not change as a result of the workshop. What evidence of change there was, revealed through the analysis, indicated a resistance on the part of the teachers to the workshop experience.

6. The teachers became significantly more positive in their responses to handicapped children. As a group they did not become more positive toward themselves, their own adjustment, or toward other individuals.

7. Each of the four schools changed in their own characteristic way on all of the instruments used for assessment. There were no consistent patterns of change among the teachers throughout the four schools; however, the changes shown by the two schools having relatively large numbers of exceptional children were closely related.

8. The teachers reported a substantial number of changes in instructional techniques and methods, classroom practices and other relationships with exceptional children as a result of the workshop experience. This evidence was used to suggest that the gains found on the General Information Inventory and the Classroom Integration Inventory were incorporated into the teachers' behavior relative to exceptional children.

9. Evidence revealed through a subjective analysis of the tape recordings from the discussion groups indicated that the results on the Activities Index were valid.

REFERENCES

1. Tukey, J. W. "Comparing Individual Means in the Analysis of Variance," *Biometrics*, V., No. 2 (June 1949).

2. Lindquist, E. F. *Design in Analysis of Experiments in Psychology and Education*. Boston: Houghton Mifflin Co., 1953.

3. Norton, Dee W. "An Empirical Investigation of Some Effects of Non-normality and Heterogeneity of the F-distribution," Ph. D. thesis in Education, State University of Iowa, 1952. Cited by E. F. Lindquist. *Design in Analysis of Experiments in Psychology and Education.*

4. Wassertheil, Sylvia. "A Study of the Need Patterns of Negative and Positive Individuals." Unpublished Master's thesis, Graduate School, Syracuse University, 1955.

CHAPTER FIVE

DISCUSSION

THE GENERAL PURPOSES OF THIS INVESTIGATION WERE:
1. to influence attitudes and understandings of teachers toward exceptional children
2. to assess the change in the attitudes, understandings and personality characteristics resulting from the workshop
3. to determine the extent to which the teachers utilized the experiences they had gained from the workshop in their relationships with exceptional children.

To accomplish these purposes, fifteen workshop meetings concerned with exceptional children were presented to all of the teachers and administrators from four schools in and near the Syracuse, New York, area. The members of the workshop were presented identical lectures in eight areas of exceptionality. After each lecture, which lasted an hour, the teachers divided into discussion groups. The discussions, also lasting an hour, were relevant to the area of exceptionality presented in the preceding lecture.

EVALUATION RESULTS

Four measuring devices were administered during the first and last sessions of the workshop. These devices were:
1. The General Information Inventory
2. The Classroom Integration Inventory
3. The Activities Index
4. The Picture Judgment Test.

A fifth instrument, the Critical Incident Technique, was given during the last session only (see Table 41).

The General Information Inventory was designed to measure the information and understanding teachers had concerning the exceptional child. The Classroom Integration Inventory, designed to measure acceptance, was analyzed in terms of the degree of acceptance teachers had

TABLE 41

Summary of Results

Instruments	School I (City)	School II (Suburban)	School III (Rural)	School IV (Parochial)	Total
GENERAL INFORMATION TEST					
Pre-test means	61.17	56.29	55.76	50.71	56.14
Post-test means	67.28	61.24	64.79	70.29	64.63
Significance level of mean gain	.01	.001	.001	.001	.001
CLASSROOM INTEGRATION INVENTORY					
Acceptance Scores					
Number of areas of gain	6	1	7	1	7
Pre-test means	145.28	170.46	170.51	155.86	165.00
Post-test means	165.17	173.64	181.94	152.79	173.47
Realism Scores					
Number of areas (increase)	0	1	2	0	1

TABLE 41 — *Continued*

Instruments	School I (City)	School II (Suburban)	School III (Rural)	School IV (Parochial)	Total
ACTIVITIES INDEX					
Significance level of vector shift	—	.01	—	—	.01
Direction of shift		Withdrawal			Withdrawal
Number of pre-test means significantly low	6	6	6	8	6
Number of post-test means significantly low	6	7	5	9	6
Dimensions showing significant increase	Nurturance	Nurturance	Affiliation, Narcissism, Play, Understanding, Impulsion	Dominance, Order	Deliberative Behavior
Dimensions showing significant decrease	Practical, Physical, Concrete or Social Action	Affiliation, Action, Counteraction			Action, Sociability

TABLE 41—*Continued*

Instruments	School I (City)	School II (Suburban)	School III (Rural)	School IV (Parochial)	Total
PICTURE JUDGMENT TEST					
Handicapped Pictures					
Pre-test means	−101.06	−116.74	− 66.42	−118.23	− 92.28
Post-test means	− 39.83	− 46.74	− 36.25	− 88.77	− 45.68
Significance level of mean gain	.4	.1	.3	.4	.05
TAT Cards					
Pre-test means	−262.95	−325.29	−279.60	−312.46	−213.96
Post-test means	−230.44	−298.53	−288.21	−337.38	−195.12
Significance level of mean gain	.3	.01	—	—	.2
CRITICAL INCIDENT TECHNIQUE					
Mean incidents involving change	2.66	1.97	2.90	2.91	2.60
TAPE RECORDINGS					
Subjective analysis of discussion groups	Restricted for first half. More expression of attitudes during last 6 meetings.	Question and answer discussion. Hostility toward workshop which lessened at the end for some individuals.	Very good discussion throughout workshop.	Restricted discussion throughout workshop. Some latent hostility.	

toward exceptional children and in terms of their ability to be realistic concerning the placement of these children. The Activities Index was administered to determine the personality structure of the teachers. The Picture Judgment Test was administered to determine the feelings and attitudes teachers had toward handicapped children, and to determine their relationships to other individuals. The Critical Incident Technique was administered to determine the extent to which the teachers used the experiences they gained from the workshop in their relationships with exceptional children.

INCREASES IN GENERAL INFORMATION AND UNDERSTANDING

The workshop proved highly effective in increasing the information and understanding that the teachers had concerning children with exceptionalities. The null hypothesis was rejected at the .01 level of significance for School I (City), and at the .001 level for Schools II (Suburban), III (Rural), and IV (Parochial). The teachers, analyzed as a total group, showed a significant increase in information at the .001 level. The pre-test and post-test means were computed for the four schools and it was found that the teachers from School I (City) had the highest mean for the pre-test and made the least gain in information. The teachers from School IV (Parochial) made the lowest mean score on the pre-test and received the highest mean on the post-test. The analysis of variance between the schools revealed that there were significant differences in the amount of gain demonstrated by the four schools.

MODIFICATION IN ATTITUDES OF ACCEPTANCE

In analyzing the scores on the Classroom Integration Inventory in terms of acceptance, wide differences were observed throughout the schools in the modification of attitudes toward greater acceptance of exceptional children. The teachers from Schools I (City) and III (Rural) made significant increases in several areas of exceptionality. School I (City) demonstrated significant increases in acceptance toward children with the following exceptionalities:

1. emotional disturbances
2. hearing handicaps
3. orthopedic and cardiac disorders
4. seizures
5. speech handicaps
6. visual handicaps.

The teachers from School III (Rural) increased significantly in their attitudes of acceptance toward children with the following exceptionalities:

1. behavior disorders
2. hearing handicaps
3. orthopedic and cardiac disorders
4. physical unattractiveness
5. seizures
6. speech handicaps
7. visual handicaps.

The teachers from School II (Suburban) showed a very slight increase which was significant for only one area of deviation: children with seizures. The teachers from School IV (Parochial) showed virtually no increase in acceptance. They increased significantly at the .05 level for children with seizures; however, this increase was offset by a significant decrease at the .001 level for children who require special toilet handling.

Although the matched-pair t tests indicated significant increases in seven areas of exceptionality for teachers as a total group, it would be misleading to conclude that each of the four schools showed an increase in acceptance. The teachers from the four schools demonstrated varying amounts of increase in acceptance. It can be observed from the pre-test and post-test means for the four schools that School I (City) had the lowest pre-test mean (145.28). The post-test mean for that school was lower than the pre-test mean for School II (Suburban) (170.46). School I (City) showed a significant increase in six areas of exceptionality, but School II (Suburban) increased in acceptance in only one area. Apparently, however, this relatively slight increase in acceptance on the part of the teachers from School II (Suburban) is not strictly a function of having had a high acceptance score prior to the workshop. This was borne out by the fact that the mean acceptance score achieved by the teachers from School III (Rural) on the pre-test was as high as that for School II (Suburban), yet the teachers from School III (Rural) increased significantly in seven areas of exceptionality (see Table 7).

It may be remembered that the lecturers, discussion leaders, and presentations were identical for each of the four schools. This variable, then, was controlled. The variables concerned with the number of exceptional children in each school, and the dynamics of the discussion groups were not controlled. Schools I (City) and III (Rural), showing the greatest gain in acceptance, had relatively large numbers of handicapped children enrolled, whereas Schools II (Suburban) and IV (Parochial) had only a few. This would appear to suggest that the workshop was most effective with those who were having concurrent experiences with exceptional children.

In addition, from a subjective analysis of the tape recordings of the discussion groups, it seemed obvious that the dynamics of the groups varied markedly. The teachers from Schools I (City) and III (Rural) were able to express their attitudes toward children with exceptionalities because they had had actual experiences with many of these children in their classrooms. The teachers' discussion in the groups from Schools II (Suburban) and IV (Parochial) was largely question and answer in nature. This may be attributable to the fact that these teachers had relatively few experiences with handicapped children.

REALISTIC PLACEMENT OF EXCEPTIONAL CHILDREN

By and large the workshop did not prove effective in increasing the abilities of teachers to become more realistic about the placement of children with exceptionalities. The significant increases in realistic placement which occurred were offset by significant decreases. Whether or not teachers had experiences with exceptional children in their classrooms seemed to make little difference in their ability to be more accurate in their judgment concerning the placement of these children.

CHANGES IN PERSONALITY CHARACTERISTICS

Although there were significant changes in the teachers' expressions of needs on a few dimensions as measured by the Activities Index, it would be highly tenuous to attribute these changes to the workshop. Although the over-all shift was in the direction of withdrawal, there were no consistent patterns of change throughout the schools. The teachers from Schools I (City) and II (Suburban) expressed significantly greater needs for participation in nurturant behavior. These two schools also decreased in their expression of the need to manipulate external objects through practical, concrete, physical or social action. The teachers from Schools II (Suburban) and III (Rural) changed significantly in opposite directions with regard to their need for affiliation. School II (Suburban) expressed a lesser need for association with others and School III (Rural) increased significantly on this dimension.

The teachers from School II (Suburban) showed a marked over-all shift in the direction of withdrawal, and decreased specifically in their desires to participate in activities involving:

1. relationships with others

2. constructive action toward the solution to conflicts
3. practical application or concrete action.

The teachers from School III (Rural), showing the greatest increase, raised their expression of activities on the following five dimensions:

1. Affiliation
2. Narcissim
3. Play
4. Understanding
5. Impulsion.

The teachers from School IV (Parochial) increased significantly in their expression of needs involving autocratic ascendancy over others and pre-occupation with orderliness.

Judging from the significant changes shown between the pre-test and the post-test, the teachers from School III (Rural) demonstrated the most noteworthy increase in their expression of activities. This is consistent with the dynamics of the group discussions in that school. The discussions seemed unrestrained throughout the workshop. The teachers were able to discuss their personal attitudes and problems more readily than any of the other groups.

Schools II (Suburban) and IV (Parochial) disclosed obvious signs of less responsiveness and greater restrictiveness toward the workshop experience. The fact that the teachers from these two schools had relatively few direct and concrete experiences with exceptional children would suggest that the presence of these children in the teachers' classrooms is an important factor in influencing teachers' receptiveness toward a workshop of this nature.

Disregarding any modification that may have occurred between the pre-testing and post-testing, the teachers, by and large, were an unusually reserved group. The pre-test and post-test means revealed a consistent pattern. Characteristically, the teachers expressed needs for activities requiring nurturant behavior. They emphasized and glorified those whom they perceived as being superior. They were somewhat defensive and attempted to justify their feelings of failure and humiliation.

The teachers were restricted in expressing hostility toward others. They seemed to have very little erotic interest in, or expression of, sexual behavior. Apparently any needs in this area have been sublimated or repressed. If not, the atmosphere of the workshop was such that they did not feel free to express the needs that existed even though they knew that their names remained anonymous throughout the testing. Their needs for voluptuous self-gratification were either restrained, suppressed or almost nonexistent. In general, they withdrew from any activity in which they would stand out from others. The teachers were opposed to superstitious, mystic or anthropomorphic ideology, indicating a tendency toward realistic objectivity.

ATTITUDES TOWARD HANDICAPPED CHILDREN

The workshop did effect changes in a positive direction with regard to the teachers' responses to handicapped children. Although the null hypothesis could not be rejected for any one of the four schools, a tendency to become more positive toward exceptional children and toward the solution to the problems experienced by handicapped children, was noted in the response of the teachers throughout the four schools to the pictures of exceptional children. Analyzing the four schools as a group, the additional degrees of freedom which were afforded made it possible to reject the hypothesis at the .05 level of significance.

ATTITUDES TOWARD OTHERS

On the TAT cards, the teachers from School II (Suburban) were the only ones who showed a significant gain in positive responses toward themselves, their life adjustment and other individuals. The teachers in Schools III (Rural) and IV (Parochial) showed a slight decrease in mean scores between the post-test and the pre-test. Irrespective of the gain shown by School II (Suburban), it may be concluded that the workshop did not influence teachers to become more positive in responding to persons other than handicapped children, as this is measured by the TAT.

MODIFICATION IN ACTUAL PRACTICE

As assessed by the Critical Incident Technique, the workshop was found to have had a strong positive influence upon the attitudes, philosophy, and teaching methods of the teachers which carried into their teaching relationships with exceptional children. A mean of 2.60 incidents of change occurred in some aspect of teaching for each of the teachers. A total of 327 incidents of modification of teaching methods or attitudes affecting teacher-child relationships occurred as a result of the workshop.

SUMMARY OF CHANGES

The changes demonstrated by the teachers, as a result of the workshop, may be summarized by the following statements:

1. The teachers from each of the four schools increased significantly in their information and understandings of exceptional children.
2. Increases in information do not necessarily effect increases in attitudes of acceptance on the part of teachers.
3. The teachers became significantly more accepting of exceptional children as a result of the workshop experiences.
4. The teachers from the two schools which enrolled the largest number of handicapped children demonstrated the greatest modification in their attitudes of acceptance toward these children.
5. The teachers did not become more realistic in their judgments of the most accurate placement of exceptional children as a result of the workshop.
6. Changes in attitudes toward exceptional children did not involve measurable changes in the basic personality characteristic of the teachers.
7. The responses of the teachers became more positive, *i.e.*, they responded with less sympathy or rejection and more concrete procedures for working with exceptional children.
8. The workshop did not effect positive responses from the teachers with regard to their own adjustment, or their adjustment to their superiors and peers.
9. The teachers were able to incorporate the increased acceptance and understanding they experienced from the workshop in their day-to-day teaching relationship with exceptional children (see Table 41).

CONCLUSIONS

The conclusions to a study of this nature are necessarily multifold. Principally, they deal with the total process of behavioral modification. Within this broad area, however, the changes of teacher attitudes were of primary importance. Specifically, this work concerns itself with the problem of effecting teachers' acceptance of the exceptional child. It is felt that the evidence presented in the body of this research effort justifies the following conclusions:

TEACHER REALISM

It has been substantiated that teacher attitudes were modified as a result of the workshop in the direction of increased acceptance toward pupils classified as exceptional. This was particularly true for the participants from those schools already providing teaching experiences for exceptional children. It was also found that the approach of the teachers with regard to the educational placement of exceptional children did not become more realistic irrespective of the increased acceptance which was demonstrated. There was still a tendency for both undercompensation and overcompensation by the teachers in their response to the problem of placement. In the areas of exceptionality where the teachers showed a highly significant increase in their attitudes of acceptance, this increase was even greater than the specialist in the area would recommend, indicating that they became overzealous in their desire to teach these children in their classroom. In areas where teachers did not increase in acceptance, or actually decreased on this dimension, they were considerably more rejecting than the specialists. It appears that their feelings of acceptance and rejection occurred on an emotional level without a particular regard to the most effective placement for children with exceptionalities.

THE PERSONALITY STRUCTURE OF TEACHERS

The workshop experience did not appear to prove effective in bringing about changes in the personality structure of the members as measured by the instruments employed in this study. The teachers appeared unusually restricted in their expression of personal needs, both before and after the workshop experience. It is heartening, however, that an effort designed to modify attitudes can be considered successful even though no major personality changes were demonstrated. Apparently it is possible to effect modification in attitudes without resultant personality changes.

THE GROUP DYNAMICS

There is an apparent relationship between the fluidity of group discussion and demonstrations of increased acceptance toward exceptional children. Conversely, where feelings, attitudes and even tensions were not openly expressed an identifiable pattern of rejection, anxiety and defensiveness appeared. It should be noted, however, that the discussions were freer and the acceptance level higher in groups where actual teaching experience with the exceptional child already existed. The unavoidable confounding of the two factors of fluidity of discussion and experience with exceptional children raises some problems in interpretation which will be discussed below, under Need for Further Research.

THE SUPPORTIVE EFFECT OF THE WORKSHOP

Teachers presented with formal lectures supported by permissive discussion sessions, films and visits to classrooms in which exceptional children were being educated increased their knowledge concerning exceptional children irrespective of their having direct and concrete experiences with these children. However, increased knowledge *per se* was not found to be a significant factor in effecting modifications of teachers' attitudes toward exceptional children. On the other hand, classroom experiences with exceptional children concurrent with a workshop appear to play a crucial role in the effectiveness of programs designed to influence teacher attitudes toward these children.

Teachers engaged in daily contact with exceptional children were most receptive to the workshop program and responded enthusiastically in the discussions. Perhaps this can be accounted for through the fact that teachers who were currently attempting to meet the daily exigencies of dealing with exceptional children have an immediate need for information, guidance and emotional release, have a wide repertoire of concrete and relevant observations bearing on the topic under discussion, and have more tangible association established through past experiences with these children. The teachers not engaged in daily contact with exceptional children seemed less receptive to a program of this nature, became defensive and resorted to thinly veiled hostility or evasive intellectualization. A possible explanation for this reaction may lie in the fact that they failed to recognize a need for an experience of this nature, responded to the ideas of the group on a purely intellectual level without the support of past experiences and association with this group of children, and were threatened or made anxious by the implied process of integration which seemed far less workable in abstraction for them than others had found it to be in actual practice.

From the reactions of those teachers who had few opportunities for actual experiences with exceptional children, it appears that the threat of having to modify behavior is more anxiety-producing than the real process of change itself. Introspection into how one might feel when asked to teach a handicapped child without having a firsthand acquaintance with that child tends to elicit rejection rather than acceptance. For teachers who are already engaged in teaching the handicapped child, the process of change is apparently perceived as being much less severe and the effect of the workshop is supportive rather than threatening.

Similar findings pertaining to attitudes toward Negroes have been reported by Weaver (1) which suggest that the successful assimilation

of Negroes as well as exceptional children requires the structure afforded by actual experience with these two groups. During World War
II the shortage of bus drivers prompted several large cities to employ
Negro streetcar platform workers and bus drivers for the first time.
Despite the high visibility of Negroes on such jobs, there was a remark-
able absence of public antagonism to colored surface transportation
workers introduced in Chicago, as compared with the difficulties encountered in Philadelphia and Los Angeles. In all three cities the decision to employ such personnel was presented to the public via the daily
press. In Chicago, the employment of the Negro traction workers took
place simultaneously with the onset of the newspaper campaign supporting the utilization of the Negro drivers. Isolated protests were expressed, but the public soon accepted the new employees.

Philadelphia and Los Angeles undertook similar newspaper cam-
paigns, but delayed the actual introduction of the Negro employees. The
public did not become more acceptant as a result of this preparatory
campaign, however, but instead appeared to become more focused in
their resistance toward the proposed change. When Negro drivers and
conductors were subsequently introduced in these two cities, considerable friction took place involving derailing of trolleys and extensive
damage to equipment. Although Negroes were eventually accepted in
such jobs, the difficulties were far greater than they had been in Chicago
where no such opportunity for developing organized resistance had
occurred.

Recent experiences with school integration in the South tend to support Weaver's observations. In those communities where integration
was put into practice despite the concomitant expression of disapproval
for the change, far less difficulty has occurred than in communities
where moves towards integration were delayed as long as possible and
accompanied by extensive public discussion.

It would appear that a similar mechanism is involved both in connection with the Negro in the community and the integration of the exceptional child. In both instances a rejected and feared minority group
is involved. The absence of specific experiences in either case causes
diffuse anxiety. The effect of a formal attempt to modify attitudes,
whether through mass media or a workshop, seems only to increase the
anxiety and to provide a specific focus for the expression of rejection
and the development of organized resistance. When specific experiences
are provided, the actual problems that arise can be dealt with directly.
The confusion of fantasied imaginary conflicts, on the other hand, associated with anxieties stemming from anticipation of the unknown is

much more difficult to resolve. This gives substance to the findings in this investigation, *i.e.*, abstractions presented by workshops or other programs designed to modify attitudes are more effective as adjuncts to experience, than as substitutes for experience. The most effective results are seemingly obtained when programs designed for implementing attitude changes are presented in conjunction with actual experiences.

IMPLICATIONS

INTEGRATION OF EXCEPTIONAL CHILDREN

The findings from this investigation strongly suggest that integration can be more effectively achieved when accompanied by the supportive experience which can be provided by a workshop. To give teachers a workshop experience six months or a year previous to placing exceptional children in the classroom seems to be less promising than having the academic experience take place in conjunction with the program of integration. Providing this experience at the time it is most needed is supportive. In addition it gives teachers an opportunity to discuss real, concrete and meaningful problems at the time they arise.

Apparently a workshop may modify the attitudes of teachers to such an extent that they will attempt integration of exceptional children without the assistance of specialists in some instances where assistance is recommended. A workshop should not only modify attitudes but should also define the types and degree of exceptionality which can be effectively taught in the regular grades. Effective integration cannot be based on the indiscriminate placement of exceptional children in regular classrooms. The successful education of exceptional children in the regular grades, in many instances, depends upon the additional services of specialists who are available on a part-time or full-time basis. Teachers can apparently become overly enthusiastic in their acceptance of the previously rejected exceptional children, welcoming certain exceptionalities in their regular classroom even though a special classroom placement would be more suitable. While many exceptional children can be fully integrated into a usual day program, not all exceptional children can be educated in the regular grades. Many children, because of extremely serious disabilities, must be provided the specialized service of the special class, the special school, or are in need of the residential school, the hospital school, or homebound teaching.

Obviously, to make integration fully effective, a mature plan for workshops organized on the local and state level is needed which incorporates such workshop programs within educational settings where integration is already in process. Preparation for integration in areas where this does not yet exist should also include planning for such workshops.

PRESERVICE EDUCATION

The implications of these findings to preservice education suggest that broad orientation courses are effective in increasing the information students have about exceptional children. By and large, however, little if any increase in the attitudes of acceptance of the trainee will take place without having actual teaching experiences with these children. Teachers who anticipate vocational placement in situations involving the teaching of exceptional children in the regular classroom or the special class, must be provided numerous concrete experiences with these children throughout their preservice program.

INSERVICE EDUCATION

The meaning of this study stands out clearly with regard to programs involving increased acceptance for exceptional children. There seems to be little doubt but that a program of this nature offers a supportive experience for teachers who are engaged in teaching exceptional children within their classroom. The ideas, assistance, and support which they gain from a workshop at the time this is needed are more apt to bring about significant changes in their attitudes and understandings.

THE NEED FOR FURTHER RESEARCH

Several reservations brought to light through this investigation should be spelled out in the event that further research of this nature is conducted. The selection of the four schools used in this study was not done on the basis of whether or not there were exceptional children attending the schools. The fact that the teachers from the two schools with exceptional children demonstrated far greater attitude changes was not anticipated at the beginning of the study. This being the case, the experimental design, although logical at the time, has weaknesses which impair the interpretation of some of the findings. These are:

1. It cannot be determined with certainty to what extent the findings regarding group differences in the modification of attitudes were a product of idiosyncratic characteristics of the four schools involved rather than a function of the existing service load with exceptional children.

2. The changes measured by instruments utilized as outside criteria do not constitute proof that changes really occurred in the actual behavior of the teachers involved. The instruments should be sup-

ported or even replaced by more rigorous situational observations of the teachers' actual behavior in their response to the exceptional children in their classrooms. Since it was found that changes in information do not necessarily involve changes in attitudes, it may also be found that changes in expressed attitudes are not reflected in behavioral changes.

Because of the above limitations of this study the following questions remain unanswered.

1. Did the changes that occurred result from the teachers having actual experiences with exceptional children?

2. What does the change in expressed attitudes really mean so far as behavior is concerned? Do teachers actually work more effectively with exceptional children as a result of attitude changes?

3. What changes in the attitudes of teachers involved in teaching exceptional children would have occurred over a period of one year irrespective of a workshop experience?

The reservations and questions raised by this research imply a need for the replication of this study involving three carefully matched groups of schools. In the first, a workshop concerned with exceptional children would be presented prior to the introduction of exceptional children into the regular grades. The second would receive the workshop at the same time exceptional children are placed into the classrooms. The third school would receive exceptional children without a workshop. The criteria for evaluating the effectiveness of the integrative teaching of exceptional children would emerge from observations of the actual teacher-child relationship and teaching practices. In using this design it could be determined with greater confidence whether or not the time element in presenting a workshop is an important factor, *i.e.*, does the workshop have greater value when presented in conjunction with the introduction of exceptional children into the classrooms? It is entirely possible that having experiences with exceptional children will cause teachers to modify their attitudes regardless of the workshop experience. From this design the additional influence of the workshop in changing attitudes could be determined. Finally, using criteria based upon direct observations for evaluation would provide evidence regarding the extent to which changes in expressed attitudes are reflected in overt behavior.

REFERENCES

1. Weaver, Robert C. *Negro Labor, A National Problem*. New York: Harcourt, 1946.

APPENDIX A

GENERAL INFORMATION INVENTORY

On the following pages you will find questions concerning general information in seven areas of the exceptional child. More than one answer may be correct; however you are to select the most appropriate answer. There will be no attempt to evaluate you on the basis of this inventory. We merely want to know what information you have now.

Directions: At the top of the answer sheet, in the spaces provided, write your code name, *General Information Inventory*, your school, and today's date. Read each item and mark the correspondingly numbered space on the answer sheet.

Mark each item clearly, filling the space between the dotted lines on the special answer sheet. Please do not make any marks in this booklet.

Understanding and General Information About Exceptional Children

1. Which of the following is a preferred method of educating mentally handicapped children? (a) to give the child work he can do with his hands. (handicraft, weaving); (b) to place the child in a vocational training school; (c) to make the program practical and less academic; (d) to present the same material presented to the average child but allowing more time for practice.

2. In educating the mentally handicapped (50-75) child, occupational training should begin (a) upon entering school; (b) the second year of high school; (c) the last year of high school; (d) when the child enters high school.

3. The major goal of training the mentally handicapped is (a) social adequacy; (b) academic proficiency; (c) occupational adequacy; (d) occupational adjustment.

4. Normal children reject mentally handicapped children because (a) of their poor learning ability; (b) of unacceptable behavior; (c) they are usually dirty and poor; (d) they do not "catch on."

5. The emotional needs of mentally handicapped are (a) stronger than normal children; (b) the same as normal children; (c) not as strong as normal children; (d) nothing to be particularly concerned with.

6. The proper placement for the slow learner (75-90) is in (a) the regular classroom; (b) special class; (c) vocational arts; (d) regular class until age of 16 and then dropped out of school.

135

.... 7. In school, the slow learner usually (a) is given a lot of successful experiences; (b) meets with a great many failures; (c) is a leader; (d) is aggressive.

.... 8. In grading the slow learner, the teacher should (a) be realistic, if the child is a failure, fail him; (b) grade him according to his achievement with relation to his ability; (c) not be particularly concerned with a grade; (d) grade him according to his IQ.

.... 9. The studies with regard to changing intelligence of preschool children indicates that (a) intellectual change may be accomplished; (b) no change can be demonstrated; (c) change may take place more readily with older children; (d) the IQ can be increased at least 20 points if accelerated training begins early enough.

.........10. The development and organization of a comprehensive educational program for the mentally handicapped is dependent upon (a) adequate diagnosis; (b) proper training facilities; (c) a psychiatrist; (d) the P.T.A.

.........11. The most value can be gained from a group achievement test (a) if the test reveals the academic achievement level of the child; (b) if the achievement test can be related to the IQ; (c) if it reveals that the child is academically retarded; (d) if each item of the test is diagnosed with respect to each child.

.........12. The mentally handicapped are physically (a) markedly taller; (b) markedly shorter; (c) heavier; (d) about the same as the average child of the same age.

.........13. The mentally handicapped child (a) looks quite different from other children; (b) is in need of an educational program especially designed for his needs and characteristics; (c) can never be self-supporting; (d) cannot benefit from any educational program.

.........14. The mentally handicapped individual usually becomes (a) a skilled craftsman; (b) a professional person; (c) a semi-skilled or unskilled laborer; (d) unemployable.

.........15. The mentally deficient are (a) potentially employable; (b) potentially unemployable; (c) educable; (d) just slightly below average in intelligence.

.........16. The educationally handicapped have (a) at least average intelligence; (b) superior intelligence only; (c) always have retarded intelligence; (d) may have somewhat retarded, average, or superior intelligence.

.........17. The most common educational handicap is (a) reading; (b) arithmetic; (c) spelling; (d) geography.

.........18. The educationally handicapped as a group commonly show all of the following characteristics but one (a) good emotional adjustment; (b) emotional problems; (c) educational problems; (d) only retarded mentality.

.........19. The mentally handicapped have (a) markedly inferior motor development; (b) superior motor development; (c) superior physical development; (d) about average motor development.

.........20. The reaction of the public toward the retarded child seems to be (a) rejecting; (b) somewhat understanding but not completely accepting; (c) accepting; (d) express feelings of acceptance but really feel rejecting.

21. Which of the following are not articulatory defects (a) thome for some; (b) wun for run; (c) perty for pretty; (d) doddie for doggie.

22. The presence of adenoidal growths may result in (a) nasality; (b) denasality; (c) hoarseness; (d) breathiness.

23. Which of the following problems is most likely to be associated with mental retardation (a) functional articulatory problems; (b) cleft palate speech; (c) ideoglossia; (d) stuttering.

24. The congenital deaf child will probably display (a) articulatory errors; (b) voice abnormalities; (c) retarded language growth; (d) all of the above.

25. The deaf, deafened, and hard-of-hearing are different categories based mainly on (a) degree of hearing loss; (b) speech development; (c) lip reading ability; (d) amount of hearing loss and age of onset.

26. Hard-of-hearing children usually have a decibel loss of (a) 0-15; (b) 20-60; (c) 70-90; (d) 90-100.

27. The criticism of the manual method of teaching the deaf is that (a) it is too difficult to learn; (b) it is difficult for these pupils to communicate with hearing people; (c) few teachers know the method; (d) it is too symbolic.

28. Educating and rehabilitating the hard-of-hearing is primarily (a) developing language; (b) fitting hearing aids; (c) giving audiometric tests; (d) teaching lip reading and speech correction and auditory training.

29. The Oral method of teaching the deaf refers to (a) teaching by means of speech and lip reading; (b) only by auditory training; (c) developing speech and language; (d) teaching of arithmetic and reading.

30. The criterion used for placement of a child in a class for the deaf is (a) speech development, intelligence, and hearing loss; (b) disease causing the loss and intelligence; (c) speech development alone; (d) hearing loss alone.

31. Speech correctionists in the public schools do all of the following but one (a) give speech correction to individual children; (b) give lip reading to hard-of-hearing children; (c) instruct teachers in methods of speech correction that they can use in their regular classes; (d) teach classes for the deaf.

32. Disorders of articulation refer to all of the following but one (a) omission of sounds; (b) pitch; (c) distortion of sounds; (d) substitutions of sounds.

33. Stuttering is often the result of (a) cleft palate; (b) emotional problems; (c) malformation of the teeth; (d) brain lesions.

34. Which of the following voice problems are likely to be more frequent in high school girls (a) nasality; (b) breathiness; (c) rapid rate; (d) insufficient loudness.

35. Which one of the following articulatory errors is the most serious contributor to speech unintelligibility (a) substitution of d for g and t for k; (b) omission of the final consonants in words; (c) distortion of sibilant sounds such as: s, z, sh, and th; (d) all of the above will contribute equally to unintelligibility.

36. With respect to chronological age, the following sounds last to be pro duced correctly by the child are (a) r and l; (b) p and b; (c) m, n, and g; (d) f and v.

37. The most common speech problem among elementary school children is (a) functional articulatory problems; (b) cleft palate speech; (c) stuttering; (d) voice problems.

38. According to contemporary research which of the following is the prin ciple etiological factor in stuttering? (a) endocrine disturbances; (b) inadequate cerebral dominance; (c) acquired anxiety relating to speech fluency; (d) hereditary predisposition.

39. The symptom most diagnostic of stuttering in the young child's speech is (a) repetition of parts of words; (b) prolonging vowel sounds; (c) attempts to avoid non-fluencies in speech; (d) hesitations between words and phrases.

40. Teachers help the stuttering child most effectively by (a) supplying him with words which he cannot say; (b) urging him to relax and speak more slowly; (c) give him as much practice as possible by calling upon him to read more often; (d) waiting for the child to finish speaking regardless of the difficulty he is experiencing; (e) have the child stop and think of what he is going to say.

41. Functional nasality is usually associated with (a) inadequate naso-pharyngeal closure; (b) blockage of the nasal pharynx by excessive adenoid tissue; (c) misuse of the vocal cords; (d) speaking on inspira tion.

42. All but one of the following choices affect the thinking and performance of brain-injured children (a) lack of ability to discriminate between essential and nonessential details; (b) evasion from reality; (c) long attention span; (d) incoherence.

43. The most important etiological factor of cerebral palsy is (a) Rh factor; (b) birth injury; (c) rubella during the first trimester; (d) heredity.

44. Which one of the following is not a clinical type of cerebral palsy: (a) spasticity; (b) athetosis; (c) poliomyelitis; (d) rigidity.

45. The intellectual ability of cerebral palsy children as a group is (a) normal; (b) above normal; (c) below normal; (d) impossible to evaluate.

46. The principle reason that severe spastics with normal intelligence are sometimes found in institutions for the feeble-minded is (a) the parents do not want them around; (b) they cannot be helped anyway; (c) it is impossible to obtain an adequate mental test on them; (d) the institution has the best training facilities for them.

47. Brain-injured children may display all of the following characteristics except one (a) disinhibition; (b) distractibility; (c) foreground and background disturbance; (d) high organization ability.

48. The mentally retarded brain-injured child is very frequently described as (a) an exogenous child; (b) a psychopathic child; (c) an endogenous child; (d) a schizophrenic child.

49. The classroom to be used for teaching brain-injured children should be (a) very colorful; (b) include much stimuli; (c) have ample window area; (d) have a minimum amount of stimuli.

50. In teaching brain-injured children, the material such as numbers, letters and figures should be (a) uniform in size and shape; (b) varied in size, shapes and colors; (c) very small; (d) all the same color.

51. The most common clinical type of cerebral palsy is (a) ataxia; (b) athetosis; (c) rigidity; (d) spasticity.

52. Anoxia is a condition in which the brain (a) receives insufficient oxygen; (b) is underdeveloped; (c) is too large; (d) has suffered from hemorrhage.

53. Which one of the following men is *not* noted for research with regard to brain injury (a) Martin Palmer; (b) W. M. Cruickshank; (c) Lewis Terman; (d) A. A. Strauss.

54. Studies have shown that the emotional adjustment of the cerebral palsied as a group is (a) normal; (b) above normal; (c) inadequate; (d) more adequate in spastics than athetoids.

55. The emotional adjustment in the home of the cerebral palsied would be expected to be (a) about the same as the average home; (b) more stable than the average home; (c) probably less stable than the average home; (d) extremely unstable.

56. The reaction of society as a whole toward the cerebral palsied is (a) somewhat rejecting; (b) as accepting as toward the normal; (c) completely accepting; (d) completely rejecting.

57. Poliomyelitis is caused by (a) heredity; (b) Rh factor; (c) a virus; (d) lack of rest.

58. Epilepsy is caused by (a) brain injury; (b) seizures; (c) Rh factor; (d) malnutrition.

59. Epilepsy occurs in approximately (a) one person in every 200; (b) one person in every 20; (c) one person in every 400; (d) one person in every 10.

60. In general the clinical type of epileptic seizures in which emotional maladjustment occurs more often is (a) petit mal; (b) psychomotor attacks; (c) Jacksonian; (d) grand mal.

61. If one of your pupils has an epileptic seizure you should (a) run out of the room for help; (b) keep him from getting into a dangerous position; (c) stick your fingers in his mouth to keep him from biting his tongue; (d) rush all of the children out of the room.

62. After a child has had an epileptic seizure in your room you should (a) reassure the child and calm his classmates; (b) see that a doctor is called; (c) point out to his classmates that he may be dangerous; (d) send the child home for a week.

63. Tuberculosis is more prevalent (a) in cities; (b) in rural areas; (c) areas near water; (d) areas of high altitude.

64. With the exception of accidents, the cause of death in children of school age by rheumatic heart disease is in (a) second place; (b) first place; (c) tenth place; (d) sixth place.

........65. The major debilitating factor in rheumatic fever (a) is the weakening of the lungs; (b) involvement of the heart; (c) weakening of the limbs; (d) weakening of the eyes.

........66. In children there are many instances, particularly in adolescence, of obesity which are most frequently caused by (a) pituitary disorders; (b) excessive intake of food; (c) lack of activity; (d) rapid development.

........67. The gland that has to do with the general metabolic activity is the (a) thyroid gland; (b) pituitary gland; (c) lymph gland; (d) pancreatic gland.

........68. Social and emotional maladjustment in physically handicapped children (a) is present in all cases; (b) can be related to their mental ability; (c) is dependent upon the number and severity of the problems; (d) is less of a problem than in normal children.

........69. Studies by means of interviews, observations, and reports of informants indicate that physically disabled persons are (a) better adjusted than normal children; (b) as well adjusted as normal children; (c) all maladjusted; (d) more frequently maladjusted than physically normal children.

........70. The attitudes of parents toward their disabled children tend to be (a) oversolicitous, rejecting; (b) accepting, understanding; (c) the same as toward their normal children; (d) more positive than toward their normal children.

........71. The attitudes of teachers toward handicapped children is (a) verbalized acceptance but somewhat rejecting; (b) completely accepting; (c) the same as toward normal children; (d) more understanding.

........72. The attitudes of disabled children toward themselves tend to be (a) not significantly different from normal children; (b) negative; (c) accepting; (d) more positive than normal children.

........73. The plan in which the blind child is enrolled with a teacher of blind children in a special room from which he goes to the regular classroom for a portion of his school day is the (a) cooperative plan; (b) itinerant teacher plan; (c) Dalton plan; (d) flexible plan.

........74. The plan in which the blind child is enrolled in the regular class in his home school where his needs are met through the cooperative efforts of the regular teacher and those of the teacher who is made available at certain times to offer this special service is the (a) cooperative plan; (b) itinerant teacher plan; (c) Dalton plan; (d) integrated plan.

........75. The plan in which the blind child is enrolled in the regular classroom, and has available to him and to his regular teachers a full-time qualified teacher of blind children plus a resource room is the (a) itinerant teacher plan; (b) cooperative plan; (c) integrated plan; (d) the sharing plan.

........76. The responsibility for the education of exceptional children should be placed upon (a) the local school districts; (b) the community; (c) the state; (d) the parents of the exceptional children.

........77. An educationally blind child is one who has a visual acuity after correction of (a) 20/70 to 20/150; (b) 20/150 to 20/200; (c) 20/20 to 20/70; (d) 20/200 or less.

78. A partially seeing child is one who has a visual acuity after correction of (a) 20/20 to 20/60; (b) 20/70 to 20/200; (c) 20/200 to 20/300; (d) 20/300 or less.

79. The blind (a) have superior sensory acuity; (b) pay attention to auditory cues more than do seeing people; (c) develop a sixth sense; (d) have markedly superior musical ability.

80. The school in which the program for the education of the blind should be one in which the enrollment (a) is made up of blind or partially sighted children; (b) is made up of sighted children; (c) is made up of crippled children; (d) is made up of mentally retarded children.

81. The realistic goal of the educational program of the blind child should be (a) to de-emphasize the handicap to the extent that attention is focused on the child; (b) to help the child forget about his blindness; (c) train the child's sixth sense; (d) integrate the child with physically handicapped children.

82. The most helpful attitude toward the blind child's achievement is (a) sympathetic; (b) nonsentimental; (c) emotional; (d) narcissistic.

83. In a school situation, the intellectually gifted differ most from the average in (a) physical development; (b) motor abilities; (c) participation in athletics; (d) academic achievement.

84. Gifted children tend to play with children who (a) are slightly older; (b) of the same age; (c) slightly younger; (d) of all ages indiscriminately.

85. Persons with superior mathematical ability usually have (a) average intelligence; (b) superior intelligence; (c) slightly retarded intelligence; (d) can do the mathematical manipulations but can put them to no practical use.

86. The most common method of handling the problem of the gifted child in the public schools today is (a) special classes; (b) acceleration; (c) multiple track programs; (d) enrichment.

87. From personality studies of the gifted, we find (a) they are better adjusted than most children; (b) they have an abnormally large number of fears; (c) they are more apt to become psychotic; (d) they adjust poorly to social conditions.

88. Which of the following methods is the *least* effective in helping a child to behave adequately in any particular situation. (a) providing more time for the effective solution of the child's problems; (b) removing psychological restraint upon his behavior; (c) giving the child good advice as to how he should behave; (d) giving him an opportunity to express his feelings.

89. The most effective method to use in preparing a child to intelligently solve problems in adult life is to (a) require the child to solve that problem in childhood; (b) give the child good examples of solutions to adult problems (c) give the child increased opportunity and freedom to differentiate the solution of his own immediate problems; (d) point out to the child the mistakes he makes in his solutions and show him how he could have made a better solution.

90. In most school room situations the chief motive of the children's behavior and learning is (a) their need for self-esteem and a feeling of personal adequacy; (b) their need for learning socially acceptable skills; (c) their need for seeking knowledge; (d) their feeling of superiority.

91. Habits that children form are a result of (a) repetition; (b) success in the satisfaction of needs; (c) practice; (d) avoidance techniques.

92. If repetition is imposed by the teacher in such a manner that the child is unable to notice progress and feels that he is failing, the result usually causes the child to (a) work harder in order to find success; (b) discover a technique of avoidance; (c) gain new insights; (d) become encouraged.

93. To the extent that the schools attempt to develop each child to maximum capacity as a productive and happy member of society, the real test of their success is (a) the degree to which the pupils can use desirable techniques in school; (b) the degree to which they voluntarily use desirable techniques in their daily living; (c) the degree to which the subject matter is meaningful to them; (d) the degree to which they can transfer the subject matter.

94. The most effective method of helping a child overcome a phobia is (a) ignoring the child's fears; (b) removing the child from the object or situation which causes his fears; (c) practical demonstrations of the harmlessness of the object he fears; (d) helping the child to develop skills so that he will be able to cope with the object of his fears.

95. It is not at all uncommon to find children having educational difficulties during adolescence. This may be a result of (a) the acceleration in the growth of the central nervous system; (b) preoccupation with gang activities; (c) increased interest in physical activities; (d) accelerated physical growth.

96. Probably the handicap which is the most widely rejected by society is. (a) visual handicap; (b) orthopedic handicap; (c) hearing handicap; (d) behavior disorder.

97. The most logical approach to understanding behavior disorders in children is to (a) understand the cause of the disorder, (b) deal with the symptom, (c) ask the child why he misbehaves, (d) find out from the child's parents why he misbehaves.

98. You have in class a child who constantly annoys his classmates by starting fights, disturbing the class and/or anything he can think of to disrupt the order of the classroom. How do you handle this problem?

99. There is another child in your class who has severe temper tantrums. How do you deal with this child?

100. You have a child in your class who seems very nervous. He rarely talks to anyone and seems to be daydreaming much of the time. How do you work with this child?

Classroom Integration Inventory

Prepared under the direction of
Dr. George G. Stern, Department of Psychology, Syracuse University

Teachers are ordinarily faced with a wide variety of problems, arising from the many different kinds of students they work with each day. On the following pages you will find brief descriptions of the behavior of a number of exceptional children. In each case you are to indicate how you would prefer to handle the situation if the decision were entirely up to you.

Directions: At the top of the answer sheet, in the spaces provided, write your code name, *Classroom Integration Inventory,* your school, and today's date. Read each item and mark the correspondingly numbered space on the answer sheet as follows:

A If you feel you could handle such a student in your regular classroom without any *fundamental* change in your present procedures.

B If you feel you could handle such a student in your regular classroom provided advice from a specialist or consultant was occasionally made available to you whenever you felt a need for such aid in dealing with some particular problem.

C If you feel you could handle such a student in your regular classroom provided there was a full-time specialist available at your school who could provide supplementary training for the student and frequent consultation with you.

D If you feel that such a student would benefit most by being assigned to a special class or school.

E If you feel that such a child cannot be handled profitably within the context of regular or special public education.

Mark each item clearly, filling the space between the dotted lines on the special answer sheet. Please do not make any marks in this booklet.

A. In regular classroom
B. With part-time aid
C. With full-time aid
D. In special class or school
E. Not for public education

1. Alfred is defiant and stubborn, likely to argue with the teacher, be willfully disobedient, and otherwise interfere with normal classroom discipline.
2. Barbara wears thick glasses, and her eye-balls jerk spasmodically from side to side; she can't see the blackboard very well, and reads poorly.
3. Chuck can get about only in a wheelchair; someone must move it for him, or carry him in their arms, because he is unable to control any of his limbs.
4. Donald is six years old and does not speak very much; what he does say is indistinct and childish, with many missing or incorrect sounds.
5. Earl is eight and wears cowboy boots to class because he hasn't learned to tie his own shoelaces; he is generally cheerful and well-behaved, but talks very little and is incapable of following any but the most simple instructions.
6. Florence is immature and oversensitive, likely to burst into tears at the slightest provocation.

7. When Alice wears her hearing aid she hears as well as any other youngster; her voice sounds flat and hollow, and is somewhat unpleasant to hear.

8. Suzy frequently gets so excited she loses control of herself and wets the floor.

9. Ruth is very much like other eleven-year-olds in most respects but occasionally, during the day, a rhythmical quiver will pass over her face and she becomes totally oblivious for a few seconds.

10. Roger's face was severely disfigured in an auto accident; although he is completely recovered physically, the surgeons do not expect to be able to make his appearance more acceptable for many years.

11. Alan wears a leg brace and walks with the aid of crutches; he gets along quite well by himself though, and ordinarily needs no help from anyone.

12. Bernard is a bully, given to teasing other children and provoking fights with them.

13. Cora is supposed to have a hearing loss, but she seems to hear all right when she sits at the right end of the front row of seats.

14. Debby cannot use bathroom facilities unless someone is there to help her; she is perfectly capable of making her needs known in ample time to avoid accidents.

15. Clara has a noticeable scar on her upper lip; her speech seems to be coming through her nose, and she is hard to understand.

16. Dotty is eight; she has difficulty following the class, and doesn't seem able to learn to read at all.

17. Eight-year-old Edward sucks his thumb all the time, apparently indifferent to the reactions of parents, teachers, or other children.

18. Every few weeks, without any warning, Stella will have a violent physical convulsion during which she may bite her tongue or lose control of her sphincters; after several minutes she returns to consciousness with a severe headache, nausea, and acute feelings of depression.

19. Sylvia's height is grotesque; she towers over every other child in elementary school and wears adult-size clothes.

20. Flora has neither bladder nor bowel control and must be taken to the bathroom at frequent intervals.

21. David squints through his eye-glasses, even when he sits at the front of the room, and cannot read the blackboard or his book quite as rapidly as many of the other children.

22. Occasionally Edward will repeat a sound two or three times before he seems able to go on; he speaks when called on, but does not volunteer much.

23. Chuck doesn't seem to catch on to things as quickly as most, and needs to have things explained over and over again; eventually, though, he appears to learn everything the others do even though it has taken longer.

24. Doris is slow, absent-minded, and a daydreamer; she seems unusually quiet and withdrawn, avoids others, and is inhibited and restrained in her behavior.

25. Every hour or so Henry stares upwards at the ceiling for several seconds and loses consciousness; he has been like this for several years but is otherwise developing normally.

26. Fred can feel the vibrations of loud music from a radio or phonograph, knows when a door has been slammed, but does not hear speech unless it is shouted.

27. Greg tires easily and needs frequent opportunities to rest; excessive stimulation or excitement must also be avoided.

28. Harold is a capable student but has a physical defect which appears to evoke laughter, ridicule, avoidance and rejection from the other children.

29. Irv is sexually precocious; masturbates in class, uses obscene language, and has made advances to several girls in his class.

30. Jane can tell the direction from which the sunshine enters her classroom; she cannot read the letters in an ordinary book.

31. Albert does not pronounce all of his speech sounds correctly, but can be understood.

32. Betty is only a little over seven but she can read the fifth grade reader very well; however, her handwriting is poor and she is about average in most other things.

33. Chester is deceitful, tells lies, and cheats in school and at play; he has been involved in several thefts, and is a persistent truant.

34. Generally speaking, Everett can control his bladder or bowel, although he is likely to have an occasional accident.

35. Jerry does perfectly good work as long as he is left alone; he becomes extremely tense and anxious, however, whenever an adult speaks to him.

36. Virginia rubs and blinks her eyes occasionally when reading, and seems to find it difficult to distinguish between certain letters of the alphabet.

37. Andy hears most, but not everything, that is said in class even though he wears a hearing aid.

38. Stan's walk is a slow shuffle; he gets along on level surfaces or moderate inclines quite well, but is unable to manage stairs at all.

39. Roy has a bright purple birthmark which covers one cheek and the side of his neck.

40. Several times a day Lester says he can smell bananas; usually this means that he will soon fall to the floor in a convulsion which may last for several minutes.

41. Carla is a persistent talker, whisperer and notepasser.

42. Bert could play songs with one finger on the piano when he was four; now, in first grade, he has begun composing little melodies to which he gives names like "Rainy Day," "Bert's Bike," or "Juice-Time."

43. June's eyes are crossed but she has adequate vision in either eye despite the muscle imbalance.

44. Laura's speech is laboriously slow, tortured, jerky and indistinct; her voice is monotonous in pitch and she cannot control its intensity.

45. Harry sulks, and sometimes gets quite noisy, whenever he loses the direct attention of the teacher.

46. William can't hear anything with his left ear, but he gets along fairly well if he can sit in one row by the window, in a room on the quiet side of the building, with the class to his right.

47. Ben is unable to walk and has been confined to a wheelchair; he manages this very skillfully and needs very little help.

48. Les was born with a malformed left hand which is withered and misshapen up to the elbow.

49. When Terry was five he was run over, losing both of his legs and genitals; he gets around quite well now but his bladder discharges into a bag which must be emptied several times a day.

50. Once or twice during the year Peter has complained of a peculiar feeling in his stomach; about a minute afterwards he has lost consciousness and his body has been first rigid and then convulsed for several minutes.

51. John has no difficulty on the playground or at the blackboard but he gets quite uncomfortable when he has to use his eyes at close range for any length of time.

52. Hugh eventually mutilates or destroys everything that gets into his hands; his books are marked and torn, his desk ink-stained and scarred, and he has even managed to crack a blackboard panel.

53. When anything happens to John the whole school knows it. A bump on the playground produces tears and wailing, an "A" for an exam brings on unrestrained shrieks of delight.

54. Sam moves about somewhat awkwardly and his limbs are in a slight but continual tremor that becomes pronounced only when he is nervous or excited.

55. Arnold is an extremely bright nine-year-old who is far ahead of the rest of the class in most subjects; he spends a good deal of his time working on a mathematical system he calls "kinestatics."

56. Bill has difficulty in starting to talk, grimaces and strains, and repeats sounds on about half the words he says in class.

57. Kate weighs enough for two children her age; it is almost impossible for her to squeeze into the standard desk.

58. Although Melvin does not really soil himself, as the day draws on he begins to smell more and more of feces.

59. A hearing aid provides no help for Harriet; she lip-reads fairly well, and can hear when she is not facing the speaker if shouted at.

60. Helen's right hand may sometimes begin to tremble uncontrollably; during the next few minutes the spasmodic movement spreads along her arm, shoulder, and head before it finally stops.

Activities Index[1]

Prepared under the direction of
DR. GEORGE G. STERN, Department of Psychology, Syracuse University

People differ in the kinds of things they enjoy, like to do or have happen to them, and in the things they dislike. The following list of activities has been obtained from a great many different persons. You are to decide which of these you like and which you dislike.

Directions: At the top of the special answer sheet write your code name, *Activities Index,* your school or organization, and today's date. Then, read each item and mark the correspondingly numbered space on the answer sheet in the *left-hand* column, if the item describes an activity or event which you would enjoy, prefer, or find more pleasant than unpleasant. Mark the *right-hand* column if the item describes an activity or event which you would dislike, reject, or find more unpleasant than pleasant.

Mark each item clearly with the pencil provided. You need not spend much time on any one item. Please go through the list quickly. Be sure to answer every item. Please do not make any marks in this booklet.

T   If the item describes an activity or event which you would enjoy, prefer, or find more pleasant than unpleasant.

F   If the item describes an activity or event which you would dislike, reject, or find more unpleasant than pleasant.

1. Having other people let me alone.
2. Helping people who are having difficulty.
3. Imagining what I would do if I could live my life over again.
4. Looking things up in original sources in order to find out for myself.
5. Winning out over someone else in a competition.
6. Reading books or seeing plays which are "take-offs" on dignified people or institutions.
7. Taking the blame for something I have not done.
8. Picking a fight when I'm in the mood.
9. Talking about how it feels to be in love.
10. Running something very soft against my skin.
11. Keeping in the background when I'm with a group of confident and boisterous people.
12. Making my work go faster by thinking of the fun I can have after it's done.
13. Being with people who are fresh, vigorous, and ready for anything most of the time.
14. Setting difficult goals for myself.
15. Toughening myself, going without an overcoat, seeing how long I can go without food or sleep, working until I'm exhausted, etc.
16. Working for tangible, clearly-defined results.
17. Dramatizing events in which I participate.
18. Working in science or mathematics rather than art or music.
19. Studying the history of present political and social problems to find out what causes them and what has been done about such problems in the past.

20. Seeking solutions to inner conflicts, moral problems, and spiritual dilemmas.
21. Sitting around and thinking.
22. Being cautious on Friday, the 13th.
23. Keeping a well-stocked medicine cabinet.
24. Concealing a failure or humiliation from others.
25. Working twice as hard to make up for a failure.
26. Washing and polishing things like a car, silverware, or furniture.
27. Deciding upon a plan of action and sticking to it.
28. Being quite changeable in my likes and dislikes.
29. Untying knots instead of cutting the string on a package.
30. Doing things leisurely, without excitement or tension.
31. Going swimming, riding, or to the movies or concert by myself rather than with a friend.
32. Discussing with younger people what they like to do and how they feel about things.
33. Seeing my name in programs, newspapers, or magazines.
34. Having my family go off on a long trip, leaving me on my own.
35. Reporting people who have broken rules.
36. Trying to copy the behavior of certain great men of the past.
37. Suffering for a good cause or for someone I love.
38. Shocking narrow-minded people by saying and doing things of which they disapprove.
39. Watching a couple who are crazy about each other.
40. Eating after going to bed.
41. Having the biggest and longest part in a play.
42. Spending most of my extra money on pleasure.
43. Exerting one's self to the utmost, almost beyond the limits of one's physical capacity, for something important.
44. Having a supervisor who makes it impossible just to get by.
45. Imaging myself accomplishing great deeds.
46. Dealing with actual situations rather than with general ideas and theories.
47. Writing about political or social issues, problems, or events, such as bills passed by Congress, revolutions, etc.
48. Studying and observing such things as rainfall, wind conditions, temperature, etc., in order to better understand and predict the weather.
49. Studying the music of particular composers, such as Bach, Beethoven, etc.
50. Leading such a full and busy life that there is little time for thought or reflection.
51. Finding the meaning of unusual or rarely used words.
52. Seeing a falling star, a white horse, or some other sign just when I'm about to make an important decision.
53. Diving off the highboard of a pool.
54. Defending myself against criticism or blame.
55. Returning to a task which I have previously failed.
56. Keeping my bureau drawers and desk in perfect order.
57. Planning my reading and outlining a reading program for myself.
58. Getting up and going to bed at the same time each day.
59. Acting impulsively just to blow off steam.
60. Having friends who are generally even-tempered and calm.

61. Leading an active social life.
62. Giving my time and energy to someone who's in need of help.
63. Doing something important to me which might be considered selfish by others.
64. Living on my own, away from home.
65. Seeing to it that other people live up to their agreements, obey rules, laws, etc.
66. Listening to a successful person tell about his past experiences.
67. Being polite or humble.
68. Doing something that might provoke criticism.
69. Talking about who is in love with whom.
70. Chewing on pencils, rubber bands, or paper clips.
71. Speaking at a club or class meeting.
72. Going to a dance.
73. Staying up all night if necessary to work at something which interests me.
74. Setting high standards for myself.
75. Reading about the lives of great people.
76. Doing things with my hands: manual labor, manipulation, or construction.
77. Taking an active part in social or political reform.
78. Reading magazines which tell about new inventions, discoveries, or scientific developments.
79. Hearing lectures or radio talks on political and social problems.
80. Imagining life on other planets.
81. Spending my time in abstract thought and discussion.
82. Making up little games or schemes that will bring luck if they come out right.
83. Selecting foods carefully for their health-giving, nutritive qualities.
84. Admitting when I'm in the wrong.
85. Quiting a job that was too big for me before anyone else finds out.
86. Keeping an accurate record of my expenses.
87. Participating in a discussion that is exceptionally logical, precise, and coherent.
88. Doing something differently for the sake of variety and change.
89. Being confronted by an emergency requiring rapid decisions and action.
90. Avoiding excitement or emotional tension.
91. Trusting people.
92. Comforting someone who is feeling low.
93. Going off by myself and thinking about my problems.
94. Having someone in the family help me out when I'm in difficulty.
95. Organizing groups to vote in a certain way in elections.
96. Going along with a chairman's decision rather than starting a fuss.
97. Trying to figure out how I was to blame after getting into an argument with someone.
98. Arguing with an instructor or superior.
99. Watching a dog or cat give birth to a litter.
100. Sleeping on a very soft bed.
101. Having the reputation of being different or unusual.
102. Getting as much fun as I can out of life, even if it means sometimes neglecting more serious things.
103. Getting to bed early, in order to have lots of sleep and rest.
104. Competing with others for a prize or goal.
105. Planning my career.

106. Learning to recognize the work of particular artists, such as Rembrant, Whistler, Van Gogh, etc.
107. Living a life which is adventurous and dramatic.
108. Doing chemical or physical experiments and research.
109. Comparing the problems and conditions of today with those of various times in the past.
110. Trying to understand the private thoughts and underlying motives of other people.
111. Deciphering codes, solving chess problems, working crossword puzzles, etc.
112. Avoiding things that might bring bad luck.
113. Riding on a roller coaster.
114. Being ready with an excuse or explanation when criticized.
115. Doing a job under pressure.
116. Arranging my clothes neatly before going to bed.
117. Stopping to read an interesting book or article found accidentally while searching for something else.
118. Being generally consistent and unchanging in my behavior.
119. Thinking carefully before speaking.
120. Having someone who is very emotional for a friend.
121. Belonging to a social club.
122. Helping newcomers learn their way around.
123. Thinking about myself and what I'm really like.
124. Knowing an older person to whom I can go for sympathy and guidance.
125. Being able to hypnotize people.
126. Following directions.
127. Admitting defeat.
128. Being with people who criticize or poke fun at the weaknesses of their superiors.
129. Flirting.
130. Noticing and trying to identify different odors.
131. Doing something which will create a stir.
132. Doing all I have to do before starting to have fun.
133. Working on tasks for long periods of time, without interruption or diversion.
134. Taking examinations.
135. Thinking about winning recognition and acclaim.
136. Working with mechanical appliances: household equipment, electrical apparatus, machinery, etc.
137. Expressing my beliefs in action.
138. Attempting to analyze data from physical, chemical, or biological experiments and formulate appropriate generalizations.
139. Studying different systems of government: the English parliamentary system, the city manager plan, civil service, communism, fascism, etc.
140. Thinking about what the end of the world might be like.
141. Devoting myself to teaching and to scholarship.
142. Reading science fiction.
143. Standing on the roof of a tall building.
144. Having someone watch me while I work.
145. Having to fight for something I want.
146. Recopying notes or memoranda to make them neat.

147. Finishing something I've begun, even if it is no longer enjoyable.
148. Starting something new.
149. Doing things on the spur of the moment.
150. Going on an emotional binge.
151. Going to parties where one is expected to mix with the whole crowd.
152. Lending things I value to a friend.
153. Catching a reflection of myself in a mirror or window.
154. Getting the opinions of others before making decisions.
155. Acting as an officer or leader in group activities.
156. Turning over leadership of a group to someone who is more capable than myself.
157. Being pushed around or taken advantage of.
158. Annoying certain people to see what they will do.
159. Reading love novels and magazines.
160. Chewing or popping gum.
161. Remaining unnoticed in a group.
162. Going with a crowd to a party, movie, or concert.
163. Taking a break or relaxing when the end of a job is in sight.
164. Working on tasks so difficult I can hardly do them.
165. Imagining situations in which I might be a hero.
166. Managing a store or business enterprise.
167. Being motivated by ideals.
168. Making careful observations to find out whether certain popular beliefs are true, such as whether red-haired people have bad tempers, whether additional vitamins in a normal diet will prevent colds, whether it is dangerous to eat fish and ice cream together, etc.
169. Talking about painting, sculpture, and other arts with people who are interested in them.
170. Seeking to explain the behavior of people who are emotionally unstable.
171. Losing myself in thought.
172. Carrying a good-luck charm.
173. Driving fast.
174. Filling in for someone in a game at which I am not yet very skillful.
175. Avoiding something at which I have once failed.
176. Cleaning up immediately after meals.
177. Starting to write a paper or essay with no clear plan in mind, letting it take shape as it's written.
178. Leading a well-ordered life with regular hours and an established routine.
179. Controlling my emotions rather than expressing myself impulsively.
180. Letting loose and having a good cry sometimes.
181. Rooming alone so no one can bother me.
182. Taking care of youngsters.
183. Keeping a diary of the things I think about.
184. Having the rest of my family make plans for themselves during the summer, leaving me on my own.
185. Organizing a protest meeting.
186. Praising people I admire.
187. Taking criticism without being able to argue back.
188. Playing practical jokes.

189. Learning more about sex.
190. Sketching or painting.
191. Speaking before a large group.
192. Giving up whatever I'm doing rather than miss a party or other opportunity for a good time.
193. Having nothing to do.
194. Doing something just to prove I can do it.
195. Imagining how it would feel to be rich and famous.
196. Fixing light sockets, making curtains, etc., for the home.
197. Trying to describe my innermost feelings to others.
198. Collecting data and attempting to formulate general laws about physical phenomena.
199. Finding out how languages have changed and grown and influenced one another.
200. Reading psychological novels.
201. Engaging in mental activity.
202. Having daydreams which almost seem real.
203. Playing rough games in which someone might get hurt.
204. Being the only novice at a table of bridge or in a golf foursome.
205. Quitting before I get fired.
206. Erasing thumb prints and marks from a book.
207. Browsing through a page or two of the dictionary while looking up a specific word.
208. Trying out new fashions, new methods, new ideas.
209. Letting my reasoning be guided by my feelings.
210. Feeling intensely about something or someone.
211. Finding a secluded place at the park or beach where I will not be surrounded by other people.
212. Carefully considering the feelings of others.
213. Having people ask me about myself.
214. Having others offer me advice.
215. Snubbing someone before he snubs me.
216. Being useful to someone I admire and respect.
217. Resisting someone who tries to coerce me.
218. Doing something which might incur the disapproval of others.
219. Being with girls who are dressed in revealing or provocative clothes.
220. Eating so much I can't take another bite.
221. Being the center of attention at a party.
222. Being with people who are always fun-loving, gay, and amusing.
223. Spending large periods of time in continuous activity.
224. Choosing difficult tasks in preference to easy ones.
225. Setting myself tasks to strengthen my will power.
226. Learning how to make lots of money.
227. Being a missionary or preacher.
228. Reading scientific theories about the origin of the earth and other planets.
229. Writing a fine book rather than being an important public figure.
230. Reviewing in my mind the impressions other people have made on me.
231. Undertaking a job for the experience it will provide regardless of pay or advancement.

232. Walking under a ladder, whistling in a bedroom, singing before breakfast, breaking a mirror, etc.
233. Climbing mountains or exploring underground caves.
234. Being closely supervised.
235. Reworking a problem that has stumped me until it is finally solved.
236. Saving string and wrapping paper from parcels.
237. Going from one activity to another according to my mood, without bothering to organize or plan things.
238. Ordering "the usual" whenever I go out to eat.
239. Speaking or acting spontaneously.
240. Being with people who seem always to be calm, unstirred, or placid.
241. Going on a vacation to a place where there are lots of other people.
242. Taking care of someone who is ill.
243. Making my handwriting decorative or unusual.
244. Having people show concern about how I'm getting along.
245. Organizing and directing the work of others.
246. Carrying out orders from others with snap and enthusiasm.
247. Taking the part of a servant or waiter in a play.
248. Giving my frank opinion, even when it is likely to prove unpopular.
249. Telling dirty jokes in mixed company.
250. Walking along a dark street in the rain.
251. Telling jokes or do tricks to entertain others at a large gathering.
252. Doing just enough work to get by, but having all the fun I can.
253. Becoming interested in something which requires intense concentration for long periods.
254. Sacrificing everything else in order to achieve something outstanding.
255. Risking my life to save someone.
256. Experimenting with plants to find out how various conditions of soil, water, and light affect their growth.
257. Being a foreign diplomat.
258. Reading about how mathematics is used in developing scientific theories, such as explanations of how the planets move around the sun.
259. Studying the development of English or American literature.
260. Thinking about the meaning of eternity.
261. Follow through in the development of a theory, even though it has no practical application.
262. Finding out which is my lucky day.
263. Deep-sea diving or hunting for big game.
264. Having my mistakes pointed out to me.
265. Avoiding jobs at which I do not expect to succeed.
266. Collecting such things as stamps, match folders, china animals, road maps, etc.
267. Doing my work efficiently, not losing a minute in digressions or interesting but irrelevant details.
268. Rereading favorite books over and over again.
269. Being guided by my heart rather than by my head.
270. Seeing sad or melodramatic movies.
271. Inviting a lot of people home for a party.
272. Providing companionship for a very old person.
273. Trying out different ways of writing my name.

274. Being with someone who always tries to be sympathetic and understanding.
275. Influencing or controlling the actions of others.
276. Having friends who are superior to me in ability.
277. Telling others about the mistakes I have made and the sins I have committed.
278. Being a model of restraint, patience, and self-control.
279. Watching a bull approach a cow, or a stallion approach a mare.
280. Reading in the bathtub.
281. Being a cheerleader at a game or rally.
282. Being able to play all the time, without a single serious care or responsibility.
283. Working hard and playing hard.
284. Picking out some hard task for myself and doing it.
285. Thinking about how to become the richest and cleverest financial genius in the world.
286. Achieving wealth and social prestige through success in practical affairs.
287. Converting or changing the views of others.
288. Studying rock formations and learning how they developed.
289. Reading and thinking about contemporary events rather than taking an active part in them.
290. Becoming thoroughly absorbed in a piece of music or a work of art.
291. Live a life of contemplation and study.
292. Learning more about astrology, phrenology, palmistry or numerology.
293. Being doubly cautious about things which are fun but which may also be physically dangerous, like sailing or hunting or exploring strange territory.
294. Concealing my mistakes from others whenever possible.
295. Playing it out, even when it's obvious I can no longer win, rather than admit defeat.
296. Keeping a calendar or notebook of the things I have done or plan to do.
297. Striving above all for precision and clarity in my speech and writing.
298. Changing my routine to avoid monotony.
299. Making up my mind slowly, after considerable deliberation.
300. Being unrestrained and open about my feelings and emotions.

Picture Judgment Test

Prepared by
PROFESSOR CARL G. ROTERS, School of Art, Syracuse University
under the direction of
DR. GEORGE G. STERN, Department of Psychology, Syracuse University

Card 1

Card 2

Card 3

Card 4

Card 5

APPENDIX B

SUMMARIES OF REMARKS MADE BY
CONSULTANTS AT WORKSHOP SESSIONS[1]

Introduction to Exceptional Children

G. Orville Johnson

The educationally exceptional child is one who deviates intellectually, emotionally, socially, educationally, physically, or in his ability to communicate to such a degree that he requires services over and beyond those that are ordinarily available for him within the regular classroom structure. During the next fourteen meetings of the workshop, eight specific areas of exceptional children will be discussed. Their problems will be pointed out and the required special considerations, understandings, planning, training, and organization of educational programs discussed. These children are: (1) children with mental retardation; (2) children with orthopedic handicaps; (3) children with speech handicaps; (4) children with hearing disorders; (5) children with visual handicaps; (6) children with academic retardation or handicaps; (7) children with emotional problems; and (8) children who are intellectually gifted.

As an introduction to the workshop, a brief description of these children who require additional planning services and organization will be given. At the same time some of the causes of the handicaps will be considered. During the course of the workshop, illustrative suggestions will be made from time to time as to what can be done for these children to increase their social, emotional, physical, and use of their intellectual abilities. Brief comments concerning their treatment and understanding, which may be helpful to them in obtaining adequate adjustment to a society made up predominantly of normal individuals, will be discussed.

One group to be considered is composed of children who have hearing disorders severe enough to cause them to be hard of hearing or deaf. Training provisions can be made for hard-of-hearing children which will include auditory training, fitting them with hearing aids, giving them speech correction and providing them with lip-reading or speech-reading instruction so that they will be able to deal more adequately with their environment. The speech correction will enable them to express themselves more adequately while the

---

[1] These summaries were made from tape recordings of lectures given by the consultants during the first half of the workshop periods. Typescripts of the lectures were then edited for inclusion here.

lip or speech reading will enable them to supplement any auditory cues they may hear with visual cues. Thus they will be able to adjust to a hearing society more easily. The hard-of-hearing are usually found in regular classes with supplementary services being provided for them by a specialist. This specialist, usually a speech correctionist, works with the child periodically and in conjunction with the regular classroom teacher in order to help the child participate more effectively in the regular classroom environment.

It is thought by most persons that the deaf child requires training in a special class for a certain period. The teacher is a specialist whose primary training has been in the area of teaching speech and teaching lip reading or speech reading in addition to providing instruction of the general academic skills. In the case of the hard-of-hearing child, supplementary services are required, while in the case of the deaf child completely different services are required, at least for a period of time.

A second group of children who are physically handicapped consists of those children who have visual impairments. Here again there are different degrees of the handicap—those children who are totally and/or educationally blind and those who have partial vision. The blind child is taught primarily through the use of tactual and auditory cues because he cannot receive adequate visual stimulation. He is taught reading through braille and learns about objects through handling them and hearing them directly as well as hearing about them.

It has been thought for a long time that blind children must be taught in special classes and residential schools provided by the community or state. There is a great deal of controversy with respect to the best method of handling the educational problem of the blind children today. That problem will be taken up by the consultant who will deal with the area of the blind.

The problem of partially seeing children who have very limited vision, who can distinguish objects, but whose vision even with correction is so limited that they find it almost impossible to read even regular textbooks and to participate in a regular classroom program, is quite different. These children need supplementary material, more adequate lighting, and special planning of such a nature that they will be able to compete with visually normal children.

Finally there is the large group of children and adults who have visual handicaps, roughly about 20 per cent of the population, whose handicap can be or has been corrected, primarily through the use of corrective lenses. As the result of correction, they can get along in society as normal seeing persons.

In conjunction with problems developed for children with auditory and visual handicaps, many of the public schools have organized hearing and sight conservation programs. These are of fundamental importance for through the hearing and sight conservation programs many children are found who have vision or hearing difficulties that are or may become acute. The necessary clinical referrals can be made so that the child may have attention before the handicap becomes so severe that it limits him in his school and total life adjustment. This is done through periodic hearing and vision surveys and referrals to opthalmologists, otologists, hearing clinics, and so on. That, too, will be covered in more detail later in the workshop.

A third group of the physically handicapped is that group referred to as the orthopedically handicapped. These are individuals that due to some bone, joint, or muscular disfunction are unable to get about or use their body as effectively as the normal person. There are many kinds of orthopedic handicaps. Additional services are provided for those children by the schools to enable them to lead full lives and to develop their physical as well as their intellectual potentials.

Some of the causes of orthopedic handicaps are diseases such as poliomyelitis and osteomyelitis; congenital defects such as congenital heart disability, congenital amputations or trauma such as an injury to the brain, severe fractures and amputations. These are the major groups of orthopedically handicapped children who need differentiated educational programs which will provide for their intellectual as well as their physical needs. The program must be one that will help them develop physically so that they can control their muscles more adequately and be able to use their bodies more effectively, as well as receive instruction in the regular academic skills. The supplementary program for these children consists of services provided by physiotherapists and occupational therapists.

There are also other kinds of physical handicaps that are disabling to a greater or lesser degree. Examples of these are the large number of cardiac cases, with rheumatic fever being a major contributing factor, and the relatively large number of epileptics. The individual who has had tuberculosis and is convalescing and regaining his strength, or any child who has been ill for a period of time and is recovering, also present somewhat the same kinds of problems as the orthopedically handicapped.

A fourth group of exceptional children involves those with problems that are largely educational and remedial—that is, they can be corrected but if left uncorrected will present a number of major problems to the schools and to the children themselves. These are the children who are potentially capable of doing work at a higher level than they are presently achieving. They often are not working up to grade level but are intellectually capable of doing more work than they are presently achieving. This problem can be remedied through special help, special services, and special kinds of instruction depending upon the particular area in which the problem is found. The case must be first diagnosed, the cause of the problem determined, and then a corrective program planned geared to the particular child and his particular problem. The cause may be emotional, it may be in terms of attitudes, it may be a result of the method of instruction or it may be as a result of a number of other factors which are causing the child not to achieve on the level of which he is capable.

Although reading is probably the primary area in which educational problems are found, there are other areas in which these problems may also be found. There are remedial problems in mathematics, languages, and physics, although these are not as common as reading. These, then, are the educationally handicapped children, those children who are not achieving educationally at the level of which they are capable.

A fifth area of exceptional children embraces those who are having problems making an adequate and acceptable social adjustment. In particular, they are having difficulty adjusting to the classroom situation. A child of this type is often called a discipline or a behavior problem. He may be treated in one of a number of different ways depending on the particular philosophy or attitude the school and teacher may have toward the child. Fundamentally it is again necessary to find out why the child has this problem, what he is reacting to that causes this kind of behavior in the classroom. Initially the problem may be one of lack of academic achievement because he is intellectually incapable of doing the work, or he may be a remedial problem and is not achieving. He is thus frustrated by the school work and reacts to these frustrations. As a result he develops all types of compensatory behavorisms to compensate for his feelings of failure and inadequacy. Behavior problems can be solved in some cases by simply providing the children with success—teaching the child to use his intelligence in terms of the academic skills. Since that will not work in every case, it is necessary to find out the "why" of the behavior and then go to the cause of the problem as a general procedure in dealing with these children. Where it is a deep-seated emotional problem, the psychologist, social worker, counselor, or psychiatrist may have to be consulted.

A sixth educational problem that faces the schools is the problem of the child who has an inadequate ability to express himself. Listeners pay more attention to how he says a thing than to what he says. This is the speech-handicapped child. He may be speech-handicapped because he is not mature. Such is the problem of some children in kindergarten and first grade. It may be due to poor speech patterns of his parents and contemporaries and consequently he has not developed correct speech. It may have an emotional cause as is found in many cases of stuttering. It may have a physiological cause as in the case of the child with the cleft lip and palate. Whatever the cause may be, in most instances it can be corrected to a large degree with adequate help. Through speech therapy the child can be aided in using his speech as a communication device much more effectively.

The area of the intellectually exceptional child requires attention at both ends of the scale. Approximately 2 per cent of the population deviate above the average to such a degree that the traditional school program is of little or no challenge to them. These children are thought of as gifted children. Many of the gifted children will have learned to read before they have started school, with no formal instruction. First grade presents little challenge to them since they either already know how or will learn easily and rapidly the initial reading skills. Similarly the other grades present no more of a challenge because the children are usually many grades in advance of their particular grade placement in terms of their ability in the basic skills. Consequently some way must be found to challenge them and provide them with a program that will encourage them to use their superior intellectual potential.

Lastly there is a whole broad group of children who have retarded intelligence. In this group there are the slow learning, comprising about 15 to 17 per cent of the school population. These children have a great deal of difficulty keeping up with the rest of the class. They are always "dragging" just a little bit behind academically. If academic standards are fixed, in terms of grade level, they have potential achievement levels of somewhere between the sixth and tenth grade by the time they ordinarily leave school at the age of 16.

They usually do not learn to read in the first grade but do in their second year. They are somewhat retarded intellectually. They are not necessarily remedial cases. Their academic problem cannot be remedied because they are working up to their intellectual potential in most instances despite the fact that they may be in the sixth grade but doing fourth grade work. This does not make a child a remedial problem because fourth grade may be and probably is the intellectual level at which he is capable of achieving at that time. If he is doing fourth grade work he is working up to his capacity and no more can or should be expected of him.

The slow learners comprise a large group. It can be anticipated that throughout the country there will be approximately one sixth of the children in every classroom who will be having a very difficult time in keeping up with the class due to slightly retarded intelligence. This group represents many of the discipline problems of the room as well. They form a large number of dropouts at the ages of 16 and 17. They leave school primarily because they feel that school is of little or no value to them.

Continuing down the intellectual scale the next group is the mentally-handicapped. The slow learners are ordinarily thought of as belonging in the regular classroom. The mentally-handicapped belong in a special class because they deviate so significantly from the normal child that they cannot make an adequate adjustment in the regular classroom. Because of their inability to adjust to a regular classroom, they need to be placed in a special class. The mentally-handicapped group of children is that group for which most states have organized special programs, have encouraged communities to organize programs and have provided support for these programs with state subsidies.

In comparing the mentally-handicapped child to the slow learner, it is found that the slow learner learns to read during his second year in school, while the mentally-handicapped child does not learn to read until he is about nine or ten years of age. He may learn to recognize a few words before that but he does not learn comprehensive reading, reading that he understands, until then. One year behind in reading makes a difference, but three or four years makes such a significant difference that it is almost impossible for these children to make the necessary academic adjustments to regular classroom situations.

This group of children, however, is educable. They can learn to employ their academic skills as usable, useful tools by reading the newspaper, acquiring information, apply for a job, reading directions, and so forth. They are potentially capable of making an independent adjustment to the society in which they live and earning a living independently in that society.

A third group of retarded children which shall be dealt with is the group often referred to as the mentally deficient or the severely retarded. These children have been ordinarily excused or excluded from school attendance. Under the present educational philosophy they are ordinarily thought to be uneducable in terms of what the school has to offer. They cannot learn the academic skills so that they will become usable tools. Occasionally there can be found one who will learn to "read" to the extent he recognizes and pronounces a few words. Very occasionally this skill is developed to a point where a child can take a book with a third or fourth grade vocabulary and read the story to the class. But if the child is asked the simplest question concerning the content of the story he often cannot answer it. He has little or no comprehension of what he has read.

The mentally deficient or the severely retarded are becoming a problem of public school education. In terms of numbers, however, the problem will not be a great one. Only in the larger communities are there enough children to have class or classes for mentally deficient children.

The Mentally Deficient

G. ORVILLE JOHNSON

The mentally deficient or severely retarded children are the group of children with the lowest intellectual abilities. Generally speaking, in the past and in most modern schools they have been and are excused or excluded from school attendance. They are ordinarily thought to be uneducable. Occasionally one will develop unusual skills in a specific academic area, such as mechanical reading, with little or no comprehension. In terms of learning any of the academic skills as potentially useful tools, however, the prognosis is very poor. Even the occasional one who has developed a fairly large sight vocabulary can merely name a group of configurations and these have relatively little meaning to him. He has formed a relationship between a configuration and a sound. He can read the word "c-a-t" because he has formed that relationship but if he reads, "The cat jumped over the wall," and is asked, "What did the cat do?" or, "What animal was in the story?" in most instances he cannot understand that much of the content or information of the material which he read. This is not reading—it is word calling. This type of "reading" is found among the severely retarded occasionally. Unless the teacher is alert, she may be fooled as to what the child's academic abilities and potentials really are. Word calling does *not* make a usable academic skill. The academic skills only are of value insofar as they become tools for the individual. Academic skills cannot become usable tools for the mentally deficient.

What do some of these severely retarded children look like? How do they compare with the normal population? It is among the severely retarded group that are found the children with physical anomalies and so-called stigmata of degeneracy that are generally associated with mental retardation. The mongol, for example, is considered as being in the severely retarded group.

The mongol is a child with a round, relatively flat looking face, large protruding tongue, the eyes apparently pulled back at the corner, giving a rather superficial similarity to the Mongoloid race. He is rather short in stature, rather heavy with poor muscular and body development, poor coordination, short and stubby fingers. His life span, until the advent of the antibiotics, was relatively short. He seemed particularly susceptible to upper respiratory infections and diseases. Their life span today, however, is much closer to that of the normal population.

There are other groups among the mentally deficient that have also been fairly well publicized. Among them are the hydrocephalics or the "water head." The head develops out of proportion to the rest of the child's physical growth. It becomes large as a result of an accumulation of the celebral spinal fluid which is not assimilated by the body as it is in the normal person. As the cerebral spinal fluid accumulates it causes a pressure upon the brain which results in its deterioration. At the same time pressure is exerted against the cranial bone causing an enlargement of the head. Occasionally a hydrocephalic is found where the condition has been arrested at an early age. For some reason or another the cerebral spinal fluid becomes assimilated by the body and no more damage occurs. The degree of intelligence of that individual will depend upon the degree and extent of the injury to the brain that occurred prior to the time that it was arrested. Occasionally a hydrocephalic child is found who is a slow learner and possibly of even higher mentality.

The majority of the hydrocephalics are in the mentally deficient group. In the progressive type, where the cerebral spinal fluid continues to accumulate, the life expectancy is very short, being anywhere from a few days to a few years. Death usually occurs as a result of complete destruction of the brain.

A third group that is referred to fairly commonly is that group of individuals called cretins. Certinism is due to lack of thyroid prior to birth where the thyroid gland is absent or completely nonfunctional. Due to the lack of thyroid the growth of the long bones is primarily affected and a dwarfed figure is found to be the result. The person's body and head is of relatively normal size but seems out of proportion to the individual's very short arms and very short legs. The cretins are usually severely retarded intellectually because the lack of thyroid also has an effect upon the intellectual development of the individual.

All dwarfs are not caused by the lack of thyroid and all dwarfs are not severely retarded. Some of them have average or above average intelligence. In these cases dwarfness is due to other glandular conditions. The dwarfness which is caused by lack of thyroid secretion, however, is also characterized by severely retarded intelligence.

A fourth group is the microcephalic. This child is often referred to as a pin head. They have been caricatured in the newspaper comics. They have a very small, peak shaped head. Usually the microcephalic is also very severely retarded.

Where are the severely retarded children found? Mental retardation is usually thought of being largely confined to the lower socioeconomic and lower cultural classes. That is not true in the cases of mentally deficient children. They come from all socioeconomic groups indiscriminately. They come from the rich, the poor, the educated, the uneducated, the doctors and the daylaborers. The incidence of severe retardation has no respect for any socioeconomic, cultural, or psychological background.

What are the causes of mental deficiency? In many cases it is not known. For the mongol there is some controversy over whether it is due to the interuterine environmental conditions of the fetus or whether it is due to some genetic factors. For cretinism it is known that it is a glandular problem. Why didn't the glands develop? That cannot be answered. It is known that marked changes can be made in the individual if he is provided with massive doses of thyroid extract starting almost at birth. These changes are very noticeable in his physical development, making it possible for him to grow into a relatively normal individual physically. Unless the thyroid therapy is started immediately after birth, irreparable damage is done to the brain. Regardless of what changes are made in his physical development at a later date, no changes can be made in his mental development once the initial damage has occurred.

There is some indication that in the case of microcephaly the condition is a result of recessive genetic factors because it seems to occur to some extent in certain families.

The causes of hydrocephaly are known to a certain degree. It is known that there are blockages in certain ventricles in the head causing the lack of absorption of cerebral spinal fluid. There has been surgery performed on some of the hydrocephalics where the ventricles were opened and the glands secreting the cerebral spinal fluid were partially destroyed in order to curb the excessive production and accumulation of cerebral spinal fluid. In many cases this operation has apparently been successful in arresting this condition. There are, however, few studies with respect to the prognoses of these individuals. The indications are that the individual will be as intelligent as permitted by the amount of undamaged brain tissue there is left at the time of the operation.

In other cases severe retardation is caused by brain injury before, during, or after birth. It may be due to asphyxiation of the mother or of the infant, preventing an adequate amount of oxygen in getting to the brain. The brain must have oxygen if it is to grow and develop properly. In infants as in adults, if the brain is deprived of oxygen for only a few minutes, irreparable damage will occur. The injury may be caused during the birth process as the result of prolonged, difficult labor, anomalies of presentation, or improper use of forceps. It may be caused by the mother having rubella during the early months of pregnancy or up to six weeks prior to conception. It is known that in 75 per cent of these cases major irreparable damage will be apparent in the child where the mother has had this disease during this time and that there will be some damage to almost 100 per cent of the children. The Rh factor is another cause of mental deficiency. These then are some of the causes of severe retardation.

In regard to the physical development the severely retarded individual is, on the average, somewhat shorter in stature than the normal child and somewhat lighter in weight. They are not as well developed physically and their motor development is more immature than that of the normal child. They learn to walk at a somewhat later age and their development of speech is markedly retarded.

What about education for this group? What kind of training should they have? What has been done for them? The public schools by and large have insisted that this is not a problem of the public schools, defining education as being for any individual who can benefit from the basic academic skills to the degree that these skills can become useful to him in his adjustment to society. Since 1949 there has been an important social movement in this area. In 1950 it became a national movement and an organization known as the National Association for Retarded Children was incorporated. This organization is getting a tremendous amount of publicity and has the help of very influential people. The Association is formed primarily of parents of retarded children who want some kind of training program provided by the public for their children. Until such a program is achieved, they are attempting to raise money so that they can provide this training themselves as a private agency. They are not going to be satisfied with what they can provide for themselves, however. They are going to work continually for the provision through public agencies for an educational program for their severely retarded children. At this date approximately one half of the states have made some kind of provision for the training of mentally deficient children in the community, usually on the basis of permissive legislation.

This has been a very brief picture of what these children look like, and what they are potentially capable of doing and a view of the problem facing parents as well as educators. These children vary in their intellectual ability all the way from being completely custodial care cases requiring bottle feeding, spoon feeding, and diaper care, regardless of their age—to having ability to dress themselves, feed themselves, help with many odd jobs around the home and earn a portion of their own spending money in protected kinds of environments, under the supervision of a kind, understanding person.

It is fairly well known that these children can learn to a degree; those of higher mental capacities can learn to associate words with certain meanings. They can associate "stop" with the red on a stoplight and know what it means to stop. They can learn protective reading. They cannot learn the academic skills as we think of them in the public schools. They can learn to help around the home by dressing themselves, feeding themselves, washing themselves and even help make the beds. They can help by sweeping, mowing the lawns, shoveling the walk, and so forth. They may even do some of these jobs for neighbors for which they may receive some pay. They can learn much better adjustment to themselves, can learn to get along with their siblings, and can be much less of a problem in the home and neighborhood. They are able to learn social skills and thus get along better in their society.

Under any conditions, however, they are as we think of them today—uneducable. They are custodial and must be cared for by some person or agency for their entire lives. Whether or not extensive community services will be provided for them is not a question of how much they can learn but what responsibility society has and through what agency society will discharge that responsibility. They have been accepted as custodial problems by society through the building and staffing of state institutions and training schools. There is one or more in almost every state. Many of these institutions are developing training programs for these groups of children to make them better institution citizens. It is anticipated that they will be able to provide a greater contribution to the life of the institution and to derive more satisfactions from their own lives. This also has economic value. As they become more independent and better personally adjusted in caring for themselves and contributing to the life of the institution, less attendants will be required.

Society, through these institutions, has assumed its responsibility, but parents are asking a different kind of responsibility from society and society is going to have to answer that request in some way. Parents are asking that society face the responsibility of providing a training program in the community where these children live so they may become better citizens at home and in that community. In this way, it is hoped that for the period of time they live at home they will be able to contribute more to the community and the home in which they are residing. It must be remembered that under any conditions the eventual solution for these individuals must be custodial care by some person or agency.

That is the problem of the mentally deficient—the problem that is present in every community, but not in many schools. It is a problem of which educators should be aware in view of the general movement to make it become a problem of the school.

The Mentally Handicapped Child

G. Orville Johnson

The mentally handicapped child is a member of the middle group of the three groups of children with retarded intelligence—the mentally deficient, the mentally handicapped, and the slow learner. The mentally handicapped child is educable. He can learn the fundamentals of the basic academic skills —reading, writing, spelling, arithmetic, and so forth—to the degree that these skills can become useful, usable tools to him in his life and in making an adjustment to the community and society. Furthermore, he has the intellectual potential to make an independent social and economic adjustment in society as an adult. He may not require custodial care. He does not need someone to watch over him and take care of him all his life as does the mentally deficient child. It is entirely possible for him actually to get a job, hold that job, participate in community activities, pay taxes, have a home, and be an independent contributing member of the society.

A mentally handicapped child, however, requires the program of a special class that is particularly designed for him if he is to receive maximum benefits from his educational experiences. The slow learners, which will be discussed at a later date, comprise an entirely different and much larger group of children. Numbers of them are found in almost every classroom. They deviate somewhat from the normal group but not to the same degree or extent. The slow learners are always at the bottom of the class but nevertheless are not so significantly retarded that the teacher is unable to differentiate the program sufficiently for them. They can be provided for within the regular classroom. Instruction must be "pitched" a grade or two below the level of the grade in which they are placed. On the other hand, the mentally handicapped child is so severely retarded that if he is to receive the maximum benefit from an educational program, it will have to be in the form of special services, usually through a special class program.

The physical development of the mentally handicapped child is relatively normal. It is impossible to diagnose the mentally handicapped child ordinarily by looking at him. He is of relatively normal height and weight, has relatively normal motor skills and motor development. Some mentally handicapped children are quite superior in their physical and motor development while some are quite inferior, the same as is found among the normal population. They are tall, short, well developed, poorly developed, well coordinated, and poorly coordinated. If the population is taken at large and compared, mentally handicapped children will be a trifle shorter, a trifle lighter, and have slightly poorer motor skills than the average of the normal group, but the differences are so small that it is impossible to diagnose the mentally handicapped children on the basis of their physical and motor development. This is not true for the mentally deficient or severely retarded child where numbers having the so-called "stigmata of degeneracy" are found. These children may have congenital deformations or amputations such as lack of a developed hand or ear, the hand may be webbed or some malformation of this type may be present. These children may have poorly developed muscles or body structure or odd shaped heads and bodily development. These characteristics are found fairly commonly among the severely retarded although not universally even among this group.

Among the mentally handicapped children, these characteristics are almost as rare as they are among the normal population. It is often said, "Oh, he looks dumb; he stands there with his mouth hanging open most of the time with a face that looks vacant." But look critically at some of the so-called normal students sometime and it will be noticed that some of them do the same things, particularly if they have enlarged tonsils, adenoids, or if they have a cold and are having to breathe through their mouths and are feeling a little bit glassy-eyed, for one reason or another. It is obvious then that it is difficult, if at all possible, to diagnose the mentally handicapped on the basis of physical development and appearance. The diagnosis must be made in terms of intellectual behavior—the way he reacts to an intellectual task, the way he talks, and the way he describes things. A listener almost immediately becomes aware of the severely retarded intelligence on the basis of the child's answers to questions, his comprehension of material and ability to carry out assigned tasks. It is somewhat more difficult to do this with many of the mentally handicapped although this is the area of their greatest disability.

The mentally handicapped child ordinarily does not receive the attention or the compassion afforded the mentally deficient child. He looks so normal and he acts so dumb that persons tend to become disgusted rather than sympathetic with him. He is told to "act his age" or "act the age he is," meaning his mental age is not up to par with his chronological age. He often is acting his age, meaning his real mental age. When a 12- or 14-year-old boy is seen, he is expected to behave as a 12- or 14-year-old boy but he may have only a mental age of 6 or 8 and therefore the behavior potential of the child of 6 or 8. Consequently, his behavior is not understood. Society tends to expect behavior of him which he is incapable of achieving.

If educators are to provide the kind of educational opportunity for the mentally handicapped child that he requires, most of it is going to have to be through a special class program rather than through an attempt to differentiate the program of the regular classroom. Differentiation of a regular class program can be done to some degree but if the best kind of program is going to be provided, it will have to be something that is outside of the kind of program that we find in the regular classroom.

In comparing the slow learner with the mentally handicapped and taking the criteria of New York State, it is found that the slow learner group has an I.Q. roughly of 75 to 90. The mentally handicapped have a 50 to 75 I.Q. The slow learning child that begins school in the first grade is approximately six years of age. At this particular time he has a mental age of about 3/4 his real six years or from four to five-plus. The basic skill that is taught in first grade is reading which requires, among other abilities and skills, a mental maturity of six-plus. In other words, the child must not only have lived six years but he must have six-plus years in mental age in order to benefit from the beginning reading program. It is obvious therefore that this child, although he has lived six years, in all probability will be unable to derive a great deal of benefit from the reading instruction that is provided for him during his first year in school. At best, by the end of that school year, he will recognize a few words, possibly read in one of the preprimers, and probably will have a sight vocabulary of under fifty words. He will be in the slowest reading group, may repeat first grade or if he is very mature socially and physically, may be passed on to second grade where the second grade teacher will have to take on much of the initial instruction in reading for the slow learning child. But during his second year in school when he is 7 he usually will accomplish his first year's work. He is retarded but only to a degree that can be compensated for and adjusted to.

Now look at the mentally handicapped child in the same kind of school picture. He enters school also at the same age of 6 but has a mental age of 3 or 4. What happens to him during his first year in school? The same thing that happens to the slow learner only to a greater degree. He has not even learned fifty sight words at the end of his first year. He either repeats the first grade or is passed on to second grade where he goes through the same experience a second time. He is again retained or receives a social promotion to third grade for his third year in school. At this time, a few of them will learn to read. When the mentally handicapped child finally begins to learn to read he is from 9 to 12 years of age with a mental age of six-plus, after having attended school from three to six years.

The mentally handicapped child deviates so significantly from the normal group that it is almost impossible to differentiate the instructional program to the degree that is necessary to provide him instruction at his ability level. Not only is this true at the first grade level, it happens as he goes along through the rest of school. Taking a child in the middle mentally handicapped group with an I.Q. of approximately 66, he starts with a normal child at the same place, that is at the age of 0 when he is born. They start off relatively even at this time. When the handicapped child is 6 years of age, however, he has a mental age of approximately 4, when he is 8 years of age he has a mental age of approximately 6, and when he is 12 years of age he has a mental age of approximately 8. So it continues. What has happened? He starts off in school with 2 years' retardation from the normal. It does not equalize as he goes along through school but it actually becomes greater so that if the first-grade teacher has trouble, what about the third-grade teacher and the sixth grade teacher? The discrepancy keeps getting greater, but even worse than that, what about the child?

Educators ordinarily think that a child should be given a chance to achieve, that every child should have an opportunity to participate in a regular class program. Is that the best practical program for this kind of child? In terms of instruction, it places a heavy responsibility upon the teacher. She is going to have to be required to instruct and make assignments for one child because the mentally handicapped group is only about 2 per cent of our population. This means that the teacher will have, ordinarily, only one mentally handicapped child in the room if the location of the school is such that the population is fairly heterogeneous. She will have a child like this in every two or three classes at the lower grade levels. This means that the teacher is going to have the one marked deviate in a group of relatively normal children. Consequently, she is not ordinarily prepared to make the kinds of academic adjustments required in terms of this specific child.

The objectives of the school program are usually described in social terms with the primary purpose of education being to help young Americans become better citizens, live more effectively in their communities, live rewarding personal lives, to become personally better adjusted, better people. These are fine ideals and all teachers are working toward them in every way possible. It is far more important for a person to be able to get along with his neighbors and with society than it is to be able to do a problem in calculus. Therefore, one of the very primary objectives of education is this whole social concept, the development of the individual. But is that the objective of the school as far as the child is concerned?

Ask a group of children, particularly first graders, why they go to school. Invariably they will respond, "I go to school to learn to read." That is also one of the school's primary objectives—to teach the children academic skills so that they may live more effectively through knowing how to use these academic skills. But the young child does not see the relationship between the skills and living. He comes to school to learn to read. "When am I going to read?" "When are you going to give me a book?"

The mentally handicapped child is given a book and everybody learns to read except him. So he tries it again the next year and again everybody except the mentally handicapped child learns to read. If he is one of the more fortunate ones he learns to read by the third or fourth year, but if he is not one of the more fortunate ones he keeps on trying to learn to read for a couple of more years. To compensate for this the teacher tries to provide him with experiences that will help him become a contributing member of society. Yet it is almost universally known that unless a person has a feeling of worthwhileness, of responsibility, that he can contribute to the group and that his contributions are worthwhile, he is going to develop antisocial compensatory behaviorisms and become an outcast from that group. When children become sufficiently deviant in their behavior, they are called delinquent.

In recognizing the mental hygiene aspects of the program, it is necessary to provide the mentally handicapped child with experiences in the classroom in which he can succeed. So teachers have him erase and wash chalkboards. He washes the boards and does a very fine job of it and is given a "pat on the back" and mention is made of the fine job he has done. He is usually taller than the rest of the class because he has invariably been retained once, twice, or three times along the way. Consequently, he can reach the curtain shades a little bit easier than the other children and so he will often be asked to do that kind of task. He will be asked to reach the things that other children cannot reach. The other children notice that he is different academically than they are and he is aware of it, too. The teacher tries to explain to the class that some children are tall and some are short, some are heavy, some are slight, some learn things more easily and others do not learn them so easily. All children are different.

Does the mentally handicapped child come to school to wash boards or to water the plants or to adjust the window shades or to turn out the lights? Does a pat on the back by the teacher substitute for the failures that the child is having in the academic areas? The reason that he is coming to school must be examined a little more carefully. He cannot be provided with these kinds of experiences all day. He needs more than these experiences; thus, the conscientious teacher goes to the teacher of a lower grade level, finds materials at the child's level of comprehension, understanding and ability, and plans lessons with these materials particularly for this child.

The mentally handicapped child is given an opportunity to succeed in these academic areas requiring skills at a lower grade level. He is in sixth grade and is doing work at the second grade level. He is being provided with graded materials at his ability level and he succeeds. He gets 100's and A's on his papers. The work is challenging, but it is not too difficult and he is being provided with academic success. Then he looks over his shoulder at the child sitting behind him, or over the shoulder of the child sitting ahead of him and he notices that their books are different and he cannot read them. He looks across the aisle in one direction and across the aisle in the other direction and everybody is doing work that he cannot do. They have a general class discussion and he can understand much of the discussion but he cannot make any worthwhile contribution to it. Anything that he has to add is something the class has had a number of years ago. How does he look at himself? He looks at himself and says, "I am a failure." What does he do? He slams the book shut and does not bother to do that work unless he is a very docile individual. After a certain amount of frustration he often does not remain relatively docile but begins to get attention in other ways. He knows that approval he received for getting 100's and A's on the papers is not legitimate in terms of the achievement of the rest of the children in the room. He knows that he cannot do the work of the rest of the children because this is infinitely more difficult. He becomes a disciplinary problem in the room, not because he is mentally handicapped but because he is reacting to the years of frustration, of inability to carry on the same kinds of academic activity as the rest of the children.

He is a failure because of having to be included with a group of children who are much better than he is and with whom he is incapable of adjusting. The school is actually helping to promote the antisocial behavior, as is the home and the community, by failing to recognize that he is a different person requiring a different kind of curriculum than the rest of the children in the classroom.

It is primarily from this social point of view that special classes are required for the mentally handicapped. It is impossible to adequately handle this problem in the regular classroom. The alert, well-trained teacher can, without a great deal of effort, adjust the instructional program for him. The sixth-grade teacher can take ten minutes out of the day to teach second-grade reading. But it is not possible for the sixth-grade teacher to prevent him from looking across the aisle and seeing the work the other children are doing or hearing the recitations of the other groups and having him say to himself, "I cannot do this; I am a failure." It is not particularly important how others look at this child in terms of his adjustment. It is important how *he* looks at *himself*. It is important how he is comparing his ability and his achievements with the other children. If he is frustrated in his school experiences then the school is due to face a real personality problem in the future. The school is due for a real discipline problem. The school is due for a real adjustment problem. The school has, as a result, a person who is going to have difficulty not only in making the adjustments in school, in the neighborhood and in the community, but who will carry the same attitudes into adult life causing innumerable adjustment problems throughout his entire life.

What about the class for the mentally handicapped? How does it differ from a regular class so that it can provide him with the kinds of security he requires for his future life? For one thing, in a class for mentally handicapped children the child has a class group with whom he can compare himself favorably. He is with a group of children who are doing the same kinds of things at approximately the same rate that he is doing them—who are having the same kinds of problems. He no longer has any unfavorable comparisons to make. Secondly, the curriculum does not have the academic emphasis which is the area of his primary disability. The school is able to provide him with the kind of program in which he not only *can* succeed but for which he can actually see some practical value.

The program for the mentally handicapped child should start at as early an age as possible, before he has had an opportunity to react to the failures and frustrations of the regular school system. In this way it is unnecessary to repair damages. The teacher can start with a fairly well adjusted individual and keep him that way. When a teacher has a group of mentally handicapped children, the readiness program can be prolonged indefinitely. There are no pressures upon him in regard to "When am I going to learn to read?" "When am I going to learn this or that skill?" The teacher has a chance to provide the necessary interpretation and explanation to his parents. The rest of the children in the class are at the same level so that he does not have to learn to read at the age of 6 or at the age of 7 or 8 or 9, but when he is ready to learn to read. The same things are true with respect to providing him with other basic academic skills. It is done at the time he is ready.

In any kind of instruction the readiness program can be prolonged past the stage at which it is thought the individual is ready to learn that specific skill. If he is not taught that skill at the time when he achieves just that degree of readiness, relatively little harm has been done, for example, in the area of reading. Studies indicate that initial instruction can be deferred for some period of time with relatively little effect upon the final competence of the individual. Much greater harm can be done by starting too early rather than too late.

There is much more to this readiness than just waiting for the individual to mature mentally, waiting for him to get older. There are specific skills and experiences that the individual must have in order to be ready to accept and benefit from certain kinds of instruction. There are a number of basic skills that are required in almost every one of the academic areas that are taught. In reading, a child must be able, for example, to discriminate between sounds. He must have auditory discrimination. He must have good visual discrimination so that he can eventually discern one letter from another. He must have good ability in language so that he will understand a sentence and know what it means. He must have speech and a number of other skills of this kind before he, as an individual, is ready to learn to read. So with the mentally handicapped a prolonged readiness program can be planned that is specific in terms of his mental characteristics, his background and his training.

For example, the mentally handicapped child has more speech problems than the normal child. Therefore, a longer time can and should be spent helping him with his speech so that he can enunciate the sounds more accurately. In all probability, he has poor language development so time must be taken to develop his language, his ability to express himself. He usually has had less experiences than the normal child so experiences must be provided to fill these gaps with trips, visual aids, and other kinds of related experiences. He has specific disabilities, and specific kinds of readiness experiences must be planned for him to bring him up to that point where he is ready to benefit from academic instruction provided him at the right time. In that way, it will be a satisfying experience, one in which he achieves, providing him with the kind of security he requires. Then he needs to be taught the academic skills, not as academic skills but as useful, usable tools.

It is known from psychological experiments that individuals transfer two kinds of learning. They transfer principles and they transfer specific skills. Normal and superior individuals can take a number of experiences and tie them together and see the continuity in them and derive a principle. They can then apply this principle to specific situations. Principles can also be taught intelligent persons who can then apply them to specific situations where they are used. This requires a certain degree of intelligence found in normal and superior individuals. The slow learner can do this to a much lesser degree and the mentally handicapped child probably has very poor ability to organize, to draw generalizations, and to apply principles to specific situations. He must be taught specifics in the kinds of situations more in which they will apply and to apply principles or generalizations to a number of specific situations to insure the use in new and novel ones.

For example, 2 and 2 equal 4. That is an abstract statement and concept. 2 what and 2 what equal 4 what? This is the kind of a thing that the mentally handicapped child has difficulty in applying without help and instruction. He can be taught to solve this problem mechanically or intelligently. When he is required to go to the store and buy 2 items costing 2 cents and use the concept of 2 and 2, how well he can use it will depend upon how it was taught. Teachers can teach him this, 2 and 2 equal 4, through a unit activity in the classroom that approaches or simulates real life situations. The teacher can establish stores or use similar types of activities in the classroom to develop a need for this concept. The initial concept should be taught as the result of a need and with materials fulfilling that need so the child manipulates, handles and uses materials and concept while he is learning it. Then he understands the 2 and 2 and can use it in similar situations. It has meaning for him.

One of the very first basic principles in teaching the mentally handicapped is that a need for the concept is developed through a unit of experience, or through an activity within the classroom, or in conjunction with the normal classroom activities. Through the development of need and with the same materials and situations, the concept itself is developed, not as an abstraction but as a solid, concrete thing. After the development of the concept, the individual must be helped to learn to use it efficiently in order to make that new useful skill of greatest value to him. He must be given practice in its use. This is the *second* step after he has developed a need for it and understands it. He has learned the concept. He has learned what it is. He must then be taught to snap off "2 and 2 equal 4." Do it any way necessary but do it. What does he do when he reaches the age of 13 and 28? Still make marks? He can, but it is difficult to make enough marks to count accurately and to come up with the correct answer. Consequently, practice is required in basic skills to make the use of the concept more accurate and more efficient. Remember, this is the second step, not the first and the children have a realization of the need for it by this time. The value in this kind of teaching is realized, for they know what the concept is and what they are doing. It does not become a mechanical sort of thing, a mere filling up of pages with busy work.

The same principle applies in the same way to spelling, writing, reading, or any one of the other basic subjects. As an example of what can be done with the mentally handicapped child in terms of an arithmetical manipulation, one teacher taught a group of boys to do this kind of problem: $6 \ 3/8 \div 15 \ 9/17$. It is a nice mathematical manipulation but they had no more concept of what one does with this type of problem or exercise, or what they were doing or why they were doing it, than if one had taught it to a pet fish. In fact, these same boys had raised the question with the teacher, "Why are we doing this kind of thing?" and she said, "It is the next thing in the book!" When asked if they had had everything in all the previous books, the teacher replied "Yes, we have gone through all the books up to this point." "What will these boys need in the community?" was the next question. What are some of the arithmetical manipulations that these boys will meet? They should be able to tell time. They should be able to use a ruler, to be able to measure, to make change, and other simple things of this sort. After a few simple arithmetic concepts that are required of all people were developed, a two-page test was made up and given the same boys who had been doing division of mixed numbers. There was not one of them that could even tell time. Of what value was this problem in fractions? It is good for those children who are going on in school, but not for mentally handicapped children who are incapable of comprehending academic skills much beyond the third-grade level. Give them the practical kinds of experiences that they require.

The *third* step is giving innumerable experiences in using the concept in life situations so that the use of the concept becomes automatic and meaningful.

These are the basic principles in teaching mentally handicapped children. The basic principle in teaching is organization and the more highly organized material, the better. The less organization in the material the less the children are going to get from it. It is necessary to teach every one of the concepts step by step, never missing one of them, teaching each step consciously and conscientiously. Many things that the normal child learns incidentally the mentally handicapped must often be taught. They must be made aware of our definitions and of the kinds of experiences that are going to be of value to them in the community. The curriculum should be geared so that the academic skills become useful to them. The shop, art, and music experiences become useful to them, helping them become well adjusted individuals, who can take a normal place in the community, get along well with others (their employers, their fellow employees), and earn a living by which they can maintain themselves in the community. A program of this type not only can be effected but is being carried out in many schools.

The Slow Learner

G. Orville Johnson

The slow learners are less handicapped intellectually than the other groups of retarded children that have been discussed. Nevertheless they present in many ways a more acute educational problem than either the severely retarded or the mentally handicapped because of their larger numbers, if for no other reason.

By definition, as was given in the first discussion in the entire area of exceptional children, the slow learner is not an exceptional child. The educational definition that was used at that time was that any child is considered to be an educationally exceptional child who deviated intellectually, emotionally, socially, educationally, physically or in terms of his ability to communicate, to such a degree that he requires services from the regular classroom teacher over and beyond those that are ordinarily available for him within the regular classroom structure. This definition does not hold for the slow learners. They do not require an educational program ordinarily beyond that which can be provided for them through regular educational programs of the schools. They do require adaptations, changes in structure, and curriculum. It is not the kind of problem that requires special classes, remedial teachers, or specialists to work with them. Nevertheless, the slow learners have constituted one of the most critical problems education has had to face in providing an optimal general educational program for all children.

One of the primary reasons that the problem of the slow learner is more acute than that of other intellectual deviate groups is because there are so many of them. It can be anticipated that in a relatively normal distribution of children in a class of thirty that there will be three, four, or five slow learners; whereas, in the case of the mentally handicapped, it can be anticipated that there will be one mentally handicapped child in any specified room every two or three years. Another reason is a general lack of understanding of who and what the slow learner is. What are his problems? What are his characteristics? What kind of curriculum does he need? The slow learner cannot be distinguished by looking at him or by even superficially observing his behavior in the classroom. It cannot be done solely in terms of the achievement he accomplishes in performing his daily assignments. He often is not recognized and teachers are not aware of his problems. Teachers are often unfamiliar with the slow learner's characteristics in terms of learning, adjustment, potential, and so forth. As a result, schools do not usually have programs designed specifically for the slow learner. Because there are so many of them, with no specific programs designed for them, they present a major educational problem to most school systems.

There are several very specific steps that must ordinarily be taken in the development of a program for all children, regardless of what their intellectual development may be. First of all, the objectives of education must be selected on the basis of a sound educational philosophy. In the early Colonial days the objectives were very simply stated. Children were to be taught the necessary skills to provide them with the academic background and understanding to go on to advanced work in one of the colleges. Any child who could not benefit from the academic instruction did not properly belong in the school and was not continued on the rolls. The training of persons who were intellectually capable, and who had a desire to learn and go on to things beyond what was offered in the public schools, was all that mattered.

As the understanding of the psychology of human development and differences in intelligence increased, resulting from the development of intelligence tests in the early part of the twentieth century, educators came to have more insight into individual differences and to realize that children and adults were not all alike, did not have all the same native intellectual endowment. So, too, the philosophy and educational objectives have changed. The educational philosophy that is most widely accepted today, voiced by Dewey in his *Democracy in Education,* actually was built and developed not by a man who was initially a philosopher but by a man who was initially a psychologist. Dewey was first a psychologist and then became a philosopher and developed an educational philosophy that was in harmony with good psychological principles.

As a result of the change in philosophy, the objectives of public schools have changed. The characteristics of the public schools have changed as characteristics of the economy have changed. As early as 1900 most states had passed compulsory education laws saying that not just the children who were financially able and intellectually capable of achievement in an academic curriculum should be included in the public school program, but that it was necessary for all children to be educated to their ability level. Consequently, as a result of the compulsory education laws, the schools have found that they are getting many children who had previously been discouraged from coming. Part of this major group that began coming in at this particular time and are in attendance today was this 15 to 17 per cent of slow learners as well as those below them in ability.

Today the general objectives of education have been voiced by many different societies and organizations. The ones that practically all modern educators will agree upon are those that have been voiced by the Educational Policies Commission of the National Education Association, namely, the objective of self-realization, the objective of human relationship, the objective of economic efficiency, and the objective of civic responsibility. These, then, have been selected as the four major objectives of education. These are broad general objectives and it is not stated specifically as to how they should be put into practice or how they should be developed. These are the objectives and they are applicable to the blind child, or deaf child, a slow learner or a highly gifted child, a normal child or any other child. Each child needs to develop a realization of his ability to relate to other people, to become economically self-sufficient and earn his own living, to acquire a sense of civic and personal responsibility beyond his own desires.

Where changes are made in terms of the education of exceptional children or children who deviate from this large normative group is not in terms of general objectives but in terms of the specific ones. One of the specific objectives for the education of the deaf child is to teach him to communicate with hearing people and to understand the communication of hearing people. He must be taught lip reading and speech. This is a specific objective for a deaf child to help him achieve better self-realization, to be able to relate to other people more effectively, because without communication he cannot do these things in a hearing society. The same principles apply to the slow learner. Here the specific objectives must be changed and the curriculum planned in terms of his characteristics. Changes must also be made in the methodology that is used for him.

The first step then in developing a program for the slow learner is an agreement upon the philosophy and over-all objectives. The second is a clarification of the specific objectives in terms of the characteristics of a certain group of children to achieve these broad objectives. The third is to implement this philosophy, to achieve these specific objectives in terms of the characteristics of the individual, the psychological, physical and social characteristics in relation to the environment in which he is living. This curriculum is planned not for the environment of the Bronx, or Queens, not for the environment of the Dakotas or Kansas, but the environment of this school, this area, this community.

There are certain things that must be known in order to plan a program intelligently for a group of children. First, there must be knowledge of the characteristics of the children and second, there must be knowledge concerning the environment. For the mentally handicapped and the severely retarded it is strongly recommended that the school psychologist be responsible for the diagnosis of the problem and placement of the children. Ideally this is also true for the slow learner but in actuality the problem is so great in terms of numbers of children that it would be impossible for most school systems to be financially able to hire a sufficient number of psychologists and social workers to provide the kind of information that is required to make the diagnosis. For most of the children the material required for the diagnosis is already contained in the folder of the child. All that is needed is a careful examination by the teacher and use of the material that is already available.

What are the materials that are available in attempting to determine the characteristics or make a diagnosis? There is the group intelligence test and the group achievement test. These are the two primary tests required. Group tests, it has been said many times, are not as valid as individual intelligence tests or individually administered tests. They are not as predictive. They cannot be used with the same degree of reliability as individual tests. But the reliability and validity of group intelligence tests can be improved tremendously.

Ordinarily group tests, and this applies to both group intelligence and achievement tests, are designed for administration at a specific grade level or a narrow range of grade levels. A primary battery and intermediate battery are for use in the first, second, and third grades or the fourth, fifth, and sixth grades. Most teachers have administered tests and have seen how they are scored and know the important data that is collected and is applicable to that restricted range of the group that the test is designed to test. Taking a very restrictive test that tests third grade, it will be noted it is broken down into scoring levels of 3.0, 3.1, up to 3.9 and 4.0. To pass this particular section of the test at a specific level, say third year level, the child may have to, out of a possible 30 items, succeed on about 8 items. He may, in order to advance this one year, have to have as high as 24 items correct to score at 3.9 or 4.0. To score at 2.0 he may be required to have only 3 items correct, and to have to score at 1.0 he may have to have only 1 correct item. The same thing occurs on the other extreme. To score 5.0 he may need 27 or 28 correct items and to score at 6.0 he may need 29 correct items. Most standard tests are set up so that the items are multiple choice in nature and a child can conceivably guess one-fourth of the questions correctly if he knows the mechanics of the test but knows nothing about the test itself. On a test such as this, out of 30 items he could conceivably guess 7 or 8 of the items correctly without knowing the answer to a single question. This means he could score somewhere between second and third year by pure chance. A very bright child who is in third or fourth grade where this test is being used might actually be doing work at the ninth grade level but by pure chance might get one or two questions incorrect because of a single arithmetical error or incorrect manipulation. Consequently, he gets 28 of the items correct, scoring at the fifth grade level when he is actually doing work at the ninth grade level.

All teachers have had unpleasant experiences with standard tests administered to children, particularly in the low intellectual levels. A child in a particular grade is given an achievement test and the remark is that the test is no good. As a poor first grade reader, for example, he cannot even read a primer well and yet this test says he is reading third grade level. The explanation is quite simple. The test is a good test but he has been given the wrong form. By pure chance he is able to guess and achieve a score which he does not deserve. Had he been given a test where he would score in the middle of the test rather than on one of the extremes, a valid evaluation of his achievement or intellectual level would have resulted. The same thing applies to both group intelligence and achievement tests.

Tests are most accurate in the middle range. If the teacher is to derive the maximum benefit from the achievement or intelligence testing program, first an estimate of the achievement level or mental age level of each child must be made. Ignore his grade placement, ignore his chronological age but estimate his achievement or mental age. Second, administer the test which applies to that achievement level or mental age level, not the test for his grade placement level or his chronological age. This means that a child in third grade who is doing first grade work should get a first grade test so that he will score in the middle of the test. Thus a more nearly accurate evaluation of his intelligence and achievement will result because the test is designed to test his level of ability. As soon as a child scores at either end or extreme of the test it is almost impossible to arrive at accurate results or an accurate evaluation. The gifted child takes the same kind of a "beating" because the test has a ceiling and he cannot show how much he is really doing. A third grader who is doing ninth grade reading must be given a ninth grade reading test to evaluate accurately the reading he is capable of doing. This means that a single achievement test or intelligence test cannot be ordinarily used to test an entire classroom. Two or three forms are required. Actually this is not a great hardship because when an entire school is to be tested, the children can be regrouped in terms of homogenous mental ages or achievement levels rather than according to grade levels and much more accurate and usable results will be available. This is the type of information necessary to select the slow learners to diagnosis the problem.

The slow learner has some characteristics other than his being in the lower

15 to 17 per cent of the intellectual scale. As a group they often show behavior deviations. Their behavior is not socially accepted by the group. Often it is said that they are discipline problems. They do not seem to know how to behave or how to react acceptably in the classroom. Academically they are extremely retarded in terms of the grade placement and chronological age. They are not performing academically at the level of the rest of the children in the class and their retarded intelligence is also reflected in their lack of understanding and lack of comprehension of directions, following directions, performing jobs on their own initiative and things of that type.

There are actually three groups of children who resemble each other very much in the public school classrooms. One group is the socially handicapped child, the emotional problem. The second group is the remedial problem of which the most prominent is reading. The third group is the slow learner. In terms of classroom behavior these three groups of children look and behave very much alike. The three groups are, as groups, behavior deviates. They are difficult to work with in terms of interpersonal relationships, getting them to cooperate with others, getting them to conform to classroom discipline methods and procedures. They are disinterested as groups in the academic material. They often have an attitude of "I don't care," "I don't want to," "I won't." Their academic achievement is well below grade placement levels.

If the available diagnostic material is carefully examined, using just the achievement tests and the group intelligence tests, the socially maladjusted child does not present any discreet picture as far as his education profile is concerned. His chronological age and mental age may be varied. He may be of average or superior intelligence or he may be retarded. His achievement may be in line with his mental age or it may be retarded. His primary problem is psychological, emotional. Factors can usually be found in and out of the school, other than academic, that are promoting this kind of behavior. Commonly found are broken homes and/or other environmental situations that have developed emotional problems in the child. It is often necessary to look outside the school for the causes of his problem.

In the remedial problem (usually reading is the best example), a specific test profile is characteristic. Taking the chronological age, the mental age, the reading age and the arithmetic computational age it is found that he has a chronological age at one level, usually relatively normal intelligence (although it may be retarded, superior, or normal), but the reading age is significantly below his mental age. In the areas that do not depend upon reading skill his achievement will again approach his mental age if he has had regular school experience. In the case of remedial problems in reading, this deficiency will also show up in his spelling, vocabulary, geography and history because all of them depend upon reading. About the only scale that does not depend on reading is arithmetical computation.

The slow learner presents a different kind of an educational profile. His chronological age is relatively the same as the rest of the students in the class but his mental age is retarded. By and large, as a group, it will be found that their reading age and their arithmetic age correspond fairly closely with their mental age. Occasionally one is found who is also a remedial problem.

Thus the slow learners and the remedial problems look alike academically, but the treatment must be considerably different because one has a potential and the other does not. One needs a corrective program and the other requires a different program, not necessarily corrective. One child has the potential to do better but the other is already working up to his potential, although he is definitely retarded as compared to the rest of the class. Consequently, it is necessary to have a diagnosis of these children. Remedial problems can be differentiated from the slow learners. Since their characteristics and causes of the problem are different, different kinds of educational programs must be planned for them. The severe emotional problem, however, is not a problem for the classroom teacher. It is a problem for the psychologist. The teacher can work with the psychologist. The teacher can work with the guidance counselor to help him but it requires more training and background in planning the program and the kinds of experiences that the child needs than can ordinarily be provided in the normal teacher preparation program.

Why does the remedial problem child misbehave? Why does he become a discipline problem in the classroom and present, on the surface, the same kinds of problems that the slow learner does? Primarily it is because he is unable to achieve academically along with the rest of the children. He develops compensatory behaviorisms that are usually of an antisocial nature and cause him to become what is called a discipline problem. But with nine out of ten of such children the behavior deviation will vanish as the problem is corrected. In about one case out of ten the primary problem is psychological and counselling and psychotherapy must be provided. The academic retardation is secondary in this case and cannot be alleviated until the psychological problem has been solved.

Why does the slow learner develop antisocial behavior? For exactly the same reason—because of his inability to perform acceptably in an academic situation. Because he cannot perform satisfactorily he develops again this antisocial behavior. The problem is not as simple in its solution as the remedial care because it is not a matter of giving him more and different kinds of reading and more and different kinds of arithmetic instruction with a fond hope and expectation of bringing him up to the level of the rest of the children. A great deal of time and work can be devoted to him but he does not have the intellectual potential to make the kind of academic adjustment required. The mental growth of a normal child and slow learner start out at about the same place but the slow learner goes along at a slower rate and never gets as high or catches up. When the normal child plateaus off at about the age of 16, the slow learner plateaus off at about the same time. Because he has been growing at a slower rate he plateaus off at a lower level and he can never be brought to a higher level by providing him with additional education. An effort can be made to teach him more but he can never catch up to the group of normal children. The main characteristics of the slow learner are retardation with respect to reading, arithmetic, and a case history all the way through school of academic slowness. In addition to over-all academic retardation he has less ability to develop high level concept formations.

In planning a curriculum for the slow learner both his psychological characteristics and his environment must be considered. The curriculum must be in terms of these characteristics, providing him with experiences that will be of most value to him in the community and in the environment in which he is living. This is necessary if he is to achieve a sense of self-realization, human relationships, economic efficiency and civic responsibility, if these are accepted as the major objectives of education.

In addition to a differentiated curriculum some differentiated methods of working with them are also required. Three or four principles of working with slow learners that are applicable, regardless of the kind of curriculum and the kind of objectives the school may have, are as follows: (1) Do not start any formalized instruction of any skill or concept until the child is ready for it. More harm than good can be done by presenting a skill or concept before the child is ready than being presented it at some later period of time; (2) there are certain factors and skills involved in all kinds of readiness—science readiness, algebra readiness, geometry readiness, arithmetic readiness and reading readiness; (3) there are certain factors that are required before a child will be able to benefit from formal reading instruction: (a) he must be mentally mature, which is approximately the mental age of 6½ years, (b) he must have speech and language and an adequate vocabulary in addition to a number of discriminatory skills, (c) he must have some motor skills so that he can control the movement of his eyes. A certain level of development in all of these is required before a child is ready to learn to read. All of these except possibly the last one are dependent to some degree, but not exclusively, on the first one—mental maturity. Without mental maturity the others cannot be achieved. On the other hand, with mental maturity it cannot be assumed the others have been achieved.

A normal child achieves this readiness with the help of the kindergarten and the first grade teacher sometime during the first year in school. By the end of first grade he has achieved or is reading a number of preprimers, a primer and a first reader. Gifted children may receive this readiness before school and may be reading when they begin school.

Reading is a form of communication and is of value only insofar as the individual can communicate by reading what some other person has written— the mere calling of words is not reading. That is the way reading is taught today—by the concept formation method. The child must be ready before he can benefit from the instruction.

What happens if it is presented too soon? The child becomes frustrated. He rebels against it and becomes antagonistic towards it. Unfortunately in many instances he not only becomes antagonistic toward it but toward everything and anything and everyone that has something to do with that situation. These attitudes can be developed in the first grade that will carry on for the rest of the child's school life. These attitudes can also be developed in any grade thereafter as the child is presented with any other new concepts or new skills, which he cannot achieve.

Continuing with the intellectual characteristics and rate of mental growth of the slow learner, if two children are examined, one of whom is 10 years old with a mental age of 8 and the other who is 8 years old with a mental age of 8, they are both ready to start academically at the same place. They both have the same intellectual maturity as far as the acquisition of academic skills and concepts are concerned. Do not make the mistake that this 10-year-old is an 8-year-old, however. He is not! He is a 10-year-old. He has lived for 10 years. He has the physical development of a 10-year-old. He has more nearly the social maturity and social development of a 10-year-old than an 8-year-old. But in terms of learning skills, he is at the same place as the 8-year-old. Re-examine them at the end of the year; one child is now 11 with a mental age of about 8 years 10 months, while the other child is 9 years of age with a mental age of 9. A slower rate of development has occurred, in one case, so that each experience is going to have to be extended for him over a longer period of time. He must be expected to learn things more slowly and consequently to require more repetition than the normal child.

The slow learner, in addition, requires a much greater amount of classroom organization and classroom routine and organization of instructional materials than do the normal and gifted children. Organization and routine provide security to children with retarded intelligence. In providing the best kind of instruction, it is necessary to take advantage of things which happen and to not necessarily offer the same thing at the same time every day, but to offer it as the need arises and insofar as it is required. This is fine for normal children and for superior children. The normal child in terms of classroom routine can understand a change, why the change occurs, and can feel secure whether or not he does the same thing at the same time every day. The slow learner is apt to have less understanding of "why" the change in routine. Consequently, any change should be explained and probably somewhat less use made of incidental learnings. Where a high organization of routine is not used in the room, the slow learners are usually last to put away their books and last to get ready for a new activity. They are lost in change from one activity to another, and always will be because they do not know what is expected of them. Under a routine program they know that after reading comes arithmetic, then geography, then spelling, and they will automatically fall into a routine or be prepared for the next subject as that subject or activity occurs. This sounds like, and in many ways is, a rather traditional method of teaching. But by providing them with the added security of routine it may be expected that behavior deviations will be somewhat reduced because along with their insecurity they become psychological problems and present various kinds of behavior deviations.

The same ideas also apply to instruction. Instruction needs to be highly organized. As an example, in the teaching of a method of word attack for children, the teacher should fall back on a highly organized method such as an analytic phonic method where it can be taught step by step. With normal children an incidental method of instruction can be used in helping them to attack new words. As the child runs into a word he does not know or the group of children meet a word they do not know, they are helped through phonics, through recognition of common words in the large words, and so forth, to attack that word so that in the future they will know how to use those skills in the learning and figuring out what new words are. Slow learners too often are not helped to pass the stage of developing an independent method, primarily because the introduction has not been organized for them and they do not have the intelligence to take the facts and organize them, generalize on them, develop a principle and then apply that principle to the situation where it is required.

There are three primary methods of teaching: (1) The verbal abstract

method, which is the least practical for mentally immature and mentally retarded children; (2) the concrete method, where concrete abstractions such as
cubes, beads, pegs, and things of that type may be used; (3) socialization
method, where an actual social need for the concept is required and the
concrete materials within that social experience are used to develop the concept. The social concept method incorporates the concrete in terms of meaning and application. This is by far the most superior method of teaching any
concept to children with any degree of retarded intelligence as well as to intellectually immature children.

These are then the steps in the developing of a program: (a) a diagnosis
of a child; (b) a developmental curriculum for the slow learner in terms of
his characteristics, needs, and environment and (c) the employment of some
of the principles that have been found applicable in working with slow
learning children.

There are, in addition, a number of issues that are present in education
today that have not been discussed here or been solved that apply particularly to the slow learner. Some of these issues that need a great deal of further discussion and solution in terms of specific situations are: "What type
of grouping should be used—homogenous or heterogenous or what?" "What
about instruction and what type should be used?" "What about promotion
and graduation?" "What about the curriculum—should it provide the same
experiences that the rest of the children receive, or should it be something
different?"

The Integration of Blind with Sighted Children

Georgie Lee Abel

It is a pleasure to discuss with you a topic which has special interest for those who have taught blind children, and I am sure will have significance for you as educators and as citizens of your community. It is understood that every person in your school has expressed enough interest in the various areas of education of exceptional children to make possible an orientation course with every teacher in the school enrolled. On this fact you are to be congratulated, and it should be added that you will be rewarded as you learn of the needs and the potentialities of those children who are blind.

Blind children have been enrolled in public school systems since the turn of the century. Prior to that time all of the blind children received their education in residential schools for the blind. You will recall that the earliest efforts to educate handicapped children were devoted to those children who had either a hearing or a visual handicap. It was natural that the only provision for the education of these two groups of children was in a special school. These schools from the beginning have made valuable educational contributions to the later programs for blind children.

The plans for educating blind children with sighted children in the public school systems resulted from the fact that blind people themselves called on the administrators of various cities in the United States and asked that blind children who would live and work with sighted adults in the future might have the opportunity to get to know these potential adults during the school year. These early programs were developed in a few large cities in the country, and they were quite different from many of the programs which you could observe today. As greater experience with this type of education revealed to the administrators the potentialities of blind children, more integration was achieved in the programs. This greater integration brought about new terminology and greater variation in descriptions of ideal programs. There was also more effective clarification of problems.

The first programs in the public schools were highly specialized and some of them were almost like little institutions with all of the classrooms for the blind children set aside in one part of the building, and with scant opportunity for the blind children to recite with the sighted children. Naturally, this early administrative caution deprived the blind children of many opportunities to derive the sociological value which prompted the blind people to ask for public school education. These programs were referred to as special classes or braille classes. Some of the earlier programs which have survived and are in existence today still use those titles.

The trend today is to provide more integration of the blind children in regular classes, i.e., to have them actually enrolled in these classrooms and return to the room provided with specialized equipment and a qualified teacher only when they need help in order to function more effectively. This (formerly referred to) "special room" or "braille class" might today be called a "resource room." The reason for this title is due to the fact that the room is a resource to the blind children. The "resource" teacher is a resource to the blind children, to the families of the children in problems which affect their education, to the teachers in the school and, at times, to the administrative or supervisory staff. The type of help given to the administrative or supervisory staff most frequently is in interpreting budgetary needs or establishing priorities in specialized equipment. There are also occasions when a close working relationship between the resource teacher and the administrators is necessary in order to develop related services, such as the use of volunteer groups, or initiating and orienting other types of professional services outside the school system.

The film which is to be shown to you today is entitled "An Integrated Program in the Stockton Public Schools." It was made by the resource teacher for the school system in Stockton, California. Miss Jeanne R. Kenmore developed this film primarily for the orientation of the people in her own school system and for the citizens in the community who were anxious to know more about the program. You will see the children functioning most of the time in the regular classrooms with the sighted children, and you will observe that as each of the eleven children returns to the resource room it is for a specific purpose. You will wish to observe the activities of the children in the resource room and the use of the specialized equipment in both the resource room and in the various regular classrooms. It is hoped that this film will not only answer some of your questions, but will provide you with an opportunity to see blind children, perhaps for the first time, and thus raise questions in your mind which will make possible a stimulating discussion period following this lecture.

It is entirely possible that any one of you may have a blind child enrolled in your room at the beginning of the next school year. Certain of the kindergartens and nursery schools in this community have blind children enrolled at the present time. These children are growing, and it is understood that their parents have asked that your public schools develop a program which will enable them to continue their education in their own communities. The school administration of this city, like any good school system, has listened to the requests from the parents and it has cooperated with Syracuse University in studying the needs of the parents and in providing orientation for key teachers and staff in order that the actual inauguration of the program will be preceded by sound planning.

You may be interested to know that, due to the fact that there has been a tremendous increase in blindness among infants born prematurely, schools throughout the country have developed a number of new programs for blind children. The eye condition of these children, known as retrolental fibroplasia, is the chief cause of blindness found in young school children today. While there has been a sufficient answer due to medical research, causing a sharp decline in this condition, for the next ten to twelve years schools will be faced with the responsibility for planning for an unusually large number of blind children. This increase in blindness has caused an increase in the number of such public school programs in the United States from some 56 programs in 25 cities some ten years ago to a total of 199 in 85 cities at the present time.

The most exciting fact to be observed in this tremendous growth is that more regular classroom teachers have had the opportunity to know blind children, and more families of these children have had the opportunity to work cooperatively with their school systems in order to receive the benefits of an education which is provided for every child on the basis of his needs.

Those who have had experience with this program often express the thought that the real inspiration comes from the fact that both the blind and sighted children profit from this educational experience and their entire lives are enriched according to their relationships in school.

As more school systems engage in this type of education, greater integration is achieved in all communities. Through the development of flexible programs, blind children are often attending their local school districts with the resource teacher in this case becoming an intinerant teacher. The trend is to provide for most of the junior and senior high school blind pupils an education which makes possible their attending their local schools and receiving the service of the itinerant teacher. This teacher provides specialized instruction, guidance and counseling in the educational program due to the fact that the child is blind, and is available for consultation with the regular teachers and the administrators of the various schools in which the itinerant teacher serves a blind child. In the large rural areas, many blind children attend their local kindergartens and, when there is sufficient itinerant teacher service, these children can often continue their elementary school education in the same school where they attended kindergarten.

The rapidly growing programs of various types in the various public school systems where blind children are enrolled presuppose a good general educational program with the addition of the service of the special teacher. Whether this teacher is a resource teacher functioning in a particular school, to which a given number of children are transported, or whether he functions in a number of schools where there is an occasional blind child enrolled, the programs draw on the creative type of education that attempts to bring into focus for the blind children all of the curriculum areas available to the sighted children. The specialist type of teacher offers to the blind children confidence in the use of all of their necessary specialized equipment, and also the orientation skill and understanding of the regular teachers who can appreciate the importance of both equipment and independent functioning in the lives of the blind children.

It is natural that you as regular teachers will feel concerned when you first know that a blind child is to be enrolled in your various classrooms. This indicates your desire to be of service to the child and your feeling of inadequacy due to lack of previous experience. You should feel free to raise all the questions that occur to you, and those who are developing the program should be able to provide you with the support and consultation which you desire in the early stages of the program. You should not have to meet the highly specialized needs which may arise because the child is blind. These needs are the responsibility of the special teacher, the administration and consultative staff. This is why the programs have to result from the combined efforts of both general education and the knowledge and ability which comes from qualified specialists in the area of education of exceptional children. Many problems are apt to arise which upon examination stem from problems in the program which can affect any child. As you gain experience with a blind child, you will grow in your ability to look at him first as a child. As you are able to do this, you will be able to know which problems should be discussed with the special teacher and which you can handle yourself because you are accustomed to working with children with problems.

It is natural also that some of you will have some difficulties in relating to certain blind children because of some of your own feelings concerning blindness. A complete loss of vision is a handicap which is confronted with many stereotype concepts both in our society and in the various types of literature which you have frequently encountered. It is often true that many teachers are able to examine these reactions quite objectively and, after they have known blind children and their families, they have been able to verbalize their change in thinking and therefore their increased ability to meet the needs of a blind child with greater objectivity. They can then look more objectively at the needs of blind children, many of which are the same as those for all children. Some of these needs can be greatly intensified because of blindness.

As you know these children, you too will be able to observe the problems in the environment of the person who is blind, and then you will see how many of the problems and frustrations stem from the feelings and reactions of those who see.

You as teachers of children should feel sure that you are able, without too much variation in your program or too much additional consideration, to provide the blind child with an opportunity to recite with his sighted classmates. In so doing, you can recognize that children have demonstrated that they can understand problems of other children without many of the inhibitions and preconceived feelings so often expressed by adults.

Experience with a large number of programs in the education of blind children has shown that the regular classroom teachers can meet the educational needs of many blind children, and that they should not have to feel too much concerned with problems they are not qualified to solve. This is the challenge of the specialist who can interpret as needs arise. Together the resource or itinerant teacher and the regular teachers can look at the child with his potentialties and his problems, whether the child be totally blind or whether he operates in the school program as a child with limited vision yet must be educated chiefly through the use of the braille system.

As you look at the film which is to be shown this afternoon, you will at times have difficulty finding the blind child and, at other times it will be quite obvious that the child is going about the hallways without the use of any vision. You will see that some other children have very limited vision, but they are permitted to look as closely at any object as they are comfortable in order to have the privilege of using vision when they can. The most important thing, however, which you will see in this film is that the blind children are obviously comfortable and happy with the sighted children, and the relationships are just as positive from the point of view of the sighted children. There is in this situation integration, and not just visiting in the regular classrooms by the blind children. In order to achieve this type of program it is absolutely necessary to have the combined efforts of the qualified resource teacher and the regular teachers in the building, who must experience strong leadership from the administrators and the consultative staff.

The Gifted Child

RUTH STRANG

It's always interesting to look at children from a different angle. When we're working with them in our own classes we don't look at them in the same way we do when we are just observing and someone else is responsible for leading the discussion. Whatever they felt free to say today, was interesting to us. I think their analysis of why some bright kids fail was very good:

1. They said that some of them thought they were brighter than they really were—that they were so bright they didn't have to study, so they didn't bother to study and didn't learn good study methods; consequently, they fell down on the examinations.

2. Many gifted children have told me that the other children don't like them, that they do not want to achieve as high as they can because they are afraid of the attitude of the other youngsters toward them.

3. Certain youngsters are tremendously interested in one or two subjects and they will spend their time on those subjects and neglect the others. The result is that they are not promoted because of their lack of attention to some subjects.

4. Another reason, as one of the youngsters said is "just monkeying around too much and not getting down to business"; such a lack of motive is often present in gifted children. They haven't sufficient motive and purpose for their school work. So, they do not put forth the maximum effort.

Usually we refer to a gifted individual as one whose performance in any line of socially useful endeavor is consistently superior. That means, then, that we are including among the gifted, not only those who are gifted verbally, but those who are socially gifted and talented in other ways. Social giftedness can be observed early. I remember one little first-grade group was building a house with big blocks. One little boy was clumsy and whenever he moved he would knock over something. One of the members of the group who was really socially gifted, instead of saying, "Jimmy, you go away. You can't play with us. You're too clumsy," said, "I'll tell you what. You be the watch dog and you sit outside the house and when anyone comes along you bark—and bark loud." That was a perfect assignment for Jimmy; he sat outside the house and everything went along happily. Perhaps you have noticed in your own classes certain youngsters who seemed to know just the right thing to do to take the tension out of situations, or to make someone else feel comfortable and happy. In a high school one time, I was giving a test of social usage. Some of these youngsters were very sensitive about what their peers, or classmates thought of them. One of the questions on the test was about the correct way of eating pie—"Do you eat pie with your fork, fingers, spoon, etc.?" And this youngster said, "You eat pie with your fingers." Before I had decided how to handle the situation, one of the youngsters in the class spoke up immediately and said, "Why, of course. You eat pie with your fingers when you're on a picnic. It wouldn't be a picnic if you didn't."

In addition to the socially gifted, you have some who are mechanically gifted, who seemed to be able to put together any kind of mechanism and make it work. Some of your "hot rodders" are of that type. They have a real mechanical sense and have a real interest in it. Then you have some who are especially gifted in mathematics. Occasionally we have an individual who is really a mathematical genius. Sometimes you have youngsters who are superior in art, music, or drama. Usually these gifts go together. That is, there's usually a rather high correlation among the different abilities. Occasionally, however, you do find some individuals who are superior in some of these special aspects and yet not quite so high as you would expect in the general tests of verbal intelligence. We should be alert to these different kinds of giftedness.

The percentage of gifted children in different studies and in different localities varies quite a bit. The Educational Policy Commission included about 10 per cent of the school population "gifted or moderately gifted"; others include only 1 or 2 per cent. In some communities the proportion of gifted is high and in others it's low. For instance, in the elementary schools of one county the percentages for the different school districts ranged from 7 to 29 per cent who were above 125 IQ. In the high schools the percentage covered a range from 4 per cent to 25 per cent. You will find a difference in the percentage of verbally, socially, mechanically, and artistically gifted in different schools and localities.

Herbert Hoover made this statement: "As a race we produce a considerable percentage of persons in each generation who have high intellectual and moral qualities. I believe we lose a large portion of those who could join these ranks because we fail to find them, to train them rightfully, to create character in them, and to inspire them to effort." Those are four very important responsibilities we have for pupils with special abilities: (1) to identify them; (2) to give them the experiences they need; (3) to help them to develop character and (4) to motivate them. You don't get exceptional performance unless you have a certain amount of persistance, purpose, and willingness to put forth effort. There are qualities of character that determine giftedness as well as the special ability.

The next question is, who are these children; how do you identify them? If we were to ask you who the gifted were in your class, how would you go about finding them? Well, you might look at the intelligence tests that have been given; that would give you some clue as to the ones who are verbally gifted. If some of these youngsters are poor readers, however, you will not discover them through the group intelligence test. If some of them are emotionally disturbed at the time they were taking the test, you will not get a true measure of their ability. So the test itself, while it is a good first step, does not always identify high ability. You depend on observation in the classroom. That is very important. When I was visiting the child research centers in England and Scotland, I was talking with the director of the schools for mentally and physically handicapped children. They had special schools for them at this time. The director of the program said that they never put a child in a special school until he had been observed for a year in a regular classroom. They didn't depend on the tests alone. They depended a great deal on the observation of the teacher in the regular school situation.

What are some of the characteristics of children of exceptional ability? You would not look for the stereotype of the gifted child—the frail, puny, bespectacled youngster. The majority of really gifted children are physically attractive and above average physically, socially, and emotionally. Since abilities tend to be postively related, you would be more likely to find your gifted children among the ones who are well developed socially, physically, and emotionally. There would be some exceptions, of course, but in general that would be true. You would also note the ones who were superior in their use of language. For instance, in one of the schools yesterday, a teacher was asked how rice was grown. One youngster gave a very inadequate and incoherent answer. Another one gave a most precise, detailed, accurate answer, using the word *evaporate* and other words that were beyond the usual third-grade ability. A child with a superior vocabulary and a superior command of language—not just using big words, but using them properly—will probably be gifted. For example, when Lord McCauley was six years old, he was at a tea his mother was giving, and someone spilt hot water on him. A little later one of the guests asked him how he was and he answered, "Thank you, Madame, the agony has somewhat abated."

Gifted children generally love to talk and discuss. Almost all of them will say that they like group discussions; they are more likely than the average to ask relative questions. They write superior compositions. They are quick to see relations and quick to learn. For instance, if you find a child in your class who gets the explanation the first time, that too is an indication of superior ability. They are good at solving problems. They like to read. Dr. Terman found that half of his group, those over 135 IQ had learned to read before they came to school. They learn by a variety of methods: by hearing stories read and identifying the words in them, by associating pictures and words, by sounding out words. There are many different ways but half of them had learned before they came to school. They usually have intellectual curiosity. They often play with children a little older than themselves. The games of children their own age seem to them a little childish. Perhaps that is one reason why we sometimes think that some of these children are immature—we see them so often playing with youngsters older than they are; they are relatively young in those groups. However, there may be some youngsters in your class that do not show these characteristics and these kinds of behavior and yet are really able children.

There are many reasons why they may not show these characteristics. They may not achieve satisfactorily, not because they can't, but because they are not interested. Some are bored by the kind of books that they have to read. Some of the books are more appropriate for girls than for boys. First and second grade gifted boys are often interested in things very different from the unexciting, amiable doings of Dick and Jane. Sometimes you find youngsters who have learned how to read and who are able to read more interesting material, being given primers that have no meaning or interest to them. I remember one little youngster after dutifully reading about three pages of such a primer, looked up at the teacher and said, "Boring, isn't it?" Another youngster under the same circumstances said to the teacher, "Take that pucillanimous primer away." And, a gifted boy who hadn't learned to read by the time he was seven years old said very disappointedly when he read his first sentence, "The boy can run. Well, I didn't have to learn to read to know that." Certainly some gifted children don't demonstrate their ability because there is nothing challenging in the reading material, nothing that seems to them to be really worth the effort of reading.

Sometimes they are not able to get the books that they want. Dr. Leta S. Hollingsworth at one time asked some gifted youngsters what their problems were. One of them said, "The librarian is my problem. I wanted a book on electricity and I found it in the library. But the librarian told me that I couldn't have it because it was for adults and I was a juvenile." So the young-ster did not get his book. Fortunately such librarians are very rare, indeed. Most of them are very cooperative and helpful.

Some gifted children do not use their ability because they do not want to be different from their classmates; they are afraid that others will call them an "eager beaver" or "a square" or "a brain." They often say, "The other kids don't like me." One very gifted boy wrote on the board one time, "The teacher stinks." He was sent to the counselor. The counselor talked it over with him and he finally decided that that wasn't the thing to write on the board. Then he said, "You know that was the first time I thought the kids liked me." Here was a boy who had been rejected by his classmates because he was bright; he wanted to do something so that he would belong with the crowd and be liked by the rest of the kids. One girl said, "If you're taller than boys it's bad enough, but if you're brighter, it's fatal."

Sometimes gifted children don't get very much stimulation at home. They are not encouraged to read; their parents are more interested in having the children help on the farm, or go to work early rather than to get a good education. Parental attitudes vary a great deal in different communities but sometimes it is the attitude of the parent that helps to explain why certain really able youngsters do not show their ability in the school situation. On the other hand we occasionally have some youngsters whose parents have put too much pressure on them; they have pushed them beyond their real ability. Some have even coached them on intelligence tests so that they would get higher scores than they ordinarily would. That is very unfortunate because such youngsters are handicapped then when they are constantly expected to live up to this false intelligence test score, and are really not capable of doing it.

The guidance people are often very helpful in identifying gifted children. For example, at Long Beach, California the counselors in each school went through the records and picked out the youngsters who had IQ's of over 120 and also youngsters who seemed to be gifted in other ways. Then they had interviews with these pupils and their parents. From the interview they obtained further information which they filed in the cumulative record. They also sent the teachers information and suggestions that would be helpful to teachers in providing experiences individual gifted children needed.

Now some of the cautions in regard to identifying gifted children are these: Sometimes the teacher confuses docility and conformity with gifted-ness. If a child is docile, tries to please, does what the teacher says, the teach-er may count him among the gifted when he is actually not so brilliant as a more obstreperous child. There's also the caution against singling out gifted children and making them feel conspicuous. If you do find a youngster who you think is genuinely gifted, you have to be careful not to call on him too often, not to give the impression that he's "teacher's pet" and not to set him apart from or superior to the others because of the effect it would have on his social relations.

There are many ways of making provisions for gifted children: (1) You can make provision for the gifted children in regular classes. (2) You can sometimes add to their program, giving them an additional course. If a genuinely gifted child is taking the regular high school course, he can carry extra class activities such as music, art, typewriting or additional subject that is not in his regular academic course. (3) You can provide some special group opportunities for them. For instance, in one sixth grade class, the best readers were given an extra library period each week during which the librarian introduced certain books to them. It might be a biography one week, or travel, or some other special kind of book. Then they would select any book they wanted and read it independently. The next week at the same period they would come together and discuss the books they had read. The youngsters appreciated this free reading and discussion very much. In compositions which I received from them, they almost always mentioned spontaneously this particular class—this library class where they had a chance to read on their own and to discuss what they had read. Other special classes such as special advanced science classes or creative writing classes may similarly be provided for the gifted. (4) Some schools make still more extensive provision for the gifted children. In the Cleveland major work program, if a boy or girl with IQ 125 or above does not seem to be working up to his potentialities, an interview with the child and his parents is arranged, and they are told, "There's opportunity to go into this special group if you want to." If the child becomes a member of one of these major work classes, he goes through the elementary years at the regular rate, but he has a very much enriched experience. (5) Another kind of provision for the gifted are honor groups in high school. For example, in the Bronx High School of Science in New York City those who are especially high in science interest and achievement in the first year may go into a special honors group for the succeeding years.

The question of whether to accelerate pupils often comes up. At one large meeting on the gifted at Atlantic City, Superintendent Spinning introduced the meeting with an original verse:

> When we have the wheat all sifted,
> And we know who are the gifted,
> Shall we accelerate, segregate, or integrate?
> Just how are the gifted lifted?

There's a great deal of debate about acceleration. In general, people who have made studies of gifted children are in favor of a small amount of acceleration, determined on an individual basis. Acceleration of one or two years, during the elementary and high school, will enable these gifted youngsters to get into college at sixteen or seventeen, and to complete their professional preparation sooner. This is a decided advantage when such long professional preparation is required for many types of work. However, this should not be a blanket rule; whether or not to accelerate should be decided on an individual basis. Only the youngsters who are physically, socially and emotionally mature should be accelerated. One child who was physically, socially and emotionally mature made a very good social and emotional, as well as intellectual adjustment when he entered college at a very early age. Another child with the same high intelligence was similarly accelerated, but made a very poor social adjustment because he was small in stature and socially immature. His classmates treated him like a little boy, and he did not engage in the normal college activities. Consequently he felt unhappy and "left out."

There are a number of good teaching techniques to help gifted children realize their potential. Basic to effective instruction is a "lush environment" with not only a wealth of reading materials but also opportunities for all kinds of creative work. I remember that Dr. Thorndike, at a service in honor of Dr. Leta S. Hollingsworth, said that perhaps one of the best things to do for gifted children was to provide well equipped laboratories, studios, and libraries, and to turn the children loose in them. Organizing group projects is an exceedingly good way to provide for individual differences. Dramatizations and other types of projects offer opportunity for varied kinds of ability. For example, in the High School and College Reading Center at Teachers College, we sometimes give a play in which gifted children who are retarded in reading take part. They do much of the creative work on the play, but all have a share in it. One boy, who couldn't read at all, played the part of the dog. All he had to say was, "Woof, Woof!" But he did it so well that he stole the show.

The newspaper is another activity in which the gifted are especially interested. In one grade the teacher discovered a boy with a special interest in science; he was reading science books far above the grade. She suggested they have a class science newspaper, and the children, recognizing his ability, elected him as editor. That gave him not only reading experience, but social experience also, because he would solicit material from the other youngsters. In one issue of the science newspaper he had placed on the front page an amusing drawing of a mosquito by the dullest boy in the class. The gifted boy had put it in that prominent position so that the other youngster would get the recognition that was so important for him. It is, however, easy to let the gifted children be in the limelight all the time. One thing they need to learn is to share their leadership experiences. There was one little girl who was always chosen to do the dances, take the lead part in the play, etc. One day when they were talking about putting on a dance in which she was going to be the chief performer, the teacher said to her, "Why don't you teach some of the other youngsters the dance?" She said, "Oh, it takes them so long to learn." The teacher replied, "It takes some people a long time to learn to share." The child gave the teacher a searching look, and a few days later she came back with the plan of teaching the other youngsters the dance. When they gave the dance she was holding up a tree in the background as part of the scenery.

Service activities are of special importance because gifted children should feel a sense of responsibility for their gifts. Advisory committees on which gifted pupils serve give them excellent opportunity for development. These advisory committees can be of assistance to the principal, the teacher, or the group can work in the direction of making some improvement in the community. For example, in one rural area there were no recreational facilities. A youth council began working on the problem. They surveyed the situation to see what possibilities existed, interviewed one of the citizens who owned a piece of land adjoining the school property, and obtained his permission to erect a recreation shelter on the site. They carried their plans to completion, exhibiting both initiative and a sense of responsibility in seeing the project through.

Gifted children usually have some very good ideas about how they like to be taught. The Office of Education is working on the question of qualifications for teachers of exceptional children. In this connection, I have read about fifty compositions on the subject, and have had several discussions with gifted children all over the country regarding teachers that appeal to them. Here are a few comments they make about the kinds of teachers they like to have.

"Mr. A had a quiet but firm way of conducting the class. Unlike most teachers he did not yell when reprimanding someone. He spoke in a quiet tone that made you feel shamed in a way, but also kept you quiet for the rest of the period. He did not have any pets. You could tell by his teaching that he was trying to help you. He tried to get the most learning out of one year pleasantly."

Here is another: "Mr. L. makes you feel that your question is one of the most important in the world. Sometimes only one or two kids at a time annoy him, and when he does get peeved at them all the other kids are on his side. My favorite teacher lets the class work together on projects most of the time, and takes over in discussion. I was always shy about speaking in front of the class and got over my shyness. In my favorite class we had projects of all sorts. When we were studying the industrial revolution, we all pretended that we were inventors and choose an invention to study. We looked up information on it and gave oral reports explaining how it worked."

Another one wrote, "I like teachers who scold only when something is unbearable. The teacher should show that she is in charge of the class. She should command respect without making speeches or asking for it." "One of my favorite teachers is Miss T., our gym teacher. I talk with her as if she were a friend and not a teacher. She has helped me to become a better sport."

A sixth grader said that she liked teachers who expected her to do her best, but not try to be a genius. "My best teacher lets me do things on my own. She respects my ideas and helps me develop them. I like teachers who mark papers according to their worth, rather than according to personal feelings they may have. In my opinion, teachers are as human as any other person who walks the earth. Sure, they lose their temper sometimes, but don't we all." The qualities that gifted children said they especially appreciated were: having a background of knowledge but not being a walking encyclopedia, a willingness to let students use initiative and responsibility, and skillful teaching.

They also recognize the importance of being helpful to the slow learner without neglecting the gifted student. That is quite important too because some people say, "The gifted can take care of themselves. You don't need to bother very much with the gifted because they will learn anyway." That isn't entirely true. They don't "just grow." They need instruction also. If we are expecting them to reach some of the higher levels of critical thinking, critical reading, higher levels of appreciation, and other superior performances in each of the subjects, we have to give instruction that will help them attain these levels. There was a freshman in college who said it was a great help to her to have some classes in high school where they had more of the kind of work that is required in college, especially instruction in reading and study methods. Some gifted youngsters go through high school without using half of their abilities and without learning efficient reading and study methods. Then when they do go to college, because of this lack they are often completely lost in their freshman year.

A summary of some of the experiences needed by able learners are these:

1. Give them the kind of instruction that they need; don't neglect them but don't expect them to do drills or listen to explanations that are not necessary.

2. Don't waste their time. They complain bitterly about having to wait for the slow learners to catch up, and wish they could go ahead on their own rate.

3. Enrich their curriculum.

4. Practice moderation in acceleration, and accelerate on the basis of a study of the individual rather than as a general policy.

5. Give the gifted child a chance to match wits. They like group discussion with others of equal ability.

6. Give them freedom to choose their reading, then turn them loose in the library. Give them opportunity for free reading when they have finished their regular assignments. Allow more time for reading in class and discussion of books they have read. Help them to evaluate their reading.

7. Help them develop their interests. Provide a wealth of suitable reading material. Help them plan a balanced daily program.

8. Give them challenging and meaningful assignments. Perhaps what bores gifted children more than anything else is doing busy work which seems to have no meaning, use, or purpose for them.

I might close with a quotation from Albert Schweitzer which I think is especially appropriate with regard to the gifted because one of the problems is to help them acquire a certain sense of destiny, a sense of responsibility for their gifts. Many gifted youngsters do not seem to have a sense of responsibility for their abilities. Albert Schweitzer says: "Whatever you have received more than others, in health, in talents, in abilities, in success, in a pleasant childhood, in harmonious conditions of homelife, all this you must not take for yourself as a matter of course. You must pay the price for it. You must render in return a great service for other lives." I think in the counseling of individual gifted children, it is very important to give them opportunities for service and some sense of responsibility for helping others.

Academic Retardation: Arithmetic

Vincent J. Glennon

That arithmetic is being taught today better than it has been taught in the past can hardly be disputed. Ample evidence of the historical type and the quantitative type is at hand to support this statement. From the historical point of view one needs only to read of the arithmetic program, or, more accurately, the lack of it, in the Dame School of colonial America. Or, a casual study of the teaching program, the teaching conditions and the general lack of professional training and competence of the Master of the early nineteenth century monitorial school will attest further to the accuracy of the statement above. From the quantitative point of view numerous studies are at hand, with data extending back to 1845, showing that in each succeeding generation more children learn more arithmetic and learn it better.

However ego-supportive this idea may be, we must hasten to say that the arithmetic program of today is not of sufficient quality to allow us to rest on our oars. There are at least three good reasons why we must continue to work at the problem of improving the quality of teaching and the quality and quantity of arithmetic learning in this year and the years ahead. First, children in the elementary and secondary schools are not sufficiently proficient in arithmetic to enable them to function effectively in real-life and school-life situations involving numbers. There is ample evidence to support this statement. Second, the change in emphasis or theory supporting the teaching of arithmetic that has occurred in the past quarter century has not filtered down through the teacher to the level of the learner. Whereas the theory has shifted from the drill theory to the meaning theory, arithmetic practices in the typical classroom are still largely based on the drill theory. We must continue to work hard at the problem of bringing practice into line with theory and thus improve both the quality and the quantity of classroom learning. Third, since the role of the teacher consists of transmitting the culture, and since arithmetic is an important part of the culture, the teacher must accept its transmission as his proper function. The improvement of arithmetic teaching can best be effected by unusually skillful initial teaching reinforced on occasion by systematic reteaching—this latter usually at the beginning of each new grade. However, due to many factors over some of which the teacher has little or no control—large class size, by way of an illustration —in far too many instances the initial teaching of arithmetic is not today being done as well as we know it can be done. The result of this situation is the child who is retarded in arithmetic.

It is the purpose of this paper to consider several of the facets of the problem of academic retardation in arithmetic: (1) What should be taught? (2) How can we identify the retarded child? (3) What may be the causes of the retardation? (4) What are some of the techniques for diagnosing the specific difficulties?

1. *What should be taught?*
Many statements of objectives of the arithmetic program have been written. Looked at historically over the past sixty years, since courses of study have been written, these objectives have changed from simple listings of compu-

tational skills or topics to comprehensive statements of both the social and mathematical phases of arithmetic teaching and learning. One of the more widely referred to statements of objectives is that by Brownell:

a) Computational skill:
Facility and accuracy in operations with whole numbers, common fractions, decimals, and per cents. (This group of outcomes is here separated from the second and third groups which follow because it *can* be isolated for measurement. In this separation much is lost, for computation without understanding *when* as well as *how* to compute is a rather empty skill. Actually, computation is important only as it contributes to social ends.)

b) Mathematical understandings:
   (1) Meaningful conceptions of quantity, of the number system, of whole numbers, of common fractions, of decimals, of per cents, of measures, etc.
   (2) A meaningful vocabulary of the useful technical terms of arithmetic which designate quantitative ideas and the relationships between them.
   (3) Grasp of important arithmetical generalizations.
   (4) Understanding of the meanings and mathematical functions of the fundamental operations.
   (5) Understanding of the meanings of measures and of measurement as a process.
   (6) Understanding of important arithmetical relationships, such as those which function in reasonably sound estimations and approximations, in accurate checking, and in ingenious and resourceful solutions.
   (7) Some understanding of the rational principles which govern number relations and computational procedures.

c) Sensitiveness to number in social situations and the habit of using number effectively in such situations:
   (1) Vocabulary of selected quantitative terms of common usage (such as kilowatt hour, miles per hour, decrease and increase, and terms important in insurance, investments, business practices, etc.).
   (2) Knowledge of selected business practices and other economic applications of number.
   (3) Ability to use and interpret graphs, simple statistics, and tabular presentations of quantitative data (as in study in school and in practical activities outside of school).
   (4) Awareness of the usefulness of quantity and number in dealing with many aspects of life. Here belongs some understanding of the important contributions of number in their evolution.
   (5) Tendency to sense the quantitative as part of normal experience, including vicarious experience, as in reading, in observation, and in projected activity and imaginative thinking.

(6) Ability to make (and the habit of making) sound judgments with respect to practical quantitative problems.

(7) Disposition to extend one's sensitiveness to the quantitative as this occurs socially and to improve and extend one's ability to deal effectively with the quantitative when so encountered or discovered.[1]

At first thought one might be inclined to think of the objectives as merely computational skill and verbal problem-solving ability, but a careful reading of the objectives above will quickly disabuse one's mind of that notion. Included among the objectives are those that might be classified in the categories of understandings, both social and mathematical, attitudes (disposition to act in a given way), appreciations (liking for and tendency to choose), habits, skills and abilities of many kinds and facts (arbitrary associations). We should add values, for surely it is within the proper function of the teacher of arithmetic to guide the learner in right thinking and right behavior and to create a learning environment that will tend to minimize negative values such as "cheating," copying the work of others, etc.

Thoughtful consideration of the problem of identifying and helping the child who is academically retarded in arithmetic, when growth in arithmetic includes the many objectives above, becomes a most complex professional undertaking. Let us now consider some general ways of identifying this child.

2. *Identifying the retarded child.*

For the purposes of this paper the academically retarded child is defined as one who is not achieving up to his estimated capacity. It is important to qualify "capacity" as "estimated" since it is quite well agreed that the exact potential of a child cannot be determined precisely. Despite this lack of precision it is still important that some attempt be made to approximate the child's level of potential if one wishes to aid him in achieving a given level of performance.

There are many sources of information that the teacher can use in identifying the academically retarded child. The most commonly used technique is that of identifying the pupil whose achievement in arithmetic, expressed in grade age terms as measured by a standard test, is significantly lower than his mental age. In the data below, pupil A, age 11 years, is above average in mental ability (mental age 14), and is performing about as well as he should be expected to perform (arithmetic age is 13.7 years or approximately equal to his mental age, 14 years). Keeping in mind the fact that the tests used would not be wholly valid or reliable, one can say that the discrepancy between potential ability to perform and actual performance is insufficient to classify this child as retarded in arithmetic.

Pupil B is also a bright child and although he is doing as well in arithmetic as the average child in his grade (A.A. is 11.1 yr.), he is definitely not doing as well as it would seem he should be doing with a mental age of 14

[1] Brownell, W. A., "The Evaluation of Learning in Arithmetic," *Arithmetic in General Education.* Sixteenth Yearbook of the National Council of Teachers of Mathematics. 1941.

TABLE I

	Chronological Age (C.A.)	Mental Age (M.A.)	Arithmetic Age	Approximate Grade of Achievement
Pupil A	11 yrs.	14 yrs.	13.7 yrs.	8.1 grade
Pupil B	11	14	11.1	5.6
Pupil C	11	8	7.9	2.5
Pupil D	11	8	6.2	lower than 1.0
Pupil E	11	11	11.3	5.7
Pupil F	11	11	7.8	2.5

years. The discrepancy between his M.A. and A.A. is about 3 years. This makes pupil B a very likely clinical case.

Pupils C and D are mentally retarded as well as academically retarded. However, whereas pupil C is doing about as well as should be expected of him (his arithmetic age is about equal to his mental age), pupil D is achieving considerably below his capacity and is therefore a child who should profit from a program of careful diagnosis and remediation.

Comparing pupils E and F we see immediately that while both are average in mental age, pupil E is achieving about up to his capacity and pupil F far below his capacity. In summary, although Pupils A, C, and E are the same chronological age but vary greatly in mental ability, each is achieving about up to his estimated ability and hence cannot be considered academically retarded in arithmetic (as academic retardation was defined above for use in this paper). On the other hand, pupils B, D, and F, also the same age but varying in potential learning ability, are not achieving up to capacity and hence are classified as academically retarded in arithmetic. These latter three children should profit greatly from a well-planned remedial program. It will be noted then that neither mental age alone nor achievement level alone provides a sufficient basis for identifying the academically retarded child. Rather, both scores are compared for a given child and when the difference or discrepancy is judged to be unduly great, let us say more than one year, that child in all probability should be considered for more extensive, intensive and specific diagnosis and remediation.

As was noted above, the discrepancy technique is the most commonly used method for identifying the academically retarded child. However, this technique alone is not sufficient. It should be supplemented by data gathered from the cumulative folders, from teacher observations of daily oral work and pencil-and-paper work, from teacher interviews with individual pupils, his parents and siblings, from observation of pupil performance in quantitative situations in the social studies unit, the science work, pupil reports, activities and projects, and from the hundred and one other less structured but perhaps more socially significant number situations that occur during the school day.

3. *What may be the causes of the retardation?*
To attempt to ascribe academic retardation in arithmetic to a single cause is to try to ascribe juvenile delinquency to a single cause. It can't be done.

Causation in both instances is usually multiple and complex. However, it is possible to consider here some of the more likely sources that contribute in varying degrees to the problem. In this paper causation will be considered as residing in any or all of these: (a) the teacher; (b) the teaching situation; (c) the teaching process (theory of arithmetic teaching); (d) the learner; and (e) the theory of curriculum organization in the school. Space allows only a brief comment on each.

   a) Causation resident in the teacher.

There is general agreement, among those who are competent to judge, that to a significant degree the teacher of arithmetic is lacking in both knowledge of the subject matter of arithmetic (as a science of numbers) and in the psychology and methodology of teaching that subject matter. This agreement is not based on superficial acquaintance with the problem through casual observation, hearsay or whatever; on the contrary, it is based in large part on the findings of research studies done over the past quarter century and on personal observation by competent authorities. This lack of scholarship and teaching competence is undoubtedly a causative factor in academic retardation, for it is difficult to see how one can teach well a body of subject matter that he only partly understands.

Newsom discusses the paucity of training in arithmetic and in the teaching of arithmetic this way:

> ...it is the writer's considered opinion that it is possible and desirable to include in the curriculum for the training of elementary school teachers a minimum of a three-hour course of background mathematics, in addition to a course on the teaching of arithmetic; moreover, a six-hour course is preferred. All too frequently teachers in the elementary grades are hardly a jump ahead of their alert students, and many teachers have confided in the writer that they lack confidence before their classes in approaching various arithmetical concepts.[2]

   b) Causation resident in the teaching situation.

By teaching situation we mean such aspects as the size of the class, the quality of the primary teaching materials (textbooks, workbooks, teachers manuals, etc.), and the quantity and quality of supplementary teaching materials (manipulative materials, play money, place value charts, and the like).

Great variation exists in the quality of the primary arithmetic teaching materials and because of this one can say that the materials of lower quality contribute to academic retardation by making the teaching more difficult for the teacher and learning more difficult for the learner. All too often the supplementary arithmetic teaching materials are entirely lacking in the classroom. Regarding size of class, it is only common sense to say that the teacher of twenty children, other things being equal, can get to know more about the arithmetical thought processes and growth of them than can the teacher of forty children. Further, when we keep in mind the scope of the objectives of arithmetic instruction listed above one can readily see that it is not possible to teach large classes as effectively as smaller classes. These several aspects of the teaching situation contribute their share to academic retardation.

---

[2] Newsom, C. V. "Mathematical Background Needed by Teachers of Arithmetic," *The Teaching of Arithmetic.* Fiftieth Yearbook of the National Council of Teachers of Mathematics, 1951.

c) Causation resident in the teaching process (theory of arithmetic teaching) .

Today there is general agreement on the verbal level that arithmetic should be taught meaningfully. However, there is not general agreement when one judges by prevailing classroom practices. By and large teachers agree that arithmetic should be taught meaningfully, but classroom practices all too often reflect a most generous use of drill procedures. Again looking back at the many objectives listed above one can see that few of these are best achieved through drill or repetitive practice.

d) Causation resident in the learner.

Since we have defined the academically retarded, for the purposes of this paper, as one who is not achieving up to his estimated capacity, we can rule out at this point lack of mental ability as a cause of academic retardation.

A most important cause of arithmetic retardation is failure to acquire those learnings which are *prerequisite* for later related learnings. As a result of this failure, which may have been due to absence from school, or others, there is a gap in the child's knowledge, and this gap makes it difficult or impossible for him to move smoothly along in acquiring the next developmental step in the learning.

Another cause might be emotional or affective. As a result of failure the child develops a dislike for school arithmetic. This attitude, at first an *effect* of some previous learning can now become a *cause* of failure in present and future learnings.

Still another cause would be his inability to keep up with the learning pace set by the teacher. This cause, however, might more appropriately be listed under section *c* above. In the classroom in which the standard teaching practice is the making of a single assignment for the whole class it is certain that the pace will not fit all of the children.

Lastly, we should mention that the whole area of neurological and physiological disabilities would be contributory to academic retardation in arithmetic.

e) Causation resident in the theory of curriculum organization.

In a number of elementary schools that are generally considered good schools the level of achievement in arithmetic, when judged in relation to the potential of the children, leaves much to be desired. It has been the experience of this writer that in a goodly number of these schools the cause for the *general* academic retardation in arithmetic resides in the fact that the arithmetic program is based to too large a degree on a psychological organization of the curriculum. More specifically, if the arithmetic is taught only when the children have a need for it, and without regard for arithmetic as a logical and systematic body of knowledge, it is more than likely that this will be an important cause of general retardation in arithmetic. Horn discusses the limitations of the psychological organization of the curriculum (integrated plan, as he calls it) and conversely the need for systematic instruction (logical organization) this way:

> It is the unanimous opinion of the present committee, however, that, after a careful appraisal of such evidence as does exist, and after giving full credit to what has been or is likely to be accomplished under integrated plans, such

plans by themselves cannot be depended upon to develop arithmetical concepts and abilities to the level and scope required in life. An especially designed program of instruction in arithmetic is essential, and such a program should include not only provision for systematic and meaningful learning in the arithmetic class but also careful attention to the mathematical needs and contributions of other areas.[3]

4. *Some techniques for diagnosing specific difficulties.*

Let us turn now to our final question. Assuming that we have identified a child who will profit by a remedial program, how do we go about diagnosing his specific areas of difficulty? What techniques do we have at our command? We will mention two references to which the reader may wish to turn for further discussion and illustrations.

The source that contains the more specific illustrations of evaluation techniques is *Arithmetic and Curriculum Organization* by Glennon *et al.*[4] In this book there are nine units in arithmetic, one for each grade level from kindergarten through grade eight. Within each unit is a section of several pages of evaluation techniques. These sections will provide the teacher with a rich source of illustrative ways of evaluating the child's growth toward the many objectives of a complete arithmetic program.

The second source is Brueckner and Bond's *The Diagnosis and Treatment of Learning Difficulties.*[5] Here they list nine categories of techniques with subcategories under most of the nine. The nine categories are listed as:

1. Analysis of written work.
2. Analysis of oral responses.
3. Interview with pupil (also teachers, associates, and parents).
4. Questionnaire.
5. Free observation in course of daily work.
6. Controlled observation of pupil when he is at work on set tasks.
7. Analysis of available records for helpful data.
8. Administration of informal diagnostic tests given in textbooks or workbooks, or prepared by the teacher to secure essential information.
9. Administration of standardized diagnostic tests intended for clinical diagnosis by some available expert or by a teacher familiar with the procedure.

Without commenting or elaborating on each procedure above it is interesting to note that Brownell says of the interview technique that "if this procedure were used commonly in connection with initial instruction, later diagnosis and remediation would be greatly reduced in amount."

---

[3] Horn, Ernest. "Arithmetic in the Elementary-School Curriculum," *The Teaching of Arithmetic*. The fiftieth yearbook of the National Council of Teachers of Mathematics, 1951.

[4] Glennon, Vincent J. *et al. Arithmetic and Curriculum Organization.* Bureau of School Services, School of Education, Syracuse University.

[5] Brueckner, L. J. and Bond, G. L., *The Diagnosis and Treatment of Learning Difficulties.* Appleton-Century-Crofts, Inc., 1955.

Concluding Statement

In the brief space of this paper we have presented some highly capsulated ideas on the problem of academic retardation in arithmetic. We have said that the objectives of a modern arithmetic program are many and complex but that it is possible to identify the child who is not achieving these objectives up to his estimated capacity. We then suggested some of the causes of retardation with which the teacher must cope if he wishes to work effectively with the child who is retarded in arithmetic. And last, we suggested some specific techniques and sources of others that could be used in diagnosing the specific arithmetic difficulties. With further study and thought the classroom teacher can feel reasonably confident of his ability to move into this area of professional work with success awaiting both the child and himself.

The Diagnosis of Reading Retardation

Rudolph J. Capobianco

Reading is considered the most basic of the tool subjects taught in the elementary years of school. Statistics reported in the literature concerning the incidence of reading retardation vary a great deal from one authority to another, estimates ranging from 1 to approximately 25 or 30 per cent. It is likely, however, that at least ten per cent of children with average and above average intelligence read so inadequately for the grade placement as to impair their total adjustment. Separate statistics concerning retardation in reading among exceptional children are unavailable. It may be assumed, however, that the typical referral to a reading clinic very often is the exceptional child with reading retardation. The normal individual with the same handicap may be overlooked in favor of those children with additional handicaps.

The importance of reading as a tool subject cannot be denied. One need only read a few of the popular magazine articles written on the topic of reading to realize its tremendous importance. The recent furor created by Rudolph Flesch in his book *Why Johnny Can't Read* is an excellent example of the concern parents have for this problem. Flesch vehemently attacks the American reading program first by attributing to certain investigators and writers the very views which they themselves have severely critized and, second, by describing a methodology of teaching reading supposedly in current use which would be a deterrence to any society. If parents believe that the methods now being used in the schools and supported by the leading scholars in the field are as Mr. Flesch describes, they would indeed be justified in criticizing these techniques.

The "cure-all" suggested by Mr. Flesch—that is, phonics—is another example of pendulum action in the field of education. Apparently, to meet the demands of critics, some educationists have utilized methods which are at opposite poles from one another—in either case resorting to extremes. At various times in the history of education, the teaching of reading has been criticized as being too visually or too phonically based. Apparently it does not occur to these critics that a combined system of teaching reading would perhaps be the best solution to the problem. Carefully conducted research by authorities in the field of reading have demonstrated that no one approach is fully adequate to teach reading to all children. Obviously a child with a visualization problem should not be presented with a visual approach to reading. Similarly, a child with an auditory handicap should not be expected to learn through a phonic method. Perhaps an examination of the learning process itself would be in order at this point.

Mass-Differentiation-Integration Sequence

Most learning has been described as following a three-stage process: mass-differentiation-integration. The mass stage may be defined as the initial impression formed by the observer in any new learning situation (the "en masse" response). The differentiation stage is defined as a process of analysis. It is in this stage that the observer isolates various components of the mass situation into meaningful parts. The integration stage, then, is the synthesis of the various component parts of the mass situation into a meaningful whole. Learning to read fits very readily into this three-stage process. In the mass stage, the child is subjected to a number of abstract stimuli, which at the pre-reading level is a meaningless mass. After the child has learned to recognize certain letters or certain words or certain phonic symbols, he has reached the stage of differentiation. The third level is not achieved until the child learns to make a meaningful whole from these separate components of the printed page, being able to accomplish purpose without going through the other two phases. Reading behavior seems to demonstrate that this mass-differentiation-integration sequence occurs in response to developmental aspects of growth. The starting point is an en masse reaction to a unit situation; the processes of seeking meaning (differentiation) and establishing meaning (integration) occur when aspects of the unit become discernible and are related to experiential background.

A few of the obvious difficulties experienced in the teaching of reading may be explained on the basis of this three-stage process. For instance, the old spelling and phonic techniques stopped at the differentiation stage. That is, they taught the individual to break down or analyze the mass but did not continue to the integration stage. Integration was left as some sort of magical process which the child should achieve automatically. The sight-word or visual approach was an attempt to skip the differentiation stage completely, as it was considered an unnecessary step in the reading process. This theory proposed to proceed directly from the mass stage to the integration level. It should be noted that children learned to read in spite of these two different approaches.

Confronted with the presentation of a phonically-based system in the teaching of reading, children learned, on their own, to integrate material into meangingful wholes. This integration occurred as a result of insightful thinking on the part of these children and/or by independently relating the material to their experiential background. When presented with a purely visual approach, the next generation of school children independently learned to analyze sounds and words before proceeding to the integration level. Assuming that it was their respective approaches to teaching, and not the improvisation on the part of pupils themselves, that led to adequate reading performance, the proponents of either system claimed total success. There was, however, a considerable number of children who did not learn to read when the phonic method was in vogue. These children were referred to reading clinics for diagnosis and remediation. The recommended treatment usually consisted of some type of visual remediation and most of the referred cases learned to read under this method. Observing the phenomenal number of successful remedial cases in the clinics, it was assumed that the sight method was superior and should be introduced into the classrooms as the *only* method for teaching reading. Unfortunately, when the sight method was introduced into the public schools and became popular, an equally large population of nonreaders were still referred to the various clinics. But for these diagnosed cases the clinics usually suggested a phonic approach to combat the reading retardation and most referred cases learned to read through the prescribed remediation.

One would assume, at this point, that the obvious inference to be drawn from the above history concerning the methodologies for teaching reading would be that a combined approach, visual and phonic, should be much superior in terms of end result than either one of the two methods mentioned above. Further, most children are capable of learning to read under either system but there is a segment of the school population which is characterized by inability in learning to read when presented with a phonic approach; similarly, there is an equivalent group of children who are unable to grasp ing these inferences from the historical data, however, the public school conreading techniques when taught by a purely visual method. Instead of making these inferences from the historical data, however, the public school continues to use this pendulum approach to teaching reading: either a total phonic approach or a total visual approach. It is an unusal teacher indeed who successfully combines these two approaches in her teaching of reading.

It is apparent then that it is a task for the researcher to present indisputable data regarding handicaps in visual and auditory discrimination with their subsequent effect upon the reading process. This statement is perhaps unfair to the researchers who have spent considerable effort in attempting to isolate some of the factors involved in reading disability cases. Studies by Bond and others have demonstrated that hard-of-hearing pupils were severely handicapped in classes where phonetic methods were stressed. Similarly other researchers have found that visually handicapped individuals had difficulty with visually oriented reading lessons. Difficulties in auditory and visual discrimination, however, are not necessarily restricted to individuals with hearing and vision imperfections per se and these discrimination difficulties are even more notorious in the production of reading disabilities than the physical handicaps themselves. Research, then, should concern itself with the diagnosis, treatment and prognosis of auditory and visual discrimination problems. This implies a psychophysiological as well as an educational experimental approach.

Diagnosis

The diagnosis of reading retardation is not fully accomplished by the administration of an achievement test, with the intention of comparing it to the mental age scored on an individually administered intelligence test. Data supplied by this "one shot" approach merely gives us information which already has been established; that is, that the child is a reading problem. Since the true function of diagnostic procedure is to supply information for the remediation of a problem, it is apparent that one should attempt to discover why the individual is not reading up to his mental age level. To answer this question of "Why," it is necessary to administer a complete diagnostic test battery. It is unfortunate, though, that the better reading diagnostic test batteries demand a professionally trained test administrator before optimum results can be achieved. It is perhaps because of this that many achievement tests have been used by less trained technicians as reading diagnostic instruments. But for many of the reading retardation cases there is a multiplicity of causes operating rather than a single cause. Careful diagnosis should appraise various factors operating so that recommended treatment will be applicable.

The utilization of an achievement test as a diagnostic procedure for determining reading retardation would necessarily overrefer children to reading clinics, especially since many of the children who would be referred as reading retardation cases would probably be working up to their mental age capacity, if not up to their grade level placement. This procedure would refer to the clinic a whole group of slow learners who may be working up to their capacity level, but would miss many of the above average pupils who are not reading up to their expected levels. Before diagnosis, it is important to obtain a mental age level on each child, attempting to relate this to an achievement level. The essence of the diagnostic procedure, however, still lies with the reading diagnostic tests which would inform the clinician: (1) What is the reading approach of the client? (2) What method of word attack does he use? (3) How do the vision and hearing functions of the child relate to the reading process? (4) What are the abilities of the child in visualization and sound blending? (5) In the analyses of the reading errors, which areas of word attack seem to give the child the most trouble? Here the utilization of vowel, consonant, and reversal errors, substitutions, sounds omitted and added, etc., would be analyzed to determine the kind of reading problem the child has.

The importance of diagnosis in the area of educational retardation is very easily seen when one examines the history of reading instruction in the public schools. It has already been suggested that the clinics handling reading retardation cases when the phonic system was in vogue utilized a visualization approach to successfully rehabilitate the reading problem in the regular classroom situation. It has been further pointed out that the reading retardation cases that were referred to clinics while the visualization approach was in common usage conversely rehabilitated the youngsters in the regular classroom situation by the utilization of a phonic approach in remediation. Without adequate diagnostics in a clinical setting, the teacher is confronted with only one alternative. Assuming that her pupils have the necessary intellectual ability to grasp the reading instruction, the teacher is left with the conclusion that it is her inability as a teacher which caused this reading retardation. Oftentimes the conscientious but naive teacher will consider it her duty to raise the child's level of reading up to his "capacity level." Hence, she spends special sessions after school hours, or perhaps weekends, with the youngster to bring about a more adequate level of reading. All too often this method is met with utter failure. The child himself, realizing his failure in reading, is further frustrated by the extra amount of time he has to spend with a subject that is obnoxious to him because of previous failure. This vicious circle of failure-frustration-more failure, etc., may be prevented by timely referrals to the reading clinic. Teachers are not professional diagnosticians; it is up to the clinician to determine why the child is a case of reading retardation. The cause may be physiological, psychological, or educational; or perhaps any combination of these factors.

The Psychoeducational Clinic

A brief description of the procedure followed in a reading or psychoeducational clinic would be in order at this point. Most of these clinics are housed and staffed in colleges and universities; there are, however, progressively more of these facilities being provided through public and private agencies throughout the states. Educational retardation surveys are not within the province of the clinic staff; facilities are offered, usually on a sliding-scale cost basis, to school, family or agency referrals. When a child is referred to a clinic, the examiner is oftentimes equipped with no more than a group intelligence rating and a very subjective judgment on the part of the teacher as to why this child is failing in reading. After establishing rapport, the examiner must first discover the functioning intellectual ability of the child. This is usually determined by an individually administered intelligence test. The choice of the instrument to be used will vary from one examiner to another, but will also depend upon the information on the nature of the child himself. That is, if a client is physically handicapped, a performance test is to be avoided. If the child is hard of hearing or deaf, obviously a verbal test is to be avoided. Usually the situation is handled by the presentation of a test which utilizes both verbal and performance measurements, such as the Wechsler Intelligence Scale for Children.

Following the establishment of a mental age level, the child is given an achievement test, if a recently administered test is not already available in the cumulative folder. The achievement test measures various aspects of the reading process, the reasoning and quantitative measurements on arithmetic, sometimes spelling and even handwriting. The diagnostician then compares the capacity level established by the intelligence test with the achievement level in the areas of reading. If the discrepancy between these two measurements is sufficient, the child is then considered for a complete diagnostic workup. Brief screening devices are then administered to determine the hearing and vision capacities of the client. Usually the hearing test consists of a "sweep" test on a puretone audiometer. There are other more informal tests of hearing capacity such as the "watch tick" and "whisper" tests; however, these latter measurements are far from precise and should be avoided when an audiometer is available. The most common vision test is the Snellen Chart, but in recent years the telebinocular (Keystone Vision Survey) test has been utilized to greater advantage. This latter test is equipped to accomplish an exhaustive survey of visual processes. Among the subjects included in the telebinocular are measurements of near and farsightedness, astigmatism indices, vertical and lateral imbalance, near and far-point fusion tests, stereopsis (depth perception), monocular and binocular visual efficiency. This test was the first one devised to appraise coordination of the eyes under conditions similar to those found in reading. The Snellen Chart is not equipped to measure completely the separate functions of vision; for instance, it misses refractive errors, farsightedness and astigmatism defects and does not simulate an actual reading situation.

Thusfar in the diagnostic setting we have established a capacity level for the child and an achievement level in reading; we have tested both the vision and hearing functions on brief screening devices. The diagnostician is now ready to administer a reading diagnostic examination. This test will answer the question: "Why is this child retarded in reading?" The three most popular reading diagnostic tests are the Durrell, Gates, and the Monroe Diagnostic. The diagnostician usually has chosen one of these tests as his favorite for the clinic setting. The test battery chosen measures such reading functions as: oral reading, oral reading comprehension (silent reading and silent reading comprehension are extracted from the achievement test records), word discrimination and recognition (auditory and visual), sound blending, visualization, and usually some measure of context clues. In addition to this battery, there is included in the diagnosis measurements of handedness and eyedness, and the clinician feels it is necessary—a projective test—to evaluate some of the emotional factors present. With the completion of this diagnostic battery, the diagnostician has collected sufficient information to accurately describe the method of word attack the child uses, make an analysis of the types of errors made and assume some measure of the visualization and sound blending competencies of the child. Armed with this information, the diagnostician can then suggest a specific therapeutic technique. The therapy may consist of a combination phonic and visualization approach (kinesthetic), either a phonic or a visualization approach, psychotherapy, or perhaps a demand for further physical evidence such as a referral for ophthalmological or audiological diagnosis, or neuological examination.

Assuming the client is diagnosed as a nonreader because of a poor method of word attack, the most productive system for his capacities would then be recommended. If he has better visualization than phonic abilities, he should obviously be given remediation with a visualization method; if the situation is reversed, then the phonic method would be to the better advantage of the child. If the diagnosis is still unclear at this stage, the diagnostician then recommends further specific testing, has more interviews with the client, his parents or teachers and/or refers the client to another agency.

Oftentimes, the therapeutic methodology recommended by the clinician is psychological rather than educational. Success has been claimed by the proponents of psychotherapeutic methods with problems in educational retardation. Other remedial specialists claim that the alleviation of the specific educational problem automatically dismisses the emotional problems involved. Time limitations prohibit the discussion of the pros and cons of these two methods. Suffice it to say, however, there is an element in these therapies that is common to both philosophical views: individual contact between client and therapist. Perhaps this common element can partially explain the high degree of successful experience with most types of remediation.

Perhaps some generalizations can be made about recommended remediation techniques. Barring other difficulties: (1) Those children with some degree of retarded mental development usually gain more through the utilization of a simple phonic approach (assuming no auditory discrimination difficulties). The Hegge-Kirk drills have been very successful with the retarded youngster particularly at the beginning stages of reading in attempting to establish a method of word attack. (2) The Dolch method of visually presented cards with pictures and words has been very successful with those children of average or above average intelligence who have not had sufficient practice to learn a method of word attack or perhaps have not been stimulated sufficiently by the atmosphere of the regular classroom situation. (3) Those children with difficulties in reversals have considerable success with the application of the Fernald kinesthetic method of remedial reading. The kinesthetic method is perhaps a misnomer. Actually it is primarily a visualization method with supplementary auditory stimulation plus the utilization of motor abilities such as writing, tracing, etc.

Complete reading diagnosis is not the task for the amateur diagnostician nor the school teacher who is unfamiliar with clinical techniques. The administration and analysis of the various reading diagnostic batteries demands a trained diagnostician. Obviously, diagnosis is not a one-shot procedure; it is a continuing process. By that, it is meant that the recommendation of a remedial process is not the goal of the diagnostician. If this process is unsuccessful, the diagnostician should be ready, willing and capable of suggesting a new technique. The task of the therapist is to continue a running diagnosis, one which may change from one day to the next or perhaps from one week to the next in the remedial setting.

The Speech Handicapped Child

LOUIS M. DI CARLO

Speech, as hearing impairments, respects neither race, creed, socioeconomic, nor intellectual status. Speech disabilities are found among children with superior intelligence, most children of retarded mental development, all deaf children, most hard-of-hearing children, crippled, emotionally disturbed, blind, and even among many nonexceptional children. Speech and language development are sociological imperatives for communication. Without the ability to communicate adequately, individuals fail to function at optimum levels. Speech has become man's most formidable communicative tool and represents a most pervasive form of human behavior. There is a good deal of question concerning the contribution of speech to mental development and some workers have come to feel that speech and intelligence are different aspects of similar behavior. Anthropologists have studied the language forms of primitive tribes and have found a positive relationship between more complex linguistic structure and higher cultural development. Speech is the one communication artery that permits interactions between individuals and groups, and a failure to develop satisfactory communication disrupts this cooperative intercourse. The child with a speech impairment is truly at a great disadvantage.

How speech first began must remain a speculative hypothesis. There are many theories concerning the origin of speech and language, but none of these theories has been scientifically corroborated. Among these theories are the onomatopoeic, interjectional, and natural expression theories. It is very questionable if any of these can explain the origin of speech and language behavior. We can study speech and language changes and we can trace language to more primitive and elementary forms but we cannot explain its origin.

Today, let us consider how speech develops among children. The idea has become prevalent that the first speech of the child is his birth cry immediately upon taking his first breath after delivery. He continues to use his voice and his vocal cries are considered a form of speech behavior. Psychologists, linguists, and anthropologists, have worked out a schema indicating specific patterns of speech development. It is my feeling that the birth cry is not speech and also that speech does not develop according to fixed temporal sequences. The first cry of the child is probably of a reflex nature and thereafter a good deal of vocalization is associated with spontaneous mass behavior. We know that a child does not have speech for about two years and then suddenly begins to use speech as communication. It would appear from observation that neurophysiological maturation is correlated with communication development.

With respect to the speech process we must consider first of all decoding linguistic phase, the association period, and finally, the encoding sequence. Hearing plays a very important part in speech reception, leading to comprehension and decoding. Experience, learning, and maturation, facilitate association behavior, and neurophysiological stability culminates in expressive communication. During the first six months the child babbles a great deal and appears to be imitating sound forms. Irwin and his co-workers have reported in their research on infant speech development, that the velar and guttural sounds predominate during the first months of the child's life. According to this group of research workers, the articulation profile of a child two and a half years of age, closely approximates that of the adult. Irwin also reported the early development of plosives and fricatives, with decreasing fricatives and increasing nasal sounds with age. Most other studies agree with these findings but some workers feel that speech continues to develop until eight years of age. By the age of seven, most children acquire satisfactory articulation. Nevertheless, speech does not develop in clearcut stages and the research unequivocally indicates that many variables and complexities operate in the development of speech as communication. Before the child can speak he must develop adequate control of silent breathing coordinations. This means that postural tonus and coordinations are satisfactory, and that he has learned to control the air column to provide the stream of breath on the expiration phase for speech. In addition, he must have developed control of the articulatory organs, the larynx, pharyngeal mechanism, the velum, soft palate, hard palate, teeth, tongue, and the lips. It is only when he is able to control all of these that he can speak. In the beginning, vocalization is an overflow of energy finding release through mass behavior. During these first few months the child uses vocalization in spontaneous play behavior and it is in this way that he sets up the circular feedback system.

The hearing now becomes important in controlling the intensity as well as the frequency patterns of the sound he produces. The first period when the child repeats sounds over and over again, is called the babbling period. There is no mystery about this phase. As the child lies on his back, and because he is a bundle of mass behavior, the vocal cords are activated and as the air column is thrown into the mouth, the changing shapes of the mouth result in the utterance of different vowels. This seems to go on incessantly even when the child is left alone but one wonders if the child is trying to speak at this time. A more rational explanation would be that this is a purely chance physiological phenomenon. As the people in his environment respond to him, they will initiate an awareness that vocalization has a communicative value. The introduction into the environment of good speech patterns will influence the child. In the beginning the child responds to the vocalization of the parents, and later when left alone, will continue vocalization. At first, as Irwin has indicated, they produce multiple backsounds. Next, with the changing shape of the resonating cavities and by the movement of the tongue and lips, many other sounds are uttered. With respect to the consonants, the procedure appears to be reversed. Nevertheless, the child's repertoire of sounds is manifold up to the first ten months and he has many more sounds than those used in his language proper. By fourteen months, the child has more than the phonetic content of his language. A very important question is, why do these many sounds eventually become restricted to the forty sounds of the language? What conditions are working to reduce the many sounds which a young child utters indiscriminately, to the forty or more sounds which the child will use in his own language?

In my opinion, the forces of social compulsion of the language itself are at work. The cultural values will eliminate from the child's behavior those elements that do not help the organism adjust to communication needs. Consequently, as the child's awareness of communication grows, many sounds are eliminated. Through the babbling stage the child is already developing feedback control of language. It is at this time also that the parent attributes meaning to the child's vocalization and the question arises as to whether the child is actually transmitting meaning or whether or not the parent is projecting meaning. Mowrer and others already expressed doubt concerning the transmission of meaning from one source to another. In a way, this is a rather startling concept because we have come to accept the idea that meaning can be transmitted. But, before meaning can be transmitted, the individual must have the meaning. If the individual has the meaning, then you elicit it rather than transmit it. Consider this for a moment in the light of the verbal behavior of a six-month-old child. You can try to transmit to him all the meaning in the world but he will not respond because his developmental level and experimental level have not permitted him to incorporate areas of meaning which may be triggered off by verbal stimuli. It takes a good deal of time for the child to build up a reservoir of information and only if he has developed meaning will the speech stimuli be elicited from him.

Authors are agreed that the child continues this babbling period until about six to nine months of age. From nine to about fourteen months of age, the child goes through a period of repeating verbal stimuli. This period may be considered as one of persistent imitation. It is called the echolalia stage, for now the child begins to echo not only his own verbalizations but also verbalization of the significant people in his environment. It is at this period also that he begins to give first word sentences. Naturally, experts are divided over this period and curiosity exists as to the meaning of the first words. As already indicated, the parents are continually attributing meaning to the child's vocalization but when the child reaches the naming stage, he now is able to participate in the communicative process because the parents fill in meaning from the different cues of the situation.

Research is quite clear that the lip consonants usually appear first and these may appear accidentally. The child closing his lips will utter the sound "ah" and verbalizes "ma-ma." The mother receives her first great thrill in interpreting this interjection as a naming activity. The father tries to get the child to say "daddy" but we know that the articulation of "daddy" requires a higher level of neurophysiological organization. The child cannot articulate "d's" until at a later time when the nervous system has become more stable in its function with respect to the integration of behavior. This simple accidental behavior may well be the battleground for the child's first conflict. Some fathers will develop shame and guilt feelings because the child has spoken "ma-ma" first, and attempts to have him produce "daddy" fail. What usually happens, however, is that in addition to "ma-ma" the child will utter other sound combinations which will permit different individuals to interpret as they would like to hear it. This period of spontaneous babbling and early first words has great predictive significance.

McCarthy has suggested that in the absence of sensitive instruments for evaluating the child's intelligence at these early levels, cues may be obtained by analyzing the child's sound production during these stages. Research reveals that mentally retarded children are delayed in the process of babbling and first word sentences. The deaf child's babbling does not include certain combinations of sounds which require hearing for control and correction. Brain-injured children may also be detected through the absence of sound production. In certain cases delayed neurophysiological maturation may retrict the amount, kinds, and types of babbling, but many authors believe that the failure to develop spontaneous babbling and first word sentences at early ages may be also symptoms of possible difficulties. McCarthy has already conducted some studies of the progress of early sound production and correlating this early vocal activity with predictive estimates of the child's intelligence. The subjects in these experiments included infants from three to seven months of age. They analyzed the type and the amount of consonants and vowels and obtained the type and amount of ratios between the consonant and vowel productions. Children who were found deficient in the sound productions at this period were studied and followed up at a later time, and in many cases mental retardation was present among those children with restricted consonant and vowel production. Consequently, it is not possible to use the amount and type of vocalization as a criteria for evaluating the child's speech production at different stages in the developmental continuum. Mentally retarded children will be delayed in speech development but nevertheless when speech begins to break through it will progress consistently with child development principles. It will be slower, it will be restricted, and it will not have many of the sounds that other children have.

A second criterion used in the child's speech, will be the amount of speech and the kinds of sentence structure. It is quite easy to see that a child can get into trouble anywhere along the developmental continuum by the disturbing influences in his environment, especially if conflict is reflected in parental struggle for power in controlling the child. Since the speech act is such a complicated one and requires so many psychological and physiological finely timed coordinations, it is vulnerable at many strategic points. For this reason parents should have some orientation with regard to the speech acquisition process and how they may help in its reinforcement. For example, parents should realize that before the child can imitate their sounds, he must first be able to produce them. This knowledge would prevent the parents from introducing strange sounds for the child to produce when he is unable to do so, but it would permit them to imitate the baby's vocal production and in this way reinforce it. As in all highly skilled acts, the child's speech becomes differentiated from the general pool of sounds if he learns to discriminate between phonetic elements in his acquisition of autocritical phonetic analysis.

We must remember that speech itself is preceded by a nonverbal communicative period when gestures carry the meaning and as speech develops, gesture communication decreases. When the child begins to use speech as a predictor, then he is using speech as true communication. A prolonged period of gesture communication may result in retarded speech development. Another cause for delayed speech development may be overprotection and oversolicitation, where the child lacks motivation since every need is anticipated for him without providing him opportunities for expressing his needs. The child may remain in the infantile gesture stage long after speech is supposed to have developed. There are children in many school systems who will not be speaking when they enter kindergarten because there has not been satisfactory motivation for the development of communication, due to the inability of the parents to provide them with growing-up experiences. Some of these children may progress through the babbling and echolalia stages satisfactorily but at a crucial point learn that they can have their needs met much more adequately without speech. At a period when they are supposed to be using words, they will stop vocalization.

Some of these children are being called aphasic. Many deaf children will go through this spontaneous vocal period undetected but since they do not have an intact auditory system, they will not be able to develop adequate speech interactions. With children whose speech progresses adequately, they hear the sound, feel the sound, and then produce the sound. As they produce the sound they hear, the feedback will exert a controlling influence. Later on, adults enter the situation and provide stimulation for them. The children now attend to stimuli which is not self-generated. As this activity continues, meaning is assigned to symbols and associations are set up. This experience now becomes a prelude to development of a vocabulary. By the time he enters kindergarten the child is supposed to have approximately two thousand words which he can use and understand, and some research indicates that the count may be as many as seventeen thousand words if prefixes and suffixes are included. At two years of age, or perhaps at eighteen months, this process of specific naming predominates. The naming activity does not appear to me to be merely one in which the child names the object, but one which indicates he is developing an ability to predict and associate it with other objects. Speech now becomes a functional tool through which he can communicate his needs and ideas. Shortly after this period, the names begin to carry qualifying words and as he grows older until he enters school, the child has a good amount of the basic language equipment for communication. Speech and language behavior continues to become more complex until he reaches the age of twelve. Some scholars believe that true communication learning occurs until the age of twelve. After the age of twelve, the learning is of a manipulative kind where symbols, either auditory, verbal, or visual, are manipulated in problem-solving behavior. If this is true it means that he does not learn new knowledge but what he does is to use it, manipulating it so that it is instrumental and operational for him in his adjustments.

Rejection, as well as overprotection, may also lead to delayed speech development. Observation of different children at the Gordon D. Hoople Hearing and Speech Center, indicates that many overprotected children of superior intelligence develop stuttering behavior while rejected children of average intelligence develop reading difficulties. Rejection may conspire to terminate in delayed speech which may retard the child permanently. Speech occurs in a social situation and presents bistimulation behavior. The speaker does not only attend to the reference but attends to the listener. Incompatibility in the reference or listeners' responses may terminate in faulty communication.

Mowrer suggested recently that learning speech behavior may be more adequately accounted for in terms of the concepts of: (1) psychoanalytical identification, and (2) modern reinforcement learning theory. He discusses the development of speech in animals, especially birds. If you bring a number of parrots or parakeets into the home, all the training you can give them will not result in speech. We know that parrots and parakeets can actually produce speech without its psychological implications. We also know if you bring a number of them into your living room you can talk yourself blue in the face and they never will respond. You may reduce the number to two and spend as much time as you wish with them, but again they will not talk. If, however, you take only one and isolate him from his species and put him into a situation where his every need depends upon you, then you may become "the love object." In this way he identifies himself with you, and in identifying himself with you he will try to be like you in some respect. If now, after you administer to his wants you speak to him, the speech will be reinforced. At first the rewards will provide primary reinforcements but later, through secondary reinforcements, any aspect of the situation which may be associated with the speaker may produce speech in his absence.

Delayed speech behavior may be present in children in a harsh environment as a revolt against authority symbols. The child will not want to identify himself with either of the speaking parents. The best way of not being like either parent, will be not speaking. By failing to speak the child also discovers that he becomes the recipient of a great deal of attention and he may use this as a means of punishing the parents. He may even learn that his failure to speak may be a way of creating a great deal of parental anxiety. Children continue to test reality all the time. In this case, the child will continue to explore the boundaries. When an environment is replete with prohibitive words, these prohibitive words may lose their value as stimuli and consequently become bad words. These words will not have any reinforcing power.

When speech does not function in an operational manner in controlling behavior, the children may become disturbed. Not only will the child be disturbed, but the language behavior itself will become more symptomatic of deeper, underlying maladjustments. Research by Johnson and his workers indicates that maladjustment may be often described as a failure to use language satisfactorily. Research further indicates that many children with speech disturbances also have reading disabilities. Under such circumstances children may fail to identify themselves with parental substitutes. When the child fails to identify himself with the significant people in his environment, the sounds which are reinforced within the dynamics of a framework of adequate learning theory, must come to him from other sources. Good patterns of speech provided by the proper people under optimum learning conditions in a framework of security relationships, make for the development of normal speech behavior. Good patterns for proper imitation expedite the learning process. While observing the classroom teacher with a group of eight-year-olds, the following incident occurred: The teacher asked for a definition of "bewitches." After some hesitation one boy in the corner raised his hand and volunteered an example: "Youse guys goes ahead, I'll bewitches later." This child's speech, as with many others in the classroom, was punctuated with many anachronisms and ungrammatical forms. The children had identified themselves with her and were imitating the models which she was providing for them.

By the time a child reaches his fourth year he has most of the sounds except the "l," "r," "w," and "y." If the child does not reproduce these adequately at four years of age, it does not mean that he is delayed in his speech development but if the child continues to substitute "w" for "r" when he is seven years of age, then it is time to understand the reason for his failure to produce such sounds. Children in the kindergarten are often heard to say, "he thaw a wabbit wun down the woad." If a child is producing this speech in the third grade, however, his speech is an indication of serious maladjustment.

Speech and voice are among the most sensitive barometers of personality structure. The child's voice will often give you a clue as to whether you are dealing with an aggressive youngster who is compensating. The examination of many children's voices indicate vocal abuse as a result of loud shouting in the home and in the playground. Consequently speech and voice analysis may often become crucial indicators of the basic difficulties in child development. Withdrawn children usually speak in a soft whispered voice, usually related to rejection in the home. Many children may develop articulation disorders because of their inability to develop listening behavior. In families where routine and regimen is too harsh or lacking altogether, the children become engrossed in daydreaming activities and fail to develop auditory attention necessary for acquiring sound discrimination. Speech development not only requires the listening process and the speech process, but reflects the total behavior on a highly integrated level.

Speech disorders not due to hearing loss may be usually classified under four categories: (1) articulation and voice disorders; (2) stuttering; (3) organic disorders; and (4) developmental failure associated with emotional madajustment. We have already indicated how maladjustment may function to delay the speech process. We have also considered the effect of hearing loss and retardation on speech development. Children in these categories usually do not have speech and consequently become of great concern to the family physician and the parents. With our better techniques for diagnosis we are finding them earlier and are providing preschool training for them. Of all the children admitted to school with speech disorders, 70 per cent of them have functional articulation problems. Their speech will be marked with substitutions, omissions, and distortions, and some children in the kindergarten have such severe articulation problems that their speech is unintelligible even when the listeners have an idea of what the child is trying to say.

The first of the articulation disorders prevalent among primary school children is the problem of substitution. These children usually substitute "th" for an "s." They will say "they would like thum ith cream for thupper." Here the "th" is substituted for the "s" and gives the child's speech an unacceptable flavor. Sometimes parents encourage this lisping, because they feel it is "cute" and in this way will continue to encourage incorrect production. The teacher may help the child overcome this lisp, by providing correct models but usually an extended period of speech therapy by the speech therapist is required because the child now has associated sound with meaning and has retarded the discrimination process. Too, the sound has now become an integrated pattern which will not disappear as a result of stimulation alone. The speech therapist's task becomes one of getting the child to identify the sound, and recognize it through excessive stimulation. The sound must then be produced in isolation so that it will not function in an incorrect pattern. When the child has achieved adequate production of the faulty sounds and can recognize his own misarticulations, production techniques are utilized in nonsense syllables, in words, and in sentences. Such instruction requires a period of time and must be conducted within the basic principles of modern learning theory. The classroom teacher should not be held responsible for providing this instruction but she can work with the therapists in setting up satisfactory conditions for transfer in the regular classroom situation.

The second kind of articulatory error that may harass a child's speech is omission. Sounds, syllables, and even words, may be omitted. The mentally retarded child's speech will have a great many omissions, not only of sounds but of total syllables. Furthermore, the mentally retarded child will telescope the syllables together. Nonmentally retarded children may leave off the endings of words. He must now be made conscious of the speech rhythms that require endings. Endings must be emphasized and instruction provided to produce and reinforce them in the proper places. Similar techniques, as for substitutions, may be utilized excepting that now identification, recognition, stimulation, and production are directed toward the omitted sounds. Again the teacher should not be responsible for this instruction but should cooperate with the speech therapist in setting up reinforcing situations.

The third type of articulatory error prevalent among children's malarticulations is distortion. Distortion represents the verbal mangling of the sound. It is not omitted or substituted but clusters about the similarity of the intended sound and yet it is too different to be recognized as the particular phoneme. When it is in context the meaning provides the cues for understanding. For example, the child in producing a "t," produces something with the movement of the tongue back of the alveolar ridge which is neither a "t" nor a "d," yet the sound unlike substitution or omission, has a certain amount of integrity. Distortions in children's speech behavior do not occur alone. They usually accompany substitutions and omissions, so that speech becomes unintelligible not because of the distortions but because of the concomitant malarticulations. Examples of this kind of speech behavior will be found in every kindergarten. The productions will range from slight to severe and in many cases the maturation factor seems to provide improvement with time, yet there are other children whose speech is so pronouncedly incorrect that maturation will not correct it. It is these children that the speech therapist and the classroom teacher should work with together.

In my visits to your school I have made recordings of some of the children's speech. I will now play a record and let you hear the kind of speech that you may get in your classroom. (A record is played here, with samples of substitutions, distortions, and omissions.) The first child you heard presented speech so unintelligible that he could not be understood. The second child had substitution and distortion. Last year he could not be understood by anyone in his environment but by attending our Clinic and with the teacher's cooperation, the child's speech behavior has shown definite improvement. He now has intelligible speech although he needs some further therapy for brushing up the rough edges. Without the teacher's help, the work at the Clinic would have had only an isolative value.

One question many of you have asked me has been "How do you test these children in order to know what sounds to work with?" We have a rather large collection of pictures which illustrate the sounds in our language in the initial, the middle, and the final positions. We want to test these sounds in their specific places. We go through the pictures and ask the child to name the object without auditory stimulation. From his responses we can construct a diagnostic profile. We can see how many sounds are distorted, which are substituted, which are omitted, and which ones contribute mostly to the unintelligibility. The test results also tell us what sounds to attack first so as to increase the child's speech intelligibility. When the sound has been determined, the therapist works with the child on one sound only until that sound has been completely corrected. In the meantime both teacher and therapist study the child to determine the conditions which are behind the articulation disorders.

As I said previously, before you can correct the speech it is necessary to break the old incorrect habit down and teach the child to supplant it with the new correct habit. The idea of breaking down a habit, or eliminating it, requires clarification. I do not believe that you really break a habit down. What you do is to build a different habit which the child continues to use through reinforcement. Because he does not use the other habit, this disappears through disusage rather than through breaking down. I have already described the correction process. The instruction is provided in the background of a game. In using game materials we resort to the principle of pleasurable behavior. First, the therapist makes the sound for him correctly and gives him an opportunity to listen to it. After he identifies it adequately she produces it correctly and incorrectly, until he is able to recognize the correct one from the incorrect one. The next step is to teach it to him in context. After he has learned to recognize it by context he learns to discriminate it, and the first step becomes one of producing it in all situations. In the beginning production stages the sound is used in nonsense syllables first before he can carry it over into his everyday speech. Our main objective in speech therapy with the child remains one of developing an autocritical phonetic analysis. In other words, we feel we have succeeded when he can become his own clinician.

The next record represents the speech of another child in your school. As you hear this child's speech (another record is played here demonstrating delayed speech and language development), you begin to wonder what kind of child he is. The feeling existed that this child might be mentally retarded. I did not know him but during the test it was my feeling that he was at least within the normal intellectual range. If he was retarded it was indeed at the borderline level. Although his speech was unintelligible, a number of characteristics identified him. First, the child was extremely attentive and persisted in his task even when he was failing. This behavior differs from the mentally retarded child who usually exhibits short attention spans and does not persist with continued failure. Secondly, this child reveals a comprehension of language beyond that of a child with mental retardation. Thirdly, he has a fair sized vocabulary. In my opinion, his teacher has done a grand job in spite of his speech difficulty. The child is learning, is profiting from his experience and his speech is improving. He is accepted by his peers and even contributes to class activities. In testing this child he was able to identify the different objects in the basic articulatory testing book. The mentally retarded child usually does not identify the objects. For example, all animals become "bow-wow" to him, which indicates that he is generaliz-ing at about the two-year level because at the two-year level everything that moves has "bow-wow" characteristics for the child. Quite often parents ac-companying their child to the Center for evaluation, insist that their child is not retarded because he comprehends even though he does not speak, but tests for comprehension usually show that the child's comprehension is very limited to a few simple commands that younger children are capable of un-derstanding. What I am actually saying is that our basic articulation test, accurately administered, provides a good deal of information concerning the intelligence of the child.

Organic difficulties may also be the causative factors for delayed speech development. Among these speech impaired children are children with cleft palates and cleft lips. These children present different correction problems and are beyond the classroom teacher's responsibility. The failure of the fusion of the hard and soft palate, and the failure of the lip to fuse creates a number of very serious distortions. It jeopardizes the child's appearance. The parents seeing this child often reject the child because of his appearance and because they feel that the child is defective. Our experience reveals that about 35 per cent of these children have defective hearing and also a good number of them are mentally retarded. The problem of speech therapy is only one aspect of a very involved series of problems. The question of early or later operation, the kind of preschool training, the amount of speech therapy, all must be considered in a habilitation program. The open cleft creates resonant deficiencies and pressure to have the child talk may culminate in a very serious incorrect speech behavior which becomes difficult to eliminate later on. Even for this type of child a classroom teacher can do a great deal. She can provide an environment of acceptance, work on his strengths, per-mit him to make contributions within his ability level, and prevent him from developing more serious speech distortions. She can work with the therapist who will demonstrate the techniques she has used and permit an under-standing for transfer. In addition to the speech program, the child's needs must be analyzed in terms of his abilities and his actual potentials. The edu-cational program should be geared to permit consistency between the aspira-tion and the achievement levels. Both the teacher and the therapist, as well as other school personnel, will find it necessary to work with the parents in promoting a greater understanding of the child.

Another group of speech impaired children are the children with cerebral palsy. These children present serious bodily motor impairments which in-volve the whole organism including the speech mechanism. Today there are elaborate preschool programs for these children. When these children are ready for school, most of them have language and speech even though this may be defective. The classroom teacher can do a great deal for these chil-dren in terms of setting up an academic program which will permit him to progress at their own pace. The speech therapist can help the classroom teacher by using her lesson plan for common elements to incorporate in her own plans. For this child speech therapy cannot be considered as a subject but as an all-day affair, requiring the perfection of the communication tool in dealing with every aspect of his living. Furthermore, this child will require the services of many specialists—the school physician, the orthopedist, the psychologist, the neurologist, the classroom teacher, and the therapist. But, those children who can go to school may make satisfactory progress although the goal for them will probably not be normalcy.

Another group of children consists of those considered to be aphasic but it is my feeling that we find very few of these in a public school situation. There are too many complicated facets to be understood before we can discuss them intelligibly. This child is one of our most serious diagnostic problems and our experience at the Clinic indicates that proper diagnosis usually eliminates them as aphasics. When such a child is in a classroom, the teacher will direct him to the proper sources for help since she should not be considered responsible for his speech development. An aphasic individual should be one who has the potentials for speech and is not mentally retarded or deaf. Furthermore, delayed speech should not be due to emotional frustration and withdrawal behavior. This type of child is usually seen in the clinic and before he goes to school he has made inroads on the solution of his difficulty.

The last group of children who are certainly handicapped by defective speech are those children who are labeled as "stutterers." This child goes through many devastating emotional crises. A good many of his experiences are saturated with emotional frustration and intellectual disillusionment. Speech for him is unrewarding and because of its nature, calls attention to itself in an unfavorable light. A good deal of research has been devoted to an understanding of "stuttering" behavior, by Doctor Johnson, his co-workers, and others. According to Doctor Johnson, "stuttering" is a form of behavior which emanates as a result of conflict between a child's desire to speak and his attempts to avoid "stuttering." In that sense, "stuttering" is a fearful experience, to be avoided. Consequently speech situations may be charged with apprehension. In speaking, the fear of "stuttering" may become so negatively changed as to negate the positive element in his desire to speak. The ambivalency may be so great as to keep the individual in a constant state of conflict. In the beginning the fear may be restricted to a few experiences but as the attempts to control these experiences fail, a generalized fear may be transferred to all speech situations. How "stuttering" begins still remains a speculative entity. An attempt to account for the origin of "stuttering" has resulted in the postulation of many theories. At one time dominance was considered important, at another time attention was given to the kind of personality that might precipitate "stuttering" behavior, and at another time neurophysiological causative variables were described. While Doctor Johnson's "semantogenic" constructs provided the best rationale for me, the profession has not yet become unanimous in accepting any one theoretical framework.

Doctor Johnson and his co-workers have studied children and adults and their research indicates that "stuttering" may not begin with the speaking act but may originate in the listening behavior of the parent or other significant individuals in the environment. This means that few "stutterers" stutter until someone labels them as stuttering individuals. His research reveals a certain similarity between children who "stutter" and children who do not "stutter," except that the children who do not "stutter" are not so labeled. These people find that young children go through a period in their speech development when their speech is characterized by prolongations, hesitations, and easy repetitions, but reactions of the significant people in the children's enrionment may call undue attention to these prolongations, hesitations, and repetitions, so that the children feeling themselves rejected, will try to avoid them. These are the usual nonfluencies of young children which are present in their early development. When, however, attention is called to these nonfluencies and spontaneous speech is substituted by efforts to control them, many antiexpectancy devices are developed. Although it would take too long to go into the psychodynamics of "stuttering" behavior, there are some things which might be mentioned that the classroom teacher can do to help the child who is stumbling in his speech. The most important one is not to label him unwittingly as others may do; the second, is to convey to him the concept that his speech will be accepted irrespective of its production. If the teacher does this, then the child will not need to find ways to overcome his nonfluencies and as he continues to speak, the more he speaks the less he will "stutter." Furthermore, if the child feels secure in the speaking situations, he will not need to learn antiexpectancy devices.

A number of questions arise here involving the handling of the "stuttering" individual. Certainly he should not be put into traumatic situations but at the same time he must not be permitted to avoid speaking. The teacher and the pupil may come to some understanding how to best handle the situation. The therapist can be the effective agent in bringing about this understanding. For the young child, the best avenue of approach is through the parent and the other people in the environment, so that a change may be brought about which will relieve the child from the fear of nonacceptance. Working with the parents becomes the most important aspect of therapy. They are instructed not to interrupt the child, not to slow him down, and not to criticize his speech production, because all of these contain the invidious rejection of the child's speech which the child may interpret as a rejection of himself. When the child feels that his speech is not accepted, then he will try to talk another way. In attempting to talk another way, he must develop compensating devices. In the beginning he finds that releasing techniques, starting devices, avoidance, circumlocution, and distractions, temporarily help him and as they are incorporated in the speech act become detrimental and disturb the speech. When this has happened, generalized fear in the form of anxiety creeps into his speaking life. An attempt to withdraw from this speech inadequacy terminates in the most fantastic kind of behavior.

There are three criteria which might identify "stuttering" behavior: (1) when someone in the environment labels the child; (2) when his speech is so deviant that it calls attention to itself; and (3) when the child actually considers himself a "stutterer." Once the child's speech behavior goes beyond the nonfluency stage and anxiety enters the speech feedback circuit, the child requires help and understanding. Our experience shows that children below the adolescent level will not profit from the direct therapy for "stuttering" behavior. The problem here is working with the teacher, the parents, and all the individuals in a child's environment, in relieving the pressures and providing security for him. With the adolescent the therapist may be more successful in helping him to overcome his "stuttering" behavior, but any therapeutic program must fit within the framework of modern learning theory and will require the cooperation of the home, school, and the community. The most important help a teacher can provide a child with "stuttering" behavior in a classroom, is adequate referral to the proper specialists. She can set the stage for him in the classroom but unless he also participates in an adequate theapeutic program, the teacher's good intentions may have only limited value.

The Hearing Handicapped Child

Louis M. Di Carlo

Our survey of a number of school systems which provide programs for exceptional children, reveals a number of very interesting phenomena. A school system may usually be evaluated in terms of the preventive measures which it advocates. For example, one index of a good system is the number of children with problems that the system detects, isolates, and helps from the very beginning. The educational atmosphere and environment of a school is very often related to the prominence of stuttering children in it. In one particular school system, we found the number of children with stuttering behavior to be below the average for schools as a whole. Furthermore, our survey also indicated that this particular community must have selective conditions functioning because the percentage of the hearing losses are quite below the norms as compared with other communities and the country as a whole. This would tend to indicate that there are variables working in another direction and these may be due to economic conditions, migration, certain types of employment, the testing program for detection, and the follow-up services for elimination and prevention of hearing losses.

The theme of this series of discussions is the place of the exceptional child in a public school. It has always been my strong conviction that education does not function in a vacuum and that education is the reflection of the intellectual, moral, social, and economic values of a community, at a specific time in history. A cursory survey of history reveals that the kind of educational treatment individuals received, is indicative of the particular type of government and culture that prevailed at the time. For example, during the "golden" days of Athens, certain ideals shaped the educational aspirations and opportunities for the people. It was a time of great intellectual activity focused around a great Greek community. Creativity, intellectual attainment, and appreciation for perfect intellectual and physical development were ideals that the Greeks strove for with singleness of purpose. The ideas of "Good," "Beauty," and "Truth" provided the matrix for their philosophical framework. At the same time a paradox existed. Notwithstanding these humanizing goals certain exceptional individuals were disregarded and denied education and political opportunities since they did not embody the criteria of the Greek culture of that time. Such an approach to the education of exceptional children did not appear consistent with their freedom for speculation. The Greek idea at the time embodied "Harmony," "Beauty," and "Truth" as the ultimate realities. Plato's philosophy provides an orientation to the culture in his comprehensive approach to the kind of standards the Greeks accepted in his "Republic." He develops and crystallizes the educational opportunities for the individuals expected to function in his society. A crippled individual was not a harmonious individual; he deviated from the concept of beauty. A retarded individual deviated from the concept of harmony. Each individual had a function in his State. The philosopher king ruled, the soldier protected, and the slaves worked. Even though Plato may not have intended that these citizens be stratified in terms of more or less desirable hierarchies, nevertheless he makes the philosopher king preferable to the slave laborer. Our own culture embraces much from the heritage of that period. Works of drama, literature, art, music, science, and philosophy continue to play a part in our educational democracy even though the culture that produced them has evaporated through the attrition of time.

Sparta also exerted a great influence in its day, although her goals differed from those of Athens. To them, the individual was created for the benefit of the State, and consequently the most important person was the warrior. The warrior received a selective type of educational and social treatment. Any handicapped individual who could not contribute to the advance of the state, was not worthy of great concern.

The Renaissance made man responsible for his own acts. The defective individual and most of the exceptional individuals suffered, since they were held responsible for behavior which was generally misunderstood. Opportunities for them were more and more restricted. With the beginning of the twentieth century in our own country, most states have provided legislation which insists that all children be given opportunity to acquire an education. Education in our democratic society fostered the concepts:

1. That the integrity of each child be preserved and above all that he be treated as an individual with his own wants, his own needs, his own goals, and aspirations.

2. That furthermore, each child should have an equal opportunity to achieve these objectives. It is not true that the handicapped or the exceptional child has been considered in terms of these two principles although there is a tendency for this to be truer now than previously. In many instances the exceptional child has been accepted for his talents, or rejected for his lack of talent. In my mind, this appears to be the important issue which faces us today. How can we provide for the exceptional child in a public school situation?

As the needs for these exceptional children became clearer in bold relief, many of our educators began projecting institutions so that those children who appeared to be at a disadvantage could obtain an equality of opportunity to grow. But with improvement in educational methodology and advances in medical science, we are now beginning to believe that many of the children who would ordinarily be in these institutions, may be handled equally well in a school system that provides special services. During the last half of the nineteenth century many residence schools for the deaf, the mentally retarded, and other kinds of exceptional children took root. Today our philosophy concerning these schools is undergoing an alteration and many of the schools that once served the needs are now becoming less efficient in providing proper educational opportunities. Hearing aids today are amplifying sound which reaches many of the children who formerly had to go to residential schools. Furthermore, better diagnostic techniques for assuaging the problem in prevention and early detection, makes it possible to give the child early training. Consequently, a number of questions arise:

1. Why does a child go to school? Does he have to go to school at all?

2. Why is the teacher important? Why is she necessary? Children would learn if they were left to the community without school attendance. Research reveals, however, that such learning occurs on a trial and error basis. Learning is not directed and no one provides guidance to prevent the unpleasant consequences of trial and error learning. We realize now, that such learning

would be accompanied by a great amount of frustration, intellectual disillusionment, and emotional maladjustment. The community would find itself in a serious state of chaos. The teacher therefore, becomes a prime citizen. It is true we have not been able to clarify our position. It is also true that we have not had recognition in terms of the dignity of our profession, but today the importance of this concept is slowly manifesting itself.

What are some of the other basic educational principles that we as teachers should develop among our children?

1. First of all we must permit the child to develop his concept of himself so that he accepts himself with persistent satisfaction. This does not mean that a child in school should be in a continuous state of self-contentment. What it means is that the child should develop enough self-critical evaluation so that his over-all experiences will give him stability. He will have moments of gladness and sadness, elation and depression, anger and rage, and will go through the gamut of emotional experiences. But, eventually, he will be able to accept these and express his emotions consistent with the realities of his living. In accomplishing this, the school permits the child to develop a concept of himself so that he will become a stable citizen. The exceptional child requires a great deal of help to attain this objective. I am now thinking of the child with a hearing or a speech impairment who is not capable of accepting himself because the derogatory attitudes of the individuals in his environment are transmitted to him so that he cannot attain security and feel capable of moving into a situation with independence and confidence.

2. The second principle would be devoted toward the development of an individual who would be accepted by his peers. A child who is happy, critical of himself, who has developed the moral sense of the group, and who has a realistic self-concept, will be accepted by his peers. A good indication as to whether a child is adjusted or not is often reflected by the children's attitudes towards him, in spite of the fact that the teacher might try to have him accepted. A teacher's persistency in trying to have the child accepted may be a projection of her own desires and aspiration levels. In a similar way the aspiration levels of parents may cause them to press the child continually and in so doing create serious problems for him. The idea of the child's acceptance by his peers can be a very crucial measure of the child's adjustment.

3. The third basic principle deals with the functioning of the child at his maximum capacity level consistent with his needs so that his aspiration levels will not be inconsistent with his achievement levels. As his capacity and achievement levels coincide, the child is able to utilize his capacities and his contribution to his group will be maximal. Many maladjusted children can be detected in a classroom by the fact that they are not utilizing their potentials. Such a child is in serious trouble and it is in this respect that children with impaired hearing are usually most deficient.

Those of us whose hearing is intact will find it difficult to appreciate the extreme complexity of the hearing process. It is only in recent years that the importance of hearing as a basic activity in child development has been realized. Hearing is an activity that we take for granted. We don't think about it and accept it at an unaware level. Yet hearing behavior is so vitally important that it may determine the basic personality structure of a child from the very beginning. Hearing is not a simple auditory activity. It is a complex type of behavior segment. Hearing takes place at different levels. While hearing behavior has come in for much scrutiny since World War II, the importance of this basic process has long been known. Even before 1915, Nitchie had devoted a good deal of study to it. Kinzie, Samuelson, and others, have considered its implications for the adult but it remained for Ramsdell to put the hearing process in a proper psychological framework.

An analysis of hearing behavior unequivocally manifests that hearing impairments have no one clinical or pathological entity. Hearing behavior varies markedly among individuals and the psychology of individual differences is fully operative in this field. There is a good deal of question as to whether the same individual responds similarly to acoustic events with each ear. According to Ramsdell, the hearing process is integrated at several different levels. These levels are not by any means isolated but contribute to the total hearing process. Nevertheless, he has called attention to the fact that hearing interactions develop from background responses at the lower levels and continue to become more complex. Specifically, he felt that hearing developed at three levels. The first level he considered the primitive level or the background level; the second level he felt to be the warning level; and the most sophisticated level was the social or the symbolic level.

Hearing at the primitive level is tremendously important. It is at this level that the child begins to develop an awareness of sound and becomes coupled to a living world. When this takes place we are not sure, but as the child hears his mother's voice he develops a feeling of identification with her and later on sounds related to significant people and events in his environment give him a feeling of aliveness. This reservoir of acoustic stimuli creates a feeling background which gives the individual an affective toneness. It provides a climate for him to develop emotional reactions of security or insecurity. It is at this level that the child responds primitively below awareness and perception. It is at this level too that hearing is more basic, least organized and the most subjective. For those who lose hearing in adulthood, this level is intimately associated with the effective disruptedness of a deadened world. Menninger has discussed this loss of affectivity according to the way the hatred of the hearing-impaired individual is directed, either toward the world without, or the world from within. Samuelson and others, have elaborated on the reactions that these hearing-impaired individuals make in their adjustment process. Research also reveals that the hearing-impaired individual has been considered in terms of deficiencies of biosocial and psychosocial makeups. Some have even held that these individuals are "not integrated on the same biological level" and have a unique psychology of their own. The evidence is overwhelmingly unequivocal that speech development depends to a large measure on an individual's hearing and that his loss of hearing will impair the speech process in terms of the amount and the type of the hearing loss. Deaf children left to themselves without the opportunity of education, would grow up to be savages. It is probably not true that these children go through the same kind of affective development as individuals with hearing who later lose it. Nevertheless, hearing is a sociological necessity and provides him with an avenue for the acquisition of meaning areas and handling activities at the nonverbal level, which help him manipulate his environment in the satisfaction of his needs and motives.

For children, hearing becomes, in the beginning, the most efficient medium for the development of their complex speech and linguistic behavior. The child's total thought structure becomes refined as his hearing and language responses include more and more of the behavior variables of the world. The development of thought structure, grammatical and syntactic rules, and also the concomitant logical compulsiveness that language and thought comprise, is performed at the symbolic level. Nevertheless, to the deaf child, the opportunity for developing warm emotional security through hearing is denied, and this task must be developed through other avenues. Profoundly deaf children would not usually be in public schools, but for the child who has a mild to moderate hearing loss the effect of distorted hearing behavior will comprise a major obstacle since he will get enough at the background level to bring confusion as a result of inadequate responses, and such responses, since they are only partial responses to partially correlated stimuli, will not provide for optimal functioning of the organism. Such failure interferes with the development of adequate security. Consequently the teacher of this child must understand the psychodynamics of this relationship, otherwise she will be inadvertently contributing to the confusion and the bewilderment which already harasses the child. By providing a warm emotional background and following mental hygiene principles, which include an understanding of the hearing loss, she can help the youngster learn to meet the usual situations of his living with a feeling of adequacy.

At the warning level these children are handicapped in a marked manner. Since the individual in a society is ready to move ahead or to withdraw, he is either ready to fight or for flight. Through hearing an individual is warned of impending events and the perception of the impending events can be quickly organized. Without this warning, the child may be in a continual state of confusion. For this reason the emotional training of a child with impaired hearing in a school situation, is imperative. An understanding of the development of the hearing process will also illustrate that the warning level is a continuation of the background level that is beginning to provide semantic cues at both the verbal and nonverbal levels. It is not my purpose to imply that a hearing loss per se is the basic etiological factor in emotional maladjustment, but it is a powerful precipitating ingredient in aggravating maladjustment. The child with a hearing loss in the regular classroom may miss certain key cues and will not understand everything in the same way as a person with normal hearing. It is in this sense also that a child with a hearing impairment will fail to develop emotional feeling of well-being, since missing key cues will isolate him in some instances from the world around him. We know that events present certain rhythmical and flux behavior patterns. The organism also presents the same kinds of fluctuations. Hearing appears to be the most effective avenue for bridging the world with the organism in terms of affectivity. The one phenomenon that makes the individual feel he is living in a live sense, is the sense of hearing. Not only does hearing couple an individual with the social world, but also with the more subtle world of movement. When this breaks down in adult life, serious repercussions in terms of his adjustment occur. Also, at both the primitive and the warning levels, an individual with impaired hearing suffers catastrophically. It is at this particular juncture in the child's development that he first senses security before the feeling becomes crystallized. Since he does not have normal hearing, his hearing interactions will not develop in a satisfactory fashion and they will not contribute to an understanding of events that take place around him, so that inner conflicts can easily be established.

Moreover, the sound level which we call the warning level might also be called the perseveration level. People are usually comparing the eye and the ear. It is my feeling that this kind of comparison has delayed the progressive development of a satisfactory psychology of deafness for many years because there is no clearcut analogy between the eye and the ear. They may behave similarly under certain conditions but the differences are so great and predominant that the superficial consideration of their similarities masks the deviations. For example, when an individual puts on his glasses the prescription actually corrects the astigmatism, but putting on a hearing aid does not correct anything. It only makes sound louder. Under certain conditions people with hearing losses do not respond satisfactorily to amplified sound and under certain conditions also the louder the sound the poorer the hearing response. Consequently, when a teacher sees a child with a hearing aid, she should not expect him to hear normally but she should understand the limitations of the child's hearing and the hearing aid, and also be aware of the possibilities of the two. Furthermore, vision is a spatial and unidirectional receptor, whereas hearing is a temperal-spatial, multidirectional receptor. It does not seem to me worth while at this time to enter into the controversy concerning which is the more efficient in learning and obtaining knowledge. Research indicates that blind children learn to speak and to get around the world without vision. They become socially coupled and make good adjustments, whereas children who fail to learn to speak are in many cases maladjusted and because they are not socially coupled withdraw into cliques and groups and live by themselves. The importance of this phenomenon can be understood in the terms that these people make in their contribution to society. Vision plays an important part in the knowledge-acquisition, but organized and sequential auditory patterns are necessary to learn communication. It is the best way for the child to learn to speak and it is his most frequently used knowledge-acquisition tool until he reaches the fourth grade. At the fourth grade the child uses his reading as much as his hearing in knowledge acquisition. In terms of a learning theory it is at the warning level where hearing reinforces the previous auditory behavior and provides the child with a well developed sense of security.

Hearing, at the higher social and symbolic level, requires that the child manipulate symbols. It may appear that it is this level which concerns us most as teachers. It should be clear now that for the emotional adjustment, the three levels are necessary. At the symbolic level the child begins to manipulate communication but to get to this level of development he goes through the three processes. It means that all hearing interactions continue to function at all times especially when the child is learning to speak. It is very important to remember that a child learning to speak cannot short-cut any of these developmental levels. Furthermore, a child who has normal hearing acuity but fails to develop speech, compels exploration of a number of personality variables. The reasons for delayed speech development are myriad and for some children the unawared simulation of hearing loss becomes a very convenient manner of adjusting. I recall one child in particular who did not develop speech, although my examination of him revealed that he had all the normal equipment for hearing interactions. The examination also indicated normality of the vocal cords and the speech organs. Nevertheless he failed to develop speech as communication. He did not fail to develop lack of understanding which may also be present in some of the children. Here was a child who refused to learn speech although he had good hearing, because it was a way of avoiding certain unpleasant adjustments. By refusing to speak he was able to evade and avoid certain adjustments that were required of him. Refusal to speak also gave him some prestige, which he found necessary. When I entered his classroom what impressed me most was how the youngster was utilizing his failure to speak by having everyone wait on him. This attention was something he did not have at home and was an excellent way of compensating. This indicates merely one of the problems that is involved in hearing at this level.

Some of the psychoanalysts feel that hearing for a child at this time permits him to recapture the presence of the parents when the parents are not present. Such behavior provides motivation for the development of speaking in specific sequences. At the sociological level a number of exciting events occur. The child is able to recreate at a later date and express his early experiences through speech and language with the refinement and the richness of the original experience itself. When language and speech develop at this level they permit the individual great mobility. His perceptions are logically and psychologically organized and he can formulate events and manipulate symbols adequately. Development of the hearing interactions with subsequent growth of language and speech, provokes the question as to what the relationship is between speaking and thinking. Even a very brief analysis of history reveals that language and speech development of the early tribes was very primitive and simple. As tribal relationships became more complicated, greater demands were made upon its members, which required a more complex communication system. Journeying into lands where primitive tribes exist will reveal the simple structure of their language behavior and a rather small vocabulary. The thought structure of these people also appears to be organized at restricted levels. A serious study of the thought and speech processes permits the speculation as to how these are interrelated. One might say that these processes are two phases of the same phenomenon. Research is quite unequivocal with respect to the deficient abstraction abilities of deaf children. It would appear that language and speech are involved in this series of behavior or events. This is another reason why it is important for teachers in the first and second grades to teach children to read because it is at this time that they appear to be ready for it and it provides reinforcement of the communication avenue. At this level language becomes more complex since the individual now is becoming assimilated in the communication matrix of the group. It is here that language becomes an instrumentation which implements his daily living, behavior, and adjustment. It permits the child to move along in the future and also provides him with the possibilities of prediction. When language becomes predictive, it is then a social technique. At the same time language through hearing makes his past available to him and allows him to elaborate his present experiences which he would have no other way of doing.

It is in this area that the deaf child is most deficient. He cannot predict things which are in the future, nor can indicate to others the events that have gone before, since his most prominent form of communication is pointing. This means that the only experience available to the deaf child is what is present and concrete. This stage would correspond to the naming stage in the development of speech in normal children. Consequently the deaf child moves very slowly and with a great deal of frustration and disillusionment. The next thing that the ability to hear permits is the development for the hearing child of grammatical structure and a logical analysis of language itself. In other words, the hearing child learns without instruction at an unawared level that the subject of sentences usually precedes the predicate and the object follows the predicate. As the requirements for communication become greater his manipulation of symbolic behavior becomes more refined and sophisticated, his adjectives and adverbial modifiers become associated with the correct antecedents. It is here that the deaf child finds himself at great disadvantage. Left to himself he would never be able to learn to speak if you did not teach him to speak. At the age of fifteen years all he would be able to do is to grunt. Of the many exceptional children, the deaf children have the greatest obstacles to overcome in the acquisition of an education. Because of the dearth of his language equipment the deaf child may often be misclassified as a mentally retarded child. In addition, continued frustration and failure to identify himself with the significant people in his environment and communicate with them, precipitates emotional behavior. Then, if he is overactive and difficult to control he may be misclassified as exhibiting prepsychotic tendencies. If he is distractible and responds with rage behavior, he may be misclassified as an aphasic individual. Such misclassification is not conducive to the provision of satisfactory educational programs, but nevertheless such misclassification is possible because he has the common characteristics of the other children: (1) failure to respond to sound; and (2) lack of speech development. Another aspect of hearing in the the development of child behavior is his acquisition of the permissions and prohibitions of his culture. Hearing children develop this through both the verbal and nonverbal aspects of communication. Hearing children continue to test the limits of reality but through hearing obtain significant cues which prescribe the boundaries. The deaf child, because of his lack of hearing, may not learn to know the cultural limits within which he can operate.

Again I must emphasize that lack of hearing or poor hearing is not the basic factor for maladjustment, but hearing deficiencies can exacerbate or aggravate the problem of adjustment for the child. If you have a hearing loss and you do not take the proper measures to overcome the deficiency, you would not understand what people are saying half the time anyway. On entering a group that is conversing someone might just begin to laugh as you enter the room; immediately you may think that they are laughing at you and it is not long before you begin to exhibit paranoic behavior. It is not a long step from this to severe maladjustment.

Moreover, if hearing does not function properly and does not operate to increase the efficiency of the individual, perceptual atrophy will occur and the child will behave as if he has greater loss than he actually has. This does not mean that physiologically his loss deteriorates but rather that his auditory perceptions do not become organized fluently. When this happens the child will learn not to attend. Many of your classrooms have children whose one indication that they have impaired hearing is their consistency in daydreaming behavior. Acoustic events do not carry meaning for them and consequently they learn to ignore them. Excessive daydreaming has the tendency of progressively isolating the child until there may be complete withdrawal from the group. For this reason it is important that the child learn to associate meaning through hearing. All deaf children in residential schools for the deaf do not have total loss of hearing. In fact, many of these children have a good deal of residual hearing. One of the problems in the past has been that a number of mentally retarded children misclassified as deaf found their way into these schools but after a period of several years' trial these children did not learn to speak and did not learn satisfactorily. Research indicates that children who fall into the idiot category rarely ever learn to speak even with a good deal of training. These children learn to grunt and the grunt becomes their major means of communication. A child at the imbecile level will learn to speak within his limits. A child whose I.Q. is between 50 and 75, will learn to speak, read, and write, up to his potentials. He will however, be delayed in the development of speech and for that reason may be misclassified. We as teachers have the responsibility of differentiating between these children so that proper educational placement will help them.

If we can learn to differentiate between children who manifest different symptoms, we may provide better educational placement early. The classroom teacher is not expected to work with deaf children but with modern hearing aids and with the provision of proper educational differentials most children with hearing losses of 60 db or less can function in the classroom quite well if they have had adequate preschool training. About 8 to 10 per cent of all the cases we see at the Gordon D. Hoople Hearing and Speech Center are children who have developed deafness and inattentivity. Examination reveals nothing wrong with their hearing apparatus; a series of learning experiences have resulted in simulated deafness. With these children, withdrawal behavior best serves their adjustment. Often such children find their way into schools for the deaf and their progress is usually not commensurate with the financial investment. If they remain in public schools they may find their way into special classes, but for these children a special class program is not the best solution. Sometimes we have a teacher who envisions the child as a challenge and discovers that by doing certain things a response is obtainable from the child. For example, many teachers discovered that looking at the hard-of-hearing child all the time, talking directly to him, would cause the child to pay attention, learn to lip read, and manage to do those things he would ordinarily not do. With modern hearing aids adequately selected, these children can be taught with the provision of some special work by hearing and speech therapists in correlation with the regular classroom teacher.

It is my conviction, based on the New Rochelle experiment, that the classroom teacher can teach the hard-of-hearing child, but that she needs help and that with the serious overcrowding she should not be responsible for his total development. In any case, whatever special services are provided, these services should be based on child development principles rather than on remedial principles. It is the hard-of-hearing child rather than deaf, that you have been working with. Today, in spite of the knowledge we have acquired, the task is no easy one. Ten years ago we did not have transistor hearing aids. We had hearing aids but we did not fully realize the help they could provide for children. Ten years ago we did not understand the full limitations of lip reading. Twenty years ago we had no experiences to indicate that severely hearing-impaired children might be educated in the public school system. That knowledge we have today, and this I believe, that while it may not be possible to handle deaf children in a regular classroom situation, the hard-of-hearing child can be so taught. The hard-of-hearing child now is one who, if detected early enough and provided with early instruction, may not need special programs, although he may have to have special services from grade to grade provided by the hearing and speech therapist, who can administer to the needs of the child in cooperation with the classroom teacher.

We are interested in the method of teaching the child. Until about fifty years ago many of these children were taught to speak with the manual or finger alphabet. I have seen children come to the Center who could not speak but who could communicate with their hands adequately even though they had large amounts of residual hearing. I remember visiting a class in one of the residential schools during an auditory training period. The children sat around the hearing aid and it was the assumption that they were going to have hearing experiences that would help them learn to refine the interpretative process, but before the class was even under way none of the children had their hearing aids on and the teacher was communicating with them in the sign language. When I asked her why she was not doing auditory training as the program had indicated, her reply was "that the language was so poetic," that she could not deprive them of it. Furthermore she also reported, that "the children do not like to use the hearing aid." She had tried one herself and found it of "no value." An examination of the hearing aid revealed that it was not in functioning order. It is my feeling that here was a situation which represented contradictory elements. First: A teacher with no sympathy for auditory training was teaching, and secondly, the instrument was not in working order. I am not objecting to the sign language or the finger alphabet, but what I am insisting is that each child with a hearing impairment should be given an opportunity to develop hearing, speech, and language behavior, if it is possible. This means that you do not teach these as subject matter, as you do geography, history, and other content material, but as continuous experiences to develop instrumentation for consummating the communication process. It is by the development of communication that the conversation of the handicapped and the reconstruction of personality may help the hearing-impaired child to function without pain and embarrassment in his society.

Placement of children with hearing impairments in the regular classroom situation will depend upon a number of factors. We know that the audiogram is no longer an infallible basis for such placement. The hearing loss per se not only implies the possibility of an impairment but what the child does with his hearing and how he uses it in meeting his needs is still the best criterion. Consequently the hearing impaired child in the regular classroom should be studied as a child with a developmental history. The method of educational treatment will depend upon the contingencies of all the factors and of the child's personality. This means that he should be studied as a developing organism and if he is detected early enough programs of desensitization and re-education will provide the bases for the orientation of the child and his parents.

In every school system where these children are being educated, the staff should include a group of people among whom should be a psychologist, a hearing and speech therapist, a counselor, and a supervisor who understands the peculiar problems associated with impaired hearing. This group would study the individual's dynamic needs and would plan for his physical, mental, emotional, and educational growth. The object of educating the hearing-impaired child in a regular classroom situation, is to provide the child with learning experiences which will help him function without pain and embarrassment in the hearing world. A meeting of minds of these people would provide for constant reappraisal and re-evaluation.

The teacher can help and be the motivating influence in the educative process. By her sympathetic understanding she can help to arrest and destroy attitudes of self-pity and encourage wholesome self-discovery. The efficacy of teaching the child will be contingent upon the cooperation of the entire school system and all the people working with the child. The testing program locates him, the health and follow-up services direct him to the specialist's care, and all of the participants contribute to the investigation, diagnosis, and educational treatment.

Notwithstanding the participation of all the specialists in helping the child, the cooperation of his classroom teacher becomes an indispensable prerequisite. If the classroom teacher is poorly oriented to the problem, she sees in the child unreasonable demands on her time and her attitude will not be conducive to progress. Where the teachers are semantically oriented they can expedite and facilitate the hearing-impaired child's education.

The hearing and speech therapists and other specialists may provide for the hearing-impaired child one or any number of specific skills such as lip reading, speech development and correction, auditory training, or language development, but the success of the program will depend upon the classroom teacher. Unless her attitude is an understanding one, and unless she sets the stage for a transfer, these skills will only have a nonreinforcing value.

The hearing and speech therapist and the classroom teacher can pool their resources and work together so each will contribute information and recommendations that will culminate in a better understanding of the child's needs. The amount of time and the necessary specific differentials will be determined by the investigation, evaluation, and recommendations of all the factors involved. If the hearing loss is slight, the child should have favorable seating and the most important concern with him would be the arresting and preservation of his hearing. If the hearing loss is sufficiently great enough to require lip reading, then this should be taught as a supplement to his hearing. The eyes and the ears will work better together than alone. Working through multistimulation the organism functions at higher levels of organization. The lip reading program should go along with the total school program and should be integrated with it. The lip reading teacher and the classroom teacher can work together in correlating their instructional materials. Futhermore, if the hearing loss requires amplification, the child should have the best kind of electrical amplification in terms of his needs. Fundamental to speech reception and production is the development of auditory discriminatory ability. Work should be devoted toward the development of auditory discriminatory ability and toward the development of differentiation between sounds. The instructions should also provide opportunities for the acquisition of comprehension through reduced cues. Auditory training should also give the individual an appreciation of not only speech sounds but of the many sound phenomena which interact in life's experiences. The classroom teacher can do a great deal to help the child associate meaning with context and encourage him to acquire success with his work.

Guidance should be reinforced for these children with impaired hearing. The guidance counselor may often help to open the doors, interpret the handicap and those forces that are crucial in a child's life, to the different participating members of the team. Individual tutoring should be provided for those children where their needs require heavy language development. This would involve the more severely impaired hearing individual. This work would be carried on with the collaboration of the regular and the special teachers and could be integrated in a uniform plan. Finally, language, voice, and speech training, would be an important form of instruction. Habilitating the child with impaired hearing through speech development may demand time and skill but in terms of giving the individual a chance to become a member of his group, through speech, such habilitation would do a great deal toward emancipating him for greater responsibilities. For the classroom teacher, the salvaging of human self-esteem and helping to realize the physical, emotional, intellectual, social, and educational growth, of children with impaired hearing, should bring rewards beyond immediate self-gratification. In my opinion, teaching of the child with impaired hearing, who can profit by existence in a regular public school classroom, becomes the responsibility of the total community.

I have spent considerable time developing the ramifications of hearing behavior. There is a great deal more that may be discovered, but the limitations of time preclude further analysis. It is important to know that hearing provides the most efficacious avenue for the development of speech. To learn speech the child must be able to identify, to discriminate, and to recall differences between phonetic elements. The most important information-bearing variables in the development of speech are: (1) frequency; (2) intensity; (3) wave complexity; and (4) temporal fluctuations.